Transforming Power

SUNY Series, Teacher Empowerment and School Reform

Henry A. Giroux and Peter L. McLaren, Editors

Transforming Power

Domination, Empowerment, and Education

Seth Kreisberg

State University of New York Press

Published by
State University of New York Press, Albany

For information, address State University of New York
Press, State University Plaza, Albany, N.Y. 12246

Production by M. R. Mulholland
Marketing by Dana E. Yanulavich

Library of Congress Cataloging-in-Publication Data

Kreisberg, Seth, 1956–   # 21969852
    Transforming power : domination, empowerment, and education / by
Seth Kreisberg.
        p.   cm. —   (SUNY series, teacher empowerment and school
reform)
    Includes bibliographical references and index.
    ISBN 0–7914-0663–6 (ch. : acid-free). — ISBN 0–7914-0664–4 (pb. :
acid-free)
    1. Education—Social aspects—United States. 2. Power (Social
sciences) 3. Teaching—Case studies. 4. Teacher–student
relationships—United States. 5. Education—Philosophy.
6. Democracy. I. Title. II. Series: Teacher empowerment and
school reform.
LC191.4.K74   1992
370. 19—dc20
                                                          90–38497
                                                          CIP

10 9 8 7 6 5 4 3 2

To my children, Daniel, Gabriel, and Rebecca

Contents

Preface

Let us teach both ourselves and others that politics ought to be a reflection of the aspiration to contribute to the happiness of the community and not of the need to deceive or pillage the community. Let us teach both ourselves and others that politics does not have to be the art of the possible, . . . but that it also can be *the art of the impossible,* that is, the art of making both ourselves and the world better.[1]

It appears to be certain for the first time that democracy and freedom, justice, and national autonomy are triumphing and that the process that has led us to that is irreversible . . . there are many difficult moments ahead. Only the real hope that we will return to Europe as free, independent, and democratic states and nations has triumphed.[2]

> Vaclav Havel, President of
> Czechoslovakia, 1990

Vaclav Havel's celebration of democracy, his dream of justice achieved through political equality, undoubtedly has resonance throughout much of the world. In 1989 and 1990 we have witnessed momentous changes: people rejecting the authority of governments, and, what is even more unheard of, even undreamed of, entire governing bodies resigning, actually relinquishing power, all in the name of democracy.

Democracy. Certainly a vital ideal in Eastern Europe. Certainly a vital ideal for Chinese students, and most certainly, an equally suspect ideal in much of the United States. Many of us who are critical of the systemic oppressions that characterize American society, including the oppressions of racism, sexism, and class exploitation, are also critical of the myth of democracy. Barbara Christian, for example, writes of the political challenge that emerges from the literature of African-American women. As African-American women tell the stories of their lives, it is clear that the ideals that supposedly shape American political life are not extended equally to all groups within the United States.

For in defining ourselves, Afro-American women writers have necessarily had to confront the interaction between restrictions of racism, sexism, and class that characterize our existence, whatever our individual personalities, backgrounds, talents. Our words, in different shadings, call into question the pervasive mythology of democracy, justice, and freedom that America projects itself to be.[3]

Christian indicts the failure of the United States to translate democratic ideals into democratic realities. Christian, Angela Davis, Bell Hooks, and many others write of the exclusion of African-American women's voices from the political life of the United States, an exclusion of women from shaping even the framing of political problems, much less the development of public policy.

The critique of democracy is expressed concretely as well. Millions of Americans do not participate in the "democratic process." The statistics are well known and telling: only 51 percent of eligible individuals voted in the last presidential election, and the percentages are often lower in state and local elections.[4] Millions of people are disenfranchised by cumbersome registration procedures and by an electoral system so influenced by money and media that the alternative candidates all seem equally removed from the realities of our lives, equally corrupt by the power games of politics.[5]

There are serious problems with democracy in the United States. Given the failures of inclusion, the lack of choice, and the corruption of the democratic process by the demands of expensive campaigns, what is there about democracy that can evoke strong passion in the rest of the world? What is there about democracy that can motivate and propel the tremendous changes in Eastern Europe? Seth Kreisberg's study of democracy and empowerment helps answer these questions. Kreisberg's analysis of democratic education and the democratic process is timely and powerful, a persuasive depiction of what it is about democracy that has allowed people throughout the world to find it a vital means of social change. Seth Kreisberg's work reminds us of the radical potential of democracy. The democratic classroom, the democratic dynamic, all are actualities that challenge the exclusions of process and finance that prevent democracy from being a reality.

The power of Kreisberg's analysis and defense of democracy has two roots: one, a thorough description of the power relations that are necessary for the actualization of democratic ideas, and two, an analysis of the practice and understanding of power in the United States that make the practice of democracy unlikely, though not impossible. It is quite clear from Kreisberg's work why we have a myth of democracy: we lack a democratic culture in the United States, an understanding and practice of the values and forms of interaction necessary to sustain the political process of democracy.

Kreisberg examines the lack of a democratic culture in two fields. First, he provides a foundational inquiry into the very understanding of power, and its radically undemocratic implications, in the work of philosophers, psychologists, and political and social scientists. It is telling that the philosophical study of power is predicated upon a definition of power as domination, what Kreisberg and others call *power over*. The ability of a society to function effectively as a democracy is decisively undercut when a culture defines effective action as coercion, when power itself is imagined as control and domination. Kreisberg demonstrates that for much of Western culture, power means domination. Democracy cannot be achieved if people regard power as fundamentally *power over*. The lack of respect and trust, the alienation and fear behind such constructions of power belie the inclusion and openness necessary for democratic participation in political processes and structures.

What makes Kreisberg's analysis so compelling is that he offers far more than critique. His thorough analysis of the predominant discourse of power is accompanied by an equally vivid account of a radically different understanding of power, the concept of empowerment and *power with*. Empowerment is the ability to make a difference, to participate in decision making, and to take action for change. Empowerment does not assume control of resisting others, but emerges from work with others who are also deciding, acting, and making a difference. Kreisberg claims that the type of power constitutive of empowerment is not *power over* but *power with*. Furthermore, it is *power with* that is required for the practice of democracy. Kreisberg argues that the exercise of democracy presumes the exercise of *power with*, a type of power characterized by mutual assertiveness and reciprocity, a process in which individuals and social systems mutually create each other. Kreisberg describes personal and political relationships in which power is a shared and expanding resource, in which the exercise of power elicits further expressions of power from others. His work is a clear description of the type of power embodied by many activists and feminists and evoked quite well in the writing of Toni Cade Bambara. Bambara writes of "sporting power" for others, and describes a complex reality in which the assertiveness of one evokes the assertiveness of others.[6] In this type of power, strength does not mean the ability to impose one's will on another; rather, strength is expressed in openness to other voices, openness to change and innovation, and trust in the growth that comes as people work together.

Kreisberg's work is itself an "insurrection of subjugated knowledges," a description of the understanding of power held by people who have been marginalized. Most of the book is devoted to the description of this positive alternative, to a careful delineation of the experience of empowerment and the role of *power with* in that experience. Kreisberg describes how empowerment was manifest in the work of a group of teachers involved in Educators for Social Responsibility. He narrates their interpretations of the empowerment they experienced as members of ESR and in their work as teachers. Kreisberg argues that there is much to be learned from these teachers, that the power they describe as central to their work—*power with*—is essential for the practice of democracy. Kreisberg explores thoroughly the interactions constitutive of democracy: the type of power required for people to become active participants in shaping the economic and social structures that affect their lives. He looks most closely at education and the type of relationship between students and teachers, between teachers and administrators, necessary if democracy is to be more than a hollow ideal.

What would happen if one woman told the truth about her life? The world would split open.[7]

Any fears that a focus on democracy will remain the privilege of the elite, or lead to an evasion of the realities of oppression, are allayed by the structure and substance of Kreisberg's work. The book itself emerged from a democratic process, a process that led Kreisberg, in many ways a privileged male, to listen to, and to learn from, the voices of silenced groups, especially women. His claims that democracy entails the nurturing of voice are not idle claims. For it is the very reality of the emergent voices of women that provides the theoretical framework for Kreisberg's work.

Kreisberg begins his book with a story written by a woman in the nineteenth century, Charlotte Perkins Gilman's "The Yellow Wall-Paper." Kreisberg states that he finds in this story a painful, accurate account of the oppression that often occurs in a culture of *power over*. Here "benevolent" control of a woman leads to her madness. What is essential for Gilman, and what is developed by Kreisberg, is that the oppressor in this case has good intentions: in fact, he "loves" the woman he controls. The point that each makes is that *power over*, in most if not all cases, is destructive.

Kreisberg has learned much from the feminist critique of patriarchal domination. Women are telling the truths about their lives, and worlds are splitting open. This book is one such opening. In his forthright analysis of male domination, in his delineation of alternative notions of power being developed by women, and in his method of research, Kreisberg demonstrates the radical changes entailed when women are heard.

Seth Kreisberg listened to women, and learned from us and with us. You will not find in this book a self-conscious discussion of men and feminism, or a discussion of whether or not men can be supporters of feminism. Rather, we see in this book how a man listened to women and, from that listening, integrated a critical perspective on his work as a teacher and a critique of political structures in the United States. Kreisberg's critique of *power over* and the ways in which it undercuts the democratic process is inseparable from his critique of patriarchal structures of domination.

From listening to women, Kreisberg also gained a clear vision of alternative ways of ordering the world, ways grounded in *power with*, ways grounded in the feminist vision of a world without hierarchical control. In his dialogue with feminist theorists, we find a clear example of the reality Kreisberg describes so vividly, the synergistic effects of mutual assertiveness and reciprocity. Mutual assertiveness can be seen in the work of women engaged in political struggles on behalf of women and in the writings of feminist poets, novelists, and theorists. Feminists have developed a clear critique of patriarchal systems of oppression. We are finding our voices and are expressing our critiques of the many forms of patriarchal control that destroy women's lives. Seth Kreisberg's response to this critique is a clear manifestation of synergy. He finds our ideas compelling and is empowered by them to participate in a critique of patriarchy. He describes patriarchal domination in education and relates that particular form of control to the patriarchal assumptions of philosophies of power. From Hobbes to twentieth-century social scientists, Kreisberg finds theories of power whose assumptions of what is natural are shaped by systems of domination. In defining power as the ability to control others, philosophers and social scientists assume a natural state of enmity toward others. In his critique of domination, Kreisberg clearly describes the way philosophical definitions of power as *power over* reinforce privilege, justifying the control of others (women, children, men of color) as part of the inexorable logic of power. Kreisberg demonstrates that in Western culture, "to be male is to be in power is to have control." His critique of *power over*, therefore, is also a critique of a patriarchal culture of hierarchy and domination.

Kreisberg's alternative conception of *power with* is equally influenced by feminist theory. Kreisberg examines the first theoretical treatment of *power with* and *power over*, the work of Mary Parker Follett, describing her theory of power and extending his description of *power with* by drawing on the work of other contemporary feminist theorists. From Jean Baker Miller, Janet Surrey, and Judith Jordan he gains insight into the types of individuation and interaction with other people intrinsic to empowerment. He discusses the theories of empowerment and social change developed by Nancy Hartsock, Starhawk, and Joanna Rogers Macy and makes an important contribution to this discussion by analyzing the theory of power emerging in these works, the understanding of power as a shared, expanding resource.

The heart of Kreisberg's book is also definitively shaped by feminist theory. By focusing on the stories of six teachers and their experiences of empowerment, Kreisberg follows the feminist methodology of grounding theory in critical reflection on women's lives. Kreisberg recounts the stories of empowerment of five women and one man, and draws from them insight into the role of empowerment in education for teachers and for students.

Kreisberg's concluding discussion of empowerment and pedagogy is both heartening and challenging. He delineates the ways teachers can help constitute a democratic culture. Kreisberg persuasively argues that by helping students find their own voices, by fostering the skills of assertion and of genuine listening to each other, teachers can develop with their students the skills needed to make democracy a reality. Kreisberg also claims that students who learn to speak with integrity, and to hear others with openness and respect, have gained the skills necessary to work for justice. His work reflects the struggle for liberation and justice at the level of daily interactions of power and knowledge that shape our lives. Kreisberg describes how people are resisting now, and advocates a further development of that resistance.

Ernst Bloch once wrote that "learned hope is the signpost for this age, not just hope, but hope and the knowledge to take the way to it."[8] Seth Kreisberg's book is a work of "learned hope," a compelling witness to the dream of democracy and a profound analysis of the power relations that make that dream a reality.

Sharon Welch
Harvard University

Notes

1. Vaclav Havel, "From a New Year's Day Speech," cited by Timothy Garton Ash, "Eastern Europe: The Year of Truth," *The New York Review of Books,* 37 (2) (15 February 1990): 22.

2. Vaclav Havel, "The Future of Central Europe," speech given to the Polish Sejm and Senate on 21 January 1990, *The New York Review of Books,* 37 (5) (29 March 1990): 18.

3. Barbara Christian, *Black Feminist Criticism: Perspectives on Black Women Writers* (New York: Pergamon, 1985), 159–60.

4. Frances Fox Piven and Richard A. Cloward, *Why Americans Don't Vote* (New York: Pantheon Books, 1989), viii.

5. See Piven and Cloward, *Why Americans Don't Vote,* for a detailed examination of the way these factors disrupt the democratic process in the United States.

6. Toni Cade Bambara, *The Salteaters* (New York: Vintage Books, 1981), 266.

7. Muriel Ruykeyser, "Kathe Kollowitz," *The Speed of Darkness* (New York: Random House, 1968).

8. Ernst Bloch, *Man On His Own: Essays in the Philosophy of Religion* (New York: Herder & Herder, 1970), 91.

Acknowledgments

Seth Kreisberg died suddenly in December 1989 at the age of thirty-three. He was a lucky man—he had touched the lives of many people and was much loved. What he wrote about in this book is what he devoted his life to—the achievement of social justice for people everywhere. Seth pursued his life's dream in big and small ways. He was on the Teaching Peace Grantmaking Board of the Peace Development Fund in Amherst, and he was actively involved in Educators for Social Responsibility since its founding. At the same time, he was a true co-parent, sharing a complex schedule of childcare, housekeeping, and other related tasks. He was committed to his teaching and struggled daily with the challenges of co-creating with his students an empowering context in which to learn. He was dedicated to the University of Massachusetts's Secondary Teacher Education Program and worked tirelessly to improve it—from providing ongoing support for student teachers to organizing a minority recruitment effort. Finally, he was generous with his time and money with whoever needed either resource.

There is much that Seth gave to others, but he received much in return. This project would not have been possible without the support of his family, friends, and colleagues. Our children, Daniel, Gabriel, and Rebecca González-Kreisberg, were unending sources of inspiration and provided an in-house laboratory in which the concepts that Seth strove to understand, particularly *power with* and empowerment, were tested on a daily basis. I can speak for Seth when I say that his family and friends provided the challenge, the love, and the laughter that made his research and writing joyous. In particular, I would like to mention Joshua and Hanna Bruno, Keith Grove, Pack Matthews, Richmond Mayo-Smith, Gene Thompson-Grove, and Zoe and Hannah Matthews Welch.

Seth often mentioned the eye-opening conversations he enjoyed with colleagues and students at the University of Massachusetts and at Harvard University, especially with David Bloome, Susan Bruno, Elyse Cann, Melissa Hoffer, Richard Katz,

Barbara Love, Sonia Nieto, Carolyn O'Grady, Donald Oliver, William Paquette, Earl Seidman, Susan Seigel, Robert Smith, and Sharon Welch. In addition, Seth's many other colleagues at the University of Massachusetts at Amherst, both within and outside the School of Education, provided feedback, encouragement, and support. I would also like to acknowledge my gratitude to the School of Education of the University of Massachusetts at Amherst for the resources, both financial and of student time and help, that were allocated to the completion of this book.

Seth was honored to have *Transforming Power* included in this series, edited by Henry Giroux and Peter McLaren, two theorists whose work and commitments he so admired. I would especially like to thank them, and Priscilla Ross, SUNY Press Editor, for their sensitivity, support, and patience, as well as for the critical perspectives they brought to this volume.

Finally, Seth's many friends within Educators for Social Responsibility, and particularly on the former steering committee of the Boston chapter, provided a community in which he developed and explored his work. Seth especially wanted to thank the six people who enthusiastically participated in his interview study: Lucile, Shelley, Gene, Rachel, Lally, and Vera. Without their willingness to reveal themselves and their experiences, this book would not have been possible. They are special people doing important work. As Seth said in the preface to his dissertation, "I hope that this [work] in some way captures their commitment, their creativity, and their hope." I also hope that it captures Seth's.

Irma V. González
Amherst, Massachusetts

Permissions

Introduction

The first thing we must acknowledge as teachers is the extent of our power, for, in large measure, the understanding (or misunderstanding) and the application (or misapplication) of that power determines our success or failure as teachers. *Power*, obviously, is a loaded word.... Many of us have the power, through a few chosen words, to bring a young person's world crashing down. We have the power, through careful selection and manipulation, to divide students against themselves and to break them into warring factions.... We have the power, through simply ignoring certain students, to make them insecure and fearful.... Conversely, we have the power to do the opposite. With a word or gesture we have the power to make a kid's day.... And, acknowledging that power, we must also admit that *not* to continually strive to use it well is almost sacrilegious. It is like having the power to heal, but never healing.

Eliot Wigginton (1986, 193, 197)

This book is about power. It is about power in the classroom, in our schools, and in our society. It is for all those educators who are striving to understand the wise and just use of power. This book is also about empowerment. It examines the empowerment of teachers and students. It explores the processes through which people develop more control over their lives and the skills and dispositions necessary to be critical and effective participants in our society. It seeks to name and understand the power that empowers and thereby uncover the nature of "transforming power."

At a time when our nation is questioning the purpose and value of our educational system and seeking new directions for restructuring our schools and educating our young people, this book seeks to offer insight into how we can create more empowering schools and classrooms. In order to do this, this book begins by looking at the larger social and theoretical context of educational theory and practice. Schools, teachers, students, and teaching exist in a churning cauldron of interrelated institutions and social forces. The manifestations of power in schools reflect these larger forces and the interconnections of our institutions. In order to understand the nature of power and the possibility of empowerment in schools, we must look at the nature of our society and the interrelationships among schools, domination, and power.

However, the heart of this book is an exploration of the nature of power in empowering relationships. What are the dynamics of power we as teachers can create in our relationships with our students that will be empowering for both our students and ourselves? What kinds of power relationships are important for teachers to experience to feel empowered?

Education is a primary vehicle of socialization—thus it is a focal point for the expression of dominant values and social relationships. It is because of this central social function that schools have historically been contested sites for competing visions of the democratic and just society. This book adds new voices to this ongoing debate. It is guided by a belief in the fundamentally political and moral nature of teaching and in the possibility of empowering and democratic change in schools and society.

1

Domination, Power,
and Empowerment

I consider the fundamental theme of our epoch to be that of *domination*—which implies its opposite, the theme of *liberation*, as the objective to be achieved.

Paulo Freire (1970, 93)

Surrounded on four sides by a swirling, patterned, yellow wallpaper, a solitary woman sits in a room. Confined to the ex-nursery of a colonial mansion, she secretly writes in her journal. The woman narrator of Charlotte Perkins Gilman's "The Yellow Wall-Paper" (1973)[1] is a young mother and wife with a "nervous condition." Through the window of her journal we witness her gradual and horrifying descent into madness.

Diagnosed by her doctor/husband, her doctor/brother, and a world-renowned male medical expert, she is ordered to stay in bed, to get plenty of rest, and to refrain from all social interactions. She is also told to give up her work—caring for her child and writing:

> If a physician of high standing, and one's own husband, assures friends and relatives that there is really nothing the matter with one but a temporary nervous depression—a slight hysterical tendency—what is one to do? . . . So I take phosphites—whichever it is, and tonics, and journeys, and air, and exercise, and I am absolutely forbidden to "work" until I am well again. (p. 10)

The narrator disagrees with the treatment prescribed for her by her husband and the medical expert:

> Personally I disagree with their ideas. Personally, I believe that congenial work with excitement and change will do me good. But what is one to do? I sometimes fancy that in my con-

dition if I had less opposition and more society and stimulus—
but John says the very worst thing I can do is to think about
my condition, and I confess it always makes me feel bad. (p. 10)

She senses that something more is wrong than a simple "nervous
condition." She senses that writing, caring for her child, and interacting with people might do her some good. Yet, infantilized by her
paternalistic husband who calls her his "blessed little goose" and
his "little darling," she is persuaded to disregard her own intuition
concerning her illness and her needs.

Trapped in her room, isolated and alone, she gradually
becomes fixated on the room's wallpaper: "One of those sprawling,
flamboyant patterns committing every artistic sin. . . . The color is
repellent, almost revolting; a smoldering unclean yellow" (p. 13).
She begins to visually trace the wallpaper's winding, weaving pattern. Gradually she comes to see a woman, imprisoned behind
bars, trying to escape. She watches the wallpaper and the woman
constantly: "Life is very much more exciting now than it used to
be" (p. 27). At the terrifying conclusion of the story she tears apart
the wallpaper, freeing the woman from her bondage. She and the
woman merge. As the story ends, she is hunched over, shoulder
against the wall, creeping around the room in circles, shouting,
"I've got out at last. . . ." (p. 36).

Written in 1899, Gilman's story seems timeless in its exposition of a fundamental dynamic of women's oppression, indeed of all
oppression: the oppressor has the overwhelming (yet never total)
ability to control and define the world of the oppressed. The narrator's husband and the distant expert, with the weight of the wisdom of the medical profession, social norms and expectations, and
male hubris on their side, have decided what is wrong with the
woman and what will make her better. The prerogatives of his gender, his profession, and his familial status enable the woman's husband to force her to give up her work and to withdraw from the
world. Against her best interests and her own sense of her needs,
he controls her world and her life.

Intuitively, the woman knows the diagnosis and treatment
are wrong. They are destroying her. Yet she is powerless to act on
her personal insight. Her voice is ignored, even viewed as irrele-
vant, by the men who control her destiny. Throughout this story
one continuously wants to shout to the husband, "Talk to your
wife, listen to her, respect what she is feeling"—in spite of the fact
that the reader knows that he is not interested in what she thinks

and that he is acting on male-defined assumptions about what it means to be a healthy woman. To the wife one wants to shout: "Speak up! Leave! Do something! You are being destroyed!" Yet we know she is alone, with nowhere to go, and no real way to break out of her male-defined reality. And this is the crux of her power-lessness: her world, her relationships, her roles and identity are circumscribed, indeed defined, by people, by institutions, by broad social forms beyond her control. Helpless onlookers, we watch her inevitable destruction.

In some ways even more disturbing is the fact that her husband "loves" her, that he is not trying to hurt her: "It is so hard to talk with John about my case, because he is so wise and because he loves me so" (p. 23). One does not sense malevolence in John; rather, a web of dominant cultural values and accepted patterns of male–female relationship make him unable to hear and respond to his wife and truly help her heal herself. The woman vaguely per-ceives this: "John is a physician, and *perhaps . . . perhaps* that is one reason I do not get well faster" (p. 10). But she is unable to act on this knowledge. The result of these twisted circumstances is that John's "treatment" is exactly the opposite of his intent. Indeed, the wall not only entraps the woman but stands between her and her husband. John's understanding of women and their needs leads him to destroy his "little darling." His action for his wife's "own good" leads to her ultimate dissolution. The story ends with the woman creeping in circles, passing over the body of her husband, who has fainted at the sight of his deranged, yet strangely liberated, wife.

This simple and moving piece of fiction, filled with building tension and horror, is a powerful unveiling of the contradictory and destructive forces manifest in traditional gender relations in the United States. But it is more as well, for the story captures fundamental dynamics that create and perpetuate powerlessness in all relationships: the relationship of domination. In the specific dynamics of the relationship between the husband and wife in "The Yellow Wall-Paper" we see reflections of relationships of dom-ination that pervade our social structures and institutions. Women are not the only people locked behind the yellow wallpaper's pat-terns of domination. There are other victims as well.[2]

Education and Domination

I remember my fifth and sixth-grade math and science teach-er: a flamboyant man with a bright red mop of hair and a thick, curled, red mustache, who always wore a bow tie. His room was a mess, with animal cages and assorted games and educational material spread around the room. He told us he had an alligator in his mustache. If we tried to untie his bow tie it would bite us. We tried often. Mr. Smith[3] cared about us, he wanted us to do our best. He was encouraging, funny, and interesting.

Mr. Smith also ritually spanked his students. When we were disruptive or otherwise disobedient, we had to submit to several gentle whacks on the buttocks—in full view of laughing and fearful fellow students. Each student expected and was expected to undergo this ritual of humiliation and submission at some point in the school year. I remember living in fear of being spanked for half of my first year with Mr. Smith—fear not of the physical pain but of the humiliation and submission I would be forced to experience.

In Mr. Smith's room there was no doubt who was in control. The act of spanking was the visible manifestation of Mr. Smith's ultimate control over his students—over our movements and activities. It was Mr. Smith who, fundamentally, defined the relationships in the classroom. Yet we all loved Mr. Smith. In him, and in our relationships with him, concern, care, humor, violence, humiliation, and submission were all mixed together in the complex web of the relationship of domination. This is domination at its most effective and most insidious, creating relationships in which people accept, even enjoy, being dominated.

I also remember my English teacher in my high school "Tragedy" course. I remember Mr. Norris[4] waving his wooden pointer at the blackboard and at us. I remember him insisting that we memorize Hamlet's soliloquies and requiring to us write out from our grammar book each grammatical rule we had broken in our essays. I remember his intimidating voice, his apparent pleasure at humiliating students for not knowing the correct answers. I remember his attitude of superiority, which was communicated through his condescending tone, his unreasonable demands, and his pompous manner. I found Mr. Norris effete and offensive. He did not engender the affection that Mr. Smith enjoyed. I often grew angry at his smugness and the pleasure he took in enforcing his rules and imposing his expectations.

Years later an endowed chair in the humanities was created for Mr. Norris. He was praised as one of the finest teachers in the school's history and quoted as commenting to parents in a commencement address:

Some of you here today—if not most of you—know me only as the central figure of a contemporary mythology created and propagated by the [Jones][5] student. I am that legendary creature, who descends each morning at eight-fifteen from some Olympian height to inflict despair, anguish and torment, and frustration upon mere mortals; that ghoul whose sole delight is draining the lifeblood from those defenseless innocents you send us each morning; that ogre whose rod and whose staff comfort none; that demi-god who is the ultimate test of mental, physical and spiritual endurance. I am he with the fist of iron, the eyes of steel, and the heart of stone. In short, I am an English teacher, the most unreasonable, the most unsympathetic, and—to students everywhere—the most unnecessary of God's creations.[6]

Beneath the self-mocking tone, it is clear that Mr. Norris takes pride in the "despair, anguish and torment" his actions and attitudes create in students. The violence in his images and language is vivid, and his underlying conception of the "productive" student–teacher relationship is clear: through submission comes academic excellence. A prominent quote on his wall reads, "If WE obey God, WE must disobey ourselves."

Nevertheless, many ex-students remember Mr. Norris as an excellent teacher, enough of them apparently for the school to position his career as a fund-raising device. One former student, now an actor, remembered: "English came to life with Norris. He instilled in me a desire to work well and accurately." Another graduate recalls that "through his teaching methods—the direct questions, the deep voice, and that dreaded wooden pointer—he has challenged us to challenge ourselves." And, in an ominous testament to the power of relationships of domination to be replicated and passed on, one ex-student, now a teacher, notes that Mr. Norris is ". . . a model that I continue to judge myself against as a teacher and an advisor."[7]

Students do not seem to remember Mr. Norris with much affection, and he would not expect them to. But they do express deep appreciation for their belief that he taught them how to write and that he made the study of English engaging. Somehow, in the playing out of the relationship of domination, the fears of humiliation and the feelings of voicelessness and inferiority are ignored and forgotten, or worse, accepted. At least in retrospect, many ex-students accept Mr. Norris's superiority, his toughness, his patronizing attitude, because they feel these attitudes were justified —they feel that what he did was for their own good.

Our culture sets up men like Mr. Smith and Mr. Norris as the models for fine teaching: as in "The Yellow Wall-Paper," care and domination are entwined. Schools are places in which relationships of domination are played out extensively every day between teachers and students, and always this domination is justified as in the best interests of students. Much as the woman in "The Yellow Wall-Paper," students are confined to places where they are told, and too often accept, that someone else knows what is good for them, where someone else controls their lives and daily choices, and where their voices are patronized or ignored. Their success in school is measured by their submission to their teachers and parents, by their willingness to accept the roles and standards that have been set for them. Those who reject these expectations are labeled "troublemakers," "problem students," "maladjusted," "unmotivated," or "culturally deprived." They are "not working to their full potential"; often they receive low grades; they are sent for psychological testing; they are kept after school. More often than not the problem is said to reside within the students or their "family backgrounds." For many students, *their* yellow wallpaper is pastel paint on cinder block walls. They are trapped figures— lacking voices that are listened to and respected, and lacking control over their lives.

Whether students accept the submission and docility that is demanded of them, or resist its imposition, all are subject to relationships of domination. Consider the average high school in the United States: every day several million adolescents between the ages of fourteen and eighteen are forced into concrete catacombs, compelled to sit in rows of desks for fifty minutes at a time, six to seven hours a day. For the most part they listen to an adult recite information at them, little of which they retain for very long. Regularly, they are asked to recite this information back on an endless stream of tests, quizzes, and worksheets. Often they must ask for a hall pass in order to go to the bathroom. They are separated by age and academic "achievement," which often falls into patterns of race, class, and gender segregation as well. When they question these patterns, they are told it is for their own good.

Throughout much of the history of U.S. education there has been persistent criticism of its authoritarian and domesticating character—of its focus on obedience and socialization to the status quo. In the past thirty years a rich and condemning literature has accumulated that unveils the class, race, and gender biases that permeate school structures, curriculum content, and pedagogy. One of the most perceptive critics of this kind of teaching is the Brazilian educator Paulo Freire. Freire (1970) describes what he calls "banking" education. An essential characteristic of banking education is the relationship between teachers and students, which Freire describes in this way:

> (a) the teacher teaches and the students are taught; (b) the teacher knows everything and the students know nothing; (c) the teacher thinks and the students are thought about; (d) the teacher talks and the students listen—meekly; (e) the teacher disciplines and the students are disciplined; (f) the teacher chooses and enforces his choice, and the students comply; (g) the teacher acts and the students have the illusion of acting through the action of the teacher; (h) the teacher chooses the content and the students, who were not consulted, adapt to it. (p. 59) [8]

The banking method is premised on what Freire calls the "teacher/student contradiction," the core of which is the pedagogical relationship of domination and submission: the teacher acts and the students are acted upon.

Freire also describes the relationship, in banking education, between the students and the knowledge they are asked to absorb:

> The teacher talks about reality as if it were motionless, static, compartmentalized and predictable. Or else he expounds on a topic that is completely alien to the experiences of the students. His task is to fill the student with contents which are detached from reality. (p. 56)

Similar to making a bank deposit, the teacher "deposits" knowledge into the student and then makes "withdrawals" in the form of tests and quizzes and methodical questioning. This knowledge is detached from the student's experience. It is someone else's understanding of what someone else thinks is important. Nevertheless it is presented as Truth, to be stored by the student and regurgitated on demand. The student experiences knowledge as imposed from above, absorbed through an act of submission.

The most profound lessons of banking education are rarely

stated explicitly, but their unspoken character does not diminish their ability to influence how people see and act in the world:

> the banking concept of education regards men as adaptable, manageable beings. The more students work at storing deposits entrusted to them, the less they develop the critical consciousness which would result from their intervention in the world as transformers of that world. The more completely they accept the passive role imposed on them, the more they tend simply to adapt to the world as it is and to the fragmented view of reality deposited in them. (p. 60)

Indeed, banking education contains a powerful hidden curriculum[9] that teaches students that the world is hierarchical, that the powerful are often arbitrary and insensitive, that they must learn their place in the hierarchy because there is no alternative to either controlling or being controlled. Banking education cultivates passivity, conformity, obedience, acquiescence, and unquestioning acceptance of authority. It makes objects out of students, it dehumanizes, it denies students' experiences and voices, it stifles creativity, it disempowers. It tells our children that there is something wrong with them; that it is they, rather than their schools and society, that need fixing.

Studies have consistently shown that the banking method of teaching is the predominant approach in United States classrooms, especially on the secondary level.[10] Ironically, despite its fundamentally antidemocratic character and effects, banking education is practiced and espoused in the name of equality, freedom, and democracy. However, banking education is not a mere anomaly, a dangling contradiction with no social function. To the contrary, banking education serves a vital function in U.S. society: it reflects, reinforces, legitimizes, and replicates those social, political, and economic structures and relationships of domination that render people powerless. In so doing, banking education helps maintain those very structures and helps perpetuate those relationships. Freire directly connects the banking method of education to wider patterns of domination, oppression, and violence in society. He writes:

> The capability of banking education to minimize or anul the students' creative power and to stimulate their credulity serves the interest of the oppressors who care neither to have the world revealed nor to see it transformed... Oppression—

overwhelming control—is necrophilic; it is nourished by love of death, not life. The banking concept of education, which serves the interests of oppression, is also necrophilic. Based on a mechanistic, static, naturalistic, spatialized view of consciousness, it transforms students into receiving objects. It attempts to control thinking and action, leads men to adjust to the world and inhibits their creative power. (p. 60)

Teachers themselves occupy a paradoxical place in the web of institutional and ideological domination in schools. Although they are central figures of authority and control in the classroom, in the larger hierarchy of the educational bureaucracy they are remarkably isolated and often strikingly powerless. John Dewey observed in 1903 that the model of educational management current in his time was to have "one expert dictating educational methods and subject-matter to a body of passive, recipient teachers" (Dewey 1940, 64). He went on to observe:

The dictation, in theory at least, of the subject-matter to be taught, to the teacher who is to engage in the actual work of instruction, and frequently, under the name of close supervision, the attempt to determine the methods which are to be used in teaching, mean nothing more or less than the deliberate restriction of intelligence, the imprisoning of the spirit. . . . It is no uncommon thing to find methods of teaching such subjects as reading, writing, spelling, and arithmetic officially laid down; outline topics in history and geography are provided ready-made for the teacher; gems of literature are fitted to successive ages of boys and girls. (Dewey 1940, 67)

He describes the general attitude toward teachers of that time period: "It is asserted that the existing corps of teachers is unfit to have a voice in the settlement of educational matters" (Dewey 1940, 67).

Observing American schools eighty years after Dewey, Theodore Sizer (1983) notes that schools and school systems are "arranged in pyramidal tiers, with governing boards and administrators at the peaks and the classrooms at the base" (p. 206). He notes:

The individual instructor or groups of instructors rarely decide what the basic outlines of their curriculum will be. That is handed down either by administratively senior colleagues or by lay boards, often with elaborate teaching guides. . . . Teachers are told the amount of time they are to spend with each class—say, fifty-five minutes, five times a week. Even though they are expected to be competent scholars, they are rarely trusted with the selection of the texts and teaching materials they are to use. . . . Teachers are rarely consulted, much less given significant authority, over the rules and regulations governing the life of their school; these usually come from "downtown." Rarely do they have any influence over who their immediate colleagues will be; again, "downtown" decides. . . . Teaching often lacks a sense of ownership, a sense among teachers working together that the school is theirs. (p. 184)

The Carnegie Task Force on Teaching as a Profession echoed Sizer's observations:

Schools . . . operate as if consultants, school-district experts, textbook authors, trainers, and distant officials possess more relevant expertise than teachers in the schools. Bureaucratic management of schools proceeds from the view that teachers lack the talent or motivation to think for themselves. ("Text of Carnegie Report" 1986, 11)[11]

The Carnegie report may signal a turning point in teachers' struggles to participate in decision making in schools. Leading educational figures with views as disparate as those of National Education Association President Mary Hatwood Futrell and former Education Secretary Terrence Bell have emphasized the need for increased teacher participation in decision making, reflecting a growing trend in education.[12]

These recent initiatives point to complex and often contradictory forces affecting schools and teachers. The issue of increased teacher control has surfaced simultaneously with increasing centralization of decision making, in part as a response to the pressure for "accountability." What seems clear is that little has changed in the basic structure of decision making in most schools in the past eighty-three years. Patterns of organizational management that take decision making away from teachers and that impose curricula and methods on teachers are a reflection of the same patterns of domination and powerlessness that characterize student–teacher relationships. Like "banking education" they too help perpetuate wider patterns of social, political, and economic powerlessness and injustice.[13]

Relationships of Domination

Across a broad spectrum of institutions that shape our lives, people have power over other people; that is, people have the ability to control, manipulate, and coerce other people for their own ends. These relationships of domination are not haphazardly and randomly developed. Rather, the very structures of our social institutions and the predominant norms, values, and beliefs of our society sanction, indeed define and reinforce, them. The ability to control and manipulate others also derives from privileged access to and control of valued resources such as education, personal wealth, housing, food, health care, and weapons of war. [14]

Relationships of domination exist in political institutions. They take the form of ruling elites who manipulate the apparatus of governance to their own advantage, whether the form of political power be totalitarian, authoritarian, or arguably democratic. The patterns of control of the few over the many are very clear and undisguised in countries such as South Africa and Haiti. However, political domination also occurs with varying degrees of complexity and subtlety in nations as diverse as the Soviet Union, Iran, Nicaragua, and the United States. In fact, throughout the world the drive to control others creates a spectrum of violent and unjust situations, ranging from war and political murder to torture, jailing of dissidents, terrorism, censorship, expropriation of property, and manipulation through propaganda and entrenched party politics. Political powerlessness is directly connected to relationships of domination generated through political activity.

Relationships of domination also thrive in our economic institutions and systems. Throughout the world, from the less industrialized nations to the highly industrialized, from capitalist to state-controlled economies, economic relationships exhibit patterns of domination that spark violence and perpetuate powerlessness. The patterns take shape in hierarchical, alienating, and exploitative economic relationships, the core of which is differentiation between those who have access to and control over wealth and those who do not. Most fundamentally, we see the results of economic domination in the vast disparities in standards of living among different nations, regions, and peoples. The powerlessness of poverty is undeniable and extensive.

We also see relationships of domination in the exploitation of illegal and legal immigrants to the United States in our factories and sweatshops and in the shrinking middle class of the United States, a country moving in the direction of an increasingly polarized society of rich and poor. We see these patterns in the rigid hierarchies of decision making in industry in the "First," "Second," and "Third" worlds alike. We see them in the actions of American companies that exploit cheap labor overseas to fuel domestic consumption.

These pervasive patterns of domination, of hierarchy and control, also characterize the dynamics of relations within the family and between the sexes across a spectrum of cultural traditions. The family is dominated by the father/husband whose "home is his castle." The male sense of entitlement to control over women and children expresses itself throughout society. It is no coincidence that men dominate politics, economics, *and* the family. Male dominance is violently evident in the statistics on rape, child abuse, and spouse battering.

These patterns of domination recur in the relationships between and among races. At its core, racism is a theory of superiority. The theory takes shape in practice when one racial group has unequal access to a society's resources and control of the society's political and economic institutions. In the United States, racism results in the economic and political marginalization and exclusion of people of color. It also is expressed in rising violence against people of color.

Similar patterns of domination can be found in the structure of relationships among members of many religious traditions. Relationships of domination within various religious traditions are modeled on a particular concept of God as father. The people are God's children, and through faith they are asked to submit to God's will, to obey the written and interpreted word. This relationship of domination is reflected in the role of the rabbi, minister, and priest and is most evident in the clergy's special access to the interpretation of scripture. Thus hierarchy, submission, and domination are perpetuated through many forms of religious practice and experience.

Domination also characterizes the Western conception of the human relationship to the natural world. At the center of this conception is the human impulse to create a more predictable and physically comfortable world. The desire to dominate nature has disturbed the delicate balance between modern societies and the environment. We see this reflected in uncontrollable urbanization and its resultant pollution and in consumer societies voraciously looking for immediate material gratification while showing little concern for the long-term impact of their waste. The desire to dominate nature has led to the reality that we are rapidly destroying that which gives us life. Three Mile Island, Chernobyl, Bhopal, the "greenhouse effect," the destruction of the rain forests, and the nuclear arms race represent the extremes of this mode of thinking, a perspective that is ultimately suicidal.

Education is characterized by the same patterns of domination as economics, politics, religion, and the family. The authoritarianism and hierarchy of these other contexts reappear in classrooms and schools with frightening frequency. What we have seen elsewhere embodied in the political leader, the capitalist, the manager, the father, the religious leader, or God, recurs in the role of the teacher, the principal, and the "central office administrator." The relationships of domination and submission that were outlined earlier in student–teacher and student–knowledge relationships and in classroom pedagogy are intricately entwined with domination throughout our culture.

So we see, across a range of societies and institutional structures within societies, the world is divided into hierarchies characterized by relations of domination. It is a battleground of winners and losers where only a few can win. Within this paradigm, relationships are vertical. Disparities in power are seen as not only inevitable, but essential for the maintenance of our institutions.

How do we explain the omnipresence of domination in our world? How are relationships and structures of domination maintained? What mechanisms produce the belief in the inevitability of domination? Three concepts are helpful for understanding the links between domination and schooling and the mechanisms through which domination reproduces itself. They are the concepts of "culture," "hegemony," and "ideology."

The concept of culture is essential for understanding the dynamics of domination. McLaren defines culture as "the particular ways in which a social group lives out and makes sense of its 'given' circumstances and conditions of life." Culture consists of the "set of practices, ideologies and values from which different groups draw to make sense of the world" (McLaren 1988, 171). The expression and preeminence of particular cultures and cultural forms within a society are directly related to the dynamics of domination in that society. In particular, culture is intimately connected to the dynamics and structure of class, gender, race, and age relations and is, in fact, a field of conflict among competing forms of knowledge and experience, indeed among competing cultures. Thus it is through the exploration of the nature and dynamics of cultures and cultural conflict that we can begin to understand the ways in which particular practices, institutions, and social structures are legitimated and conspire to perpetuate domination.

The pervasiveness of domination within, among, and across cultures suggests that domination is maintained through more subtle processes than the exercise of brute force. Domination is perpetuated through the ability of those who dominate to gain the consent of the oppressed *without the awareness of the oppressed that they are participating in their own oppression.* For instance, often domination's one-sidedness is hidden behind a veil of espoused benevolence. It is stated and believed, by the dominator and by the dominated, that the relationship is in the best interests of both.[15] Thus the colonizer always has arguments ready as to why colonization is in the interests of the colonizer *and* the colonized—e.g., the colonizer brings Christianity, development, literacy, hygiene, etc., to the colonized. The capitalist argues that the free market improves the standard of living for all economic levels of society. The parent argues that his or her violence and control are for the child's own good. Teachers believe that their wisdom and experience entitle them to impose their beliefs on students without challenge.

And quite often the dominated accept, on a surface level at least, these rationalizations. They internalize and accept the dominator's image of them. Many students believe that they need teachers to tell them what to do and that they are not capable of making choices themselves. Some women believe that every family needs a head of the house and that men have the appropriate genetic and psychological makeup to rule the family, while women have the appropriate dispositions to submit to and support the male prerogatives.[16]

The conclusion to be made here is not that the dominated get what they deserve, nor that domination is justified if the oppressed accept their subjugation. Rather, this discussion points to a more complex analysis of domination, one that helps explain the collusion of dominator and dominated in accepting and maintaining relationships of domination. It directs us to look more deeply at how specific relationships of domination are situated within a web of supporting ideological and structural forces that form a pattern so pervasive and persistent across continents and cultures that many, if not most, people believe that relationships of domination are inevitable, unchangeable, appropriate, and natural—an inherent part of what it means to be human.

This saturation of consciousness and experience with domination is captured in the concept of hegemony. As defined by Antonio Gramsci, hegemony is the process through which dominant groups impose their conception of reality on all subordinate groups. Raymond Williams describes hegemony as

> a whole body of practices and expectations; our assignments of energy, our ordinary understanding of man and his world. It is a set of meanings and values which as they are experienced as practices appear as reciprocally confirming. It thus constitutes a sense of reality for most people in the society, a sense of absolute because experienced [as a] reality beyond which it is very difficult for most members of society to move in most areas of their lives. (Apple 1979, 5)

McLaren has described hegemony as "the cultural encasement of meanings, a prison house of language and ideas" (McLaren 1988, 173). It is the process through which the dominant culture supplies the symbols, representations, morality, and customs that frame, form, and constrain what we do and say, the principles that underlie our thoughts and actions and the broader structures that shape our experiences in the various institutions in which we live (e.g., family, school, workplace, government, and religious institutions). Gramsci (1972) argues that this saturation of consciousness and experience is so deep that the reality of domination constitutes a common sense view of reality.

To accomplish this saturation, hegemony works on both the individual's mind and body. The concept of ideology is crucial to understanding this process. A dominant ideology is a controlling set of representations, beliefs, values, ideas, and assumptions that are conveyed through a culture's intellectual heritage, its popular culture, and its "common sense" understandings of the world represented in various forms of mass media, folk knowledge, and everyday forms of communication. That is, a pervasive set of ideas and ways of looking at reality constitute individual consciousness and both justify and conceal domination.

However, ideology and hegemony work directly on the body as well—that is, on the level of our everyday unconscious experience. On fundamental levels, who we are, what we want, what we need, and thus what kinds of social relationships we seek out and create are shaped by the patterns and daily routines of our everyday lives. In part this occurs through the process by which ideology seeps deep within our personalities, into the depths of our unconscious, shaping our personalities, needs, and desires. I want to argue, though, that the process by which social practices become sedimented and reproduce themselves, while connected to ideological processes of reproduction, are also distinct from these processes. People tend to relate to others in the same ways others have related to them. We tend to act in the ways we see and experience others' actions. Patterns of relationship reinforce and replicate themselves. Experience solidifies into habit. In fact, hegemony is most encompassing when a dominant ideology reflects and is expressed in everyday experience and in a range of social practices and structures in a society. In this society, relationships of domination are maintained by just such a correspondence of consciousness and experience, which, while never total and static, is still powerful and broadly encompassing.[17]

Beyond the Limits of Domination

A fundamental conviction undergirding this book is that, despite the pervasiveness of patterns of domination, we as individual human beings, acting with others, can be agents of social change. This belief in human agency, in the individual's ability to make a difference, drives my commitment to education and is the central impetus behind the writing of this volume. Patterns of domination are not the inevitable outgrowth of human nature. Dominating behavior is a social phenomenon. Stubbornly persistent as they are, patterns of domination are ultimately shaped by humans and thus transformable by human action.[18]

Recent work in critical pedagogy, as well as in fields other than education, has pointed out that domination in schools and society does not function as a seamless web. Rather, a more complex analysis is emerging that reveals the ways in which schools not only reproduce domination, but produce resistance to domination as well.[19] Schools are, in fact, sites of ongoing contestation and struggle for control. Resistance theorists offer important insights into the possibility of human agency and educational and social transformation.

Resistance is readily apparent in most situations of domination. While the mechanisms of hegemony are powerful, they are

not all-encompassing, and they are always characterized by contradictions and conflict. The dominated rarely consent fully to
their own domination. Many reject the dominator's theories of
their inferiority, and they resist the notion that their submission is
for their own good. Many of the colonized reject colonization, and
many people of color reject exclusion or marginalization. Women
reject objectification, workers reject arbitrary work rules, and students reject their infantilization. The woman in "The Yellow Wall-
Paper" writes despite her husband's attempt to stop her. And I,
too, refused to let Mr. Smith spank me. My parents supported my
stand, and I do not ever remember being struck by him.

Indeed, in schools students resist doing homework and delay
the beginnings of classes. They develop intricate systems of cheat-
ing and psyching out teachers. They smoke cigarettes and mari-
juana in school bathrooms and sell drugs in school stairwells. They
are opinionated with teachers and wear clothes that offend adults.
They refuse to participate in some classes and organize to change
unfair rules. In fact, there seems to be no imposition of domination
that does not simultaneously create forms of resistance. Hegemony
is never complete. In the moment of rejection of domination lies
the seeds of transformation and liberation.[20]

Clearly, then, schools do not merely replicate domination
with systematic precision. On the contrary, they are places in
which there is an ongoing struggle for control. They are what
Aronowitz and Giroux (1985) call "contested public spheres" that
have the potential to contribute to social transformation. The
Deweyian conception of schools as primary forces of change, and
early Marxist conceptions of schools as mere reflections of more
fundamental economic class relations, have been replaced by a
more subtle and complicated notion of domination and resistance,
one that recognizes the interconnectedness of institutions, the possibilities for human agency, and the real but limited potential for
action in any one place to spark social change.

The pervasiveness of domination as the common mode of
relationship, its extensive presence in a range of cultures and dominant ideologies, and its connection to violence and injustice, suggest two central challenges for those who seek to develop pedagogies of empowerment. First, we must develop a critical
understanding of domination. This calls for the development of a
critical cultural literacy, one that can uncover what Maxine
Greene has called the "taken for granted world" and the ways in
which domination functions in society and in our lives. Most

importantly, it means we must identify and explore the situations that present opportunities for resistance and change.

Second, and I believe even more fundamentally, we must find new modes of relationship which are not based on domination and submission and are not organized into hierarchies of the powerful and powerless. For although thought and action are intricately connected in praxis, we must not confuse our realization of the need for alternatives to domination and our critiques of how domination works with the transformative project of imagining and *creating* new forms of human relationships. This calls for alternative ways of *thinking* about ourselves, our communities, and our world. More profoundly, it calls for developing new ways of *being* with other people that can nourish emerging critical awareness and nurture a new set of needs and desires in everyday experience. This does not mean that models for these alternative ways of thinking and relating do not already exist. Rather, it acknowledges the need for identifying where alternatives to domination are being developed and extending their spheres of practice, as well as for exploring and struggling to develop radically new modes of relationship. This search is the central focus of this book: to identify and explore, in theory and experience, forms of relationship that can nourish self and social empowerment.

Empowerment

In the past twelve years, empowerment has emerged as a important theme in the women's movement, in community organizing and the rise of the "new populism," and in the progressive movements for peace and social justice of the '70s and '80s. In the past decade, and particularly in the last five years, the concept and process of empowerment have emerged as a focus of research in the social science and educational literature as well.[21] Most discussions of empowerment state or imply that large numbers of people in this society are disempowered and that the experience of powerlessness must be emphasized in grappling with social problems. The idea and term *empowerment* emerged as a direct response to analyses of powerlessness and critiques of social structures and social forms that perpetuate domination and the corresponding urge to understand, identify, and describe processes through which individuals and communities create alternatives to domination. Thus empowerment is seen as a process that demands both personal and institutional change. It is a personal transformation out of silence and submission that is characterized by the development of an authentic voice. It is a social process of self-assertion in one's world.

Despite the fact that the term *empowerment* has an expanding presence in a broad range of fields and contexts, it has too often been used as a rhetorical device without being carefully defined by its wielders. However, several theorists have taken the time to more carefully develop the idea of empowerment to make it a substantive concept. Perhaps the purest and simplest definition running throughout this literature is that *empowerment is a process through which people and/or communities increase their control or mastery of their own lives and the decisions that affect their lives.* Alone, however, this definition is incomplete and leaves out several important aspects of empowerment.

On one level empowerment is described as a psychological process. It is intimately connected with individual's feelings of self-worth and self-confidence and sense of efficacy. But empowerment is also inseparably linked to the social and political conditions in which people live. In his discussion of empowerment as it relates to healing, Richard Katz points to the central issue of empowerment being access to and control of valued resources. Thus he suggests not only that empowerment involves a psychological process, but that it is directly related to the allocation and distribution of resources as well. The link between the psychological and the social is also explored by Barbara Solomon (1976), who writes with regard to social work with oppressed groups. She stresses that empowerment is a process through which people increase skills at exercising interpersonal influence and performing valued social roles. Charles Kieffer (1981), in his study of community activists, builds on this by showing that empowerment is a process through which individuals develop "participatory competence." Empowerment involves individuals gaining control of their lives and fulfilling their needs, in part, as a result of developing the competencies, skills, and abilities necessary to effectively participate in their social and political worlds. An essential component in this process is the development of a critical awareness of one's social condition and society in general: that is, the development of a critical cultural literacy, the ability to critically analyze one's social and political world on multiple levels as a prelude to and integral component of action.[22]

Julian Rappaport (1981) notes that empowerment marks a movement away from a paternalistic notion of "helping" as a way of addressing individuals' needs and deficiencies to a notion of *change* that focuses on assuring individuals and communities of their *rights and responsibilities*. It moves from an imagery and symbolism that relies on others to solve our problems to one that fosters a belief in our capacities to help ourselves and others.

Virtually all serious discussions of empowerment emphasize the importance of community—of support and shared struggle in the process of empowerment. Empowerment comes through mutual dialogue and shared work to improve the lives of particular individuals while at the same time trying to improve the lives of all individuals in a particular community. Individual empowerment is tied to community empowerment. Thus the empowerment of an individual teacher is tied to the empowerment of all teachers in her or his school community. The empowerment of an individual assembly-line worker is connected to the empowerment of all co-workers in the same factory and to changing the structure of decision making in the workplace they share. Thus empowerment is often described as a process of individual *and* group transformation in which individuals and groups come to develop "mastery of their lives" and "control of valued resources" and to develop skills in "interpersonal influence" and "participatory competence" through group problem-solving and collective action. Most empowerment theorists see individual and community destinies as interdependent and mutually reinforcing.

While it was frequently mentioned by progressive educators for many years, empowerment has only in the past five years begun to appear with any regularity in educational literature. More lately, in the past few years, the term *empowerment* has begun to saturate the rhetoric of school reform across the political spectrum. For the most part in the educational literature, the focus has been on the empowerment of teachers and much less frequently on the empowerment of students. The term has become a mainstay of the Association for Supervision and Curriculum Development, of teachers' unions, of the school reform movement, and of the teacher education reform movement. The journal *Language Arts* devoted a special issue to empowerment, and professional conferences have focused on empowerment as an overriding theme. Recently, Leslie Ashcroft (1987) has gone so far as to call for "empowering" to be the basis of a philosophy of education. And in recent discourses in critical and feminist pedagogy the term is increasingly invoked and developed directly.[23]

Not surprisingly, as the theme of empowerment has begun to enter into mainstream discourses of educational change, it has begun to be drained of its critical edge. That is, in groups such as ASCD, empowerment retains its participatory meaning but loses its connection to critiques of domination and oppression. Deprived of this social/historical context, empowerment is transformed from a generative theme for democratic and liberatory change into a technique for the "effective" delivery of educational services. [24]

The Problem of Power in Empowerment

The diverse and compelling body of work that has emerged on empowerment in the past ten years has opened up an exciting and contested new area of research. The empowerment theories cited above are provocative contributions to our understanding of the processes and conditions that help individuals and groups move toward freedom and equality. In the early 1980s, as I began to develop an interest in the concept of empowerment, I was struck by the fact that *power* is its root word. This presented an apparent contradiction: the pervasive conceptions of power in our culture and emerging definitions and descriptions of empowerment seemed to be in conflict. Predominant theories of power define power in terms of the ability to control others, to impose one's will on others. Power is viewed in terms of relationships of domination. This is the conception of power as *power over*. [25]

Empowerment theories, in specifically addressing the problem of powerlessness and racism, in seeking to maximize the power of individuals and groups (particularly oppressed groups), in criticizing paternalism and arguing for collaboration and participation, in seeking to equitably distribute resources, and in seeking to enhance individuals' capacities for full participation in a reinvigorated democratic process, reject modes of relationship based on domination. They distinguish self-assertion from self-imposition. Rosenman puts it well: "Empowerment for an individual means the development and use of mechanisms which allow control over individual and community destinies to be exercised without the oppressive and unjust restraint of others" (Rosenman 1980, 252). In rejecting relationships of inequality, control, and domination as antithetical to empowerment, theories of empowerment seemed to reject power as an integrally positive dimension of empowerment. The contradictory implication is that empowerment means transcending power.

Moreover, a closer examination of discussions of empowerment yields few direct explorations of how our conceptions of power fit into the process of empowerment.[26] While it is useful to see empowerment as the process by which people come to have control over their lives, the avoidance of dealing directly with the issue and concept of power points to a failure of many empowerment theories to substantively address the nature of relationships among people who are in the process of becoming empowered and in the actions of empowered people. This points to a theoretical gap in developing discussions of empowerment: empowerment is a theory in search of a compatible conception of power.

The conflict between the common conceptions of power and theories of empowerment raises fundamental questions: How can a theory of empowerment be incompatible with predominant notions of power? Must power be conceived in terms of domination? In terms of coercion and force? As *power over?* Are there alternative conceptions of power that may be more consistent with emerging empowerment theories?

In relation to education, a central pedagogical question that emerges from this discussion is: What are the nature and dynamics of power relations in empowering classrooms? More specifically, how do teachers and students relate to one another in empowering classrooms? How do students relate to their peers? Put differently, what is the nature of power that empowers and is empowering?

Aronowitz and Giroux (1985) are concerned with empowerment as a central dynamic of "emancipatory" education. They argue for the importance of going beyond critique and developing a "language of possibility" that can offer new possibilities for democratic social relations and educational theory and practice that can play a role in the creation of these new possibilities. They note the limits of the conception of power "defined primarily as a negative force that works in the interests of domination" (p. 154). Such a conception of power is only able to contribute to analyses that explain how school practices reproduce domination. They accurately observe that if schools are truly to be seen as places in which teachers and students can develop approaches to teaching and learning that contribute to the struggle for a more democratic and just society, then the predominant conception of power as domination will have to be "rescued." They go on to argue that power must be seen as both a positive and negative force, "something that works both on and through people. . . . Its character will have to be viewed as dialectical . . . as both enabling and constraining" (p. 216).

Jean Baker Miller (1976) offers encouragement in this search for alternative concepts of power:

We need to raise the question of the nature and psychological meaning of power and self-determination, lest we misconstrue both women's advantages and liabilities for this struggle. The words "power" and "self-determination" have acquired certain connotations, that is they imply certain modes of behavior more typical of men than women. But it may be that these modes are not necessary or essential to their meaning. Like all the concepts and actions of a dominant group, "power" may have been distorted and skewed. (p. 115)

Indeed, the challenge of disentangling the concept of power from its patriarchal moorings is the central focus of this book. In this I am deeply indebted to feminist theorists, both inside and outside the field of education, who have led the way in challenging our dominant notions of power. Loosed from the reigns of patriarchal perspectives and armed with courageous honesty, fierce insight, and the experiences of millennia of suffering and subjugation, feminists have not only presented us with searing analyses of the nature of domination, but they have also brought to our awareness both the reality and possibility of power relationships not based on relationships of domination.

In the following pages I seek to more clearly understand the nature of power that empowers and to more carefully explore the interpersonal dynamics of power in empowering relationships. This effort is synonymous with the larger quest to identify and explore the nature, dynamics, and possibilities of human power relationships that are not defined by relationships of domination. It is my hope that the discussion that follows will contribute to an emerging language of possibility in education and to the development of pedagogies of empowerment that can sow and cultivate the seeds of liberatory and democratic social change.

Notes

1. "The Yellow Wall-Paper" was originally written in 1899 by Gilman and brought from obscurity in 1973 when it was republished by the Feminist Press.

2. I am not saying that all forms of domination—e.g., racism, sexism, classism, anti-semitism, ableism, heterosexism—are characterized by the identical dynamics of domination as described in "The Yellow Wall-Paper." Foucault notes that "quite specific relations of domination ... have

their own configuration and relative autonomy" (Foucault 1980b, 188). He argues that each relation of domination needs to be analyzed in its particularity—as well as for its similarities to other forms of domination. Many women, because of their roles as wives and mothers, are in unique positions of intimacy with men. This intimacy is one particular specificity that creates conditions for particular technologies and dynamics of domination that may not exist in other relationships of domination. Nevertheless, it is my contention that there is a fundamental commonality in power dynamics among all forms of domination. I believe "The Yellow Wall-Paper" compellingly captures many of these dynamics.

3. The name is a pseudonym.

4. The name is a pseudonym.

5. The name is a pseudonym.

6. From a fund-raising brochure, "Jones Alumni Humanities Chair."

7. See note 6.

8. Several theorists quoted in this paper use the term *man* and male pronouns ostensibly to refer to all humans, male and female. While these quotations may at times be difficult to read because of their gender-exclusive language, I have chosen to leave them as they were written. I have done this because this is the way they *were* written. The quotations represent the words the theorists chose to write and therefore represent the writers' thinking and bias more accurately than any altered language might. I choose, however, to use gender-inclusive language in my own writing.

9. The concept of the "hidden curriculum" as developed by a range of theorists over the past twenty years is a powerful concept for understanding and describing the unstated and often hidden ways schools and schooling affect students (Giroux and Purpel 1983).

10. Silberman 1970, Goodlad 1983, and Sizer 1984 are three examples of extensive on-site observational studies that revealed similar realities in schools.

11. The degree of centralization of decision making in schools varies by state and region, as well as along urban and suburban lines. For instance, social studies teachers in affluent suburban Massachusetts schools for the most part have wide latitude to choose curriculum materials and teaching methods, while in a Boston high school all students in U.S. History must take the same tests. A recent survey of urban teachers (Olson 1988) reflects these observations and points to increasing feelings of powerlessness among urban teachers. Nevertheless, while teachers' experiences of powerlessness may vary by degrees, the overwhelming evidence of teachers' experiences and recent research clearly indicates that to

an extremely high degree teachers have not been included as full partners in the fiscal, personnel, and curriculum decisions that affect their professional lives.

12. Recent innovations in "school-based management" such as in the Dade County, Florida, public schools (Fiske 1988) reflect this trend, as does the fact that *teacher empowerment* was one of the most repeated phrases at the 1988 Association for Supervision and Curriculum Development (ASCD) annual convention in Boston.

13. However, increased teacher participation in school decision making is not a panacea for pedagogical change in U.S. education. Even in those schools in which teachers have been, or are becoming, invested with real decision-making power, the possibility of pedagogical change and innovation is often limited by teachers' own educational experiences. The strength and pervasiveness of predominant cultural norms creates obstacles to teachers' transcending their traditional roles as banking educators. For the most part we have been educated with banking methods and teacher education programs that rarely explore alternatives to banking education with any real depth or substance. In addition, the widespread contempt of U.S. teachers for educational theory, especially theory that connects schooling to the wider social and political culture and sees education as a vehicle for social change, creates barriers to the development of pedagogical alternatives. As a result, while increasing teacher participation in decision making is an important step forward for many reasons, it is unclear, even doubtful, whether increased teacher participation in school management and curriculum decision making *inherently* leads to the development of approaches to teaching that are not based on the premises of banking education. This is not meant to "blame" teachers for banking education, but rather to point to their complex and often contradictory roles and experiences within the pervasive web of banking education.

14. John Brenkman has defined domination as: "the socially organized forms of exploitation, coercion, and non-reciprocity which structure the uses that one individual or group make of another for the satisfaction of its own need." (Brenkman 1987, 128).

15. Reaganomics and the "trickle down" theory are perfect examples of this kind of thinking. The selfishness and individualism of the policies are veiled in a cloak of a rhetoric of social benevolence.

16. Phyllis Schlafly (1977) articulates this perspective in unusual depth.

17. There is a tendency in critical pedagogy, however, to reduce experience to ideology—to fail to fully distinguish human practices and experiences from human consciousness of practices and experiences. Intertwined as they are, experience and consciousness are distinct, and

each must be explored on its own terms to fully understand the dynamics of domination. Feminists in particular have explored the power of relationships of domination to reproduce themselves, in particular in traditional family structures and their psychodynamics of interpersonal relationships. In particular see the works of Chodorow (1978), Dinnerstein (1976), and Miller (1983). Bowles and Gintis (1986) discuss how similar dynamics of reproduction occur in other sites of domination as well.

18. Many other theorists have been developing and expanding theories of human agency and the potential for individual (and group) action for change. Gramsci's discussion of hegemony includes the possibility of such action. Some more contemporary theorists addressing these issues include Bowles and Gintis (1986), Giroux (1983, 1988) and Freire (1970). It is not within the scope of this book to outline a theory of change and human agency.

19. In critical educational theory Giroux 1983, Willis 1977, Apple 1979, and McRobbie 1978 are important works on resistance. Outside the field of education, particularly powerful work on resistance is emerging in feminist applications and extensions of Michel Foucault's work. For instance see Welch 1985 and Diamond and Quinby 1988.

20. Apple (1979, 1982), Willis (1977), and Giroux (1983) have eloquently pointed out some of the complex relationships between domination and resistance in schooling.

21. For important early discussions of the concept see Berger and Neuhaus 1977, Solomon 1976, Rappaport 1981, Katz 1983/84, Kieffer 1983/84, and Gross 1985.

22. See Berger and Neuhaus 1977, Rappaport 1981, Rosenman 1980, Solomon 1976, and Kieffer 1981.

23. See Shor and Freire (1987), McLaren (1988), Giroux (1988a and b), Weiler (1988), Gore (1989), and Simon (1957).

24. In her discussion of the rhetoric of teacher empowerment, Jennifer Gore (1989) identifies three emerging discourses on empowerment: empowerment as constructed by discourses of professionalism, empowerment as constructed by discourses of liberal humanism, and empowerment as constructed by discourses of critical educational theory. She is particularly insightful in her analysis of Maeroff 1988, which she argues does not significantly challenge existing power relations in schools, encourages competition among teachers, lacks a vision of the future, and essentially blames teachers and their "self-imposed" low self-esteem for the current "crisis" in education. She argues that empowerment here is essentially reduced to "superficial changes to existing arrangements which boil down to making teachers 'better' at implementing goals of authorities" (Gore 1989, 7).

25. As far as I can determine, Mary Parker Follett (1924, 1942) was the first to develop *power over* as a specific construct for the analysis of power.

26. Gross 1985 and Ashcroft 1987 are two recent exceptions. Ashcroft's article in particular is an important contribution to our understanding of the nature of power in empowerment in the field of education.

2

Power Over: The Predominant Conception of Power

(Captions to a series of nine drawings of a man dressed as a beach lifeguard.)

> I walk around the beach all day—
> In a pith helmet, sweat shirt, red trunks and a whistle—
> So everybody thinks I'm a lifeguard—
> Which I am not—
> And any time I see some guy bigger, better looking and more muscular than me making out with a girl—
> I blow my whistle at him—
> And I yell 'Hey you, get away from there'—
> And I let him off with a tongue-lashing and a warning—
> and *I* take the girl.—
> *POWER.*
>
> Jules Feiffer quoted in Woodhead (1970, 150)

Recently I asked a group of tenth-grade students to state the first words or images that came to mind when they heard and saw the word *power*. Their responses included: money, parents, life, Mike Tyson, football coaches, happiness, authority, greed, selfishness, overbearing, commanding, control, force, strength, light switch, sun, earth, kings and queens, nuclear arms, bullying people around, Adolph Hitler. I also asked the same question of a group of undergraduate and graduate students who were studying to become teachers. Their responses were remarkably similar, although perhaps a bit more negative. They included: domination, abuse, greed, control, fist, elites, football, authority, nuclear, superiority, anger, scared, destruction, powerlessness, bad, strength, inequality, bolt of lightning.

I have asked this question of many students, teachers, and administrators over the past several years with similar results. We overwhelmingly associate power with relationships of domination, conflict, violence, evil, selfishness, hierarchy, and victimization. In fact, the first meaning of power given in *Webster's Third International Dictionary of the English Language* (1981, 1778) is "A position of ascendancy; ability to compel obedience; CONTROL, DOMINION." This conception of power permeates our lives. Indeed, our most common meanings and associations are accurately captured in the Feiffer cartoon: power is the ability to get one's way, to intimidate, to manipulate, to "take the girl," to win.

Our multiple forms of mass media overflow with similar images of power as force and violence. Television is a particularly effective conveyer of images, meanings, and messages. For example, professional wrestling represents our modern-day morality plays in which the forces of good and evil are represented by 275-pound men pounding one another mercilessly to the mat. The underlying message of professional wrestling is that, whether "good" or "evil," power is represented by brute physical force and the ability to assert oneself, mentally and physically, over another. "Good" power resides in the person who plays "by the rules" until goaded beyond self-control, at which point breaking the rules is seen as perfectly justified. Professional football functions in a similar vein, projecting vivid images and messages about the nature of power: of its inherent violence, its necessary pain, and the unceasing struggle to win. Boxing, too, and its glorification of brute bloody conquest mixed with pervasive racism, is perhaps the purest expression of the link between violence and power.

But sports television is only one aspect of the medium that transmits electronic images of power. Afternoon and evening soap operas, from "Dallas" and "Dynasty" to "Days of Our Lives," are psychological battlefields for control, presenting perpetual competition for self-fulfillment, often at the expense of others. Dallas's J. R. Ewing embodies the ruthless, selfish, and isolated man of power. His pathetic loneliness is overshadowed by his ability to get what he wants by whatever means at his disposal. Then too, there is the pervasive presence of "crime-time television," which depicts a world on the verge of chaos in which only the organized might of the police ("Miami Vice," "Hill Street Blues") or the isolated effort of the vigilante (the "Enforcer," the "A-Team," "Dirty Harry") can impose any order. Perhaps even more disturbing is how deeply these images of power and violence seep into children's television as well. The extremely popular war cartoons such as "G.I. Joe," "Rambo," "Transformers," and "Captain Power and the Soldiers of the Future" contain an average of forty-eight violent acts each half hour. These shows communicate and legitimize a view of social relationships characterized by mutual aggression and violence grounded in a battle for control, superiority, and the "good." They communicate stark messages about the nature of power and viable methods of conflict resolution in our society.

These images of power are not reserved for viewers of sports, dramatic, and children's television programming alone. Television news thrives on "reporting" on battles for political, economic, and military control to the masses through shows such as the evening news, "20/20," and "60 Minutes," not to mention new syndicated shows such as "A Current Affair." A PBS miniseries called "The Power Game" was billed as a "riveting and candid look at the real Washington. The famous and the faceless. The players and the pawns. And the power games they play." We were invited to meet "people you've never heard of who are calling the signals on power plays that affect you every day" (*New Republic*, 1988). Reports on the workings of government, the realities of wars, the intricacies of corporate takeovers, and negative political campaigns are news, and it is important to know about them. However, by reflecting these aspects of our society back to us, usually uncritically, television plays a major role in shaping and reinforcing our images and ideas of power as *power over*.

But television is only one medium for communicating these cultural messages. Popular movies, magazines, newspapers, books, video games, rock videos, advertising, and popular music all perform similar functions. It is no exaggeration to say that our ears, eyes, minds, and hearts are surrounded and continuously bombarded by a steady and pervasive stream of images of power as a relationship of domination.

In his best-selling book *Power: How to Get It, How to Use It,* Michael Korda (1975) describes our culture's "power game":

> All life is a game of power. The object of the game is simple enough: to know what you want and get it. The moves of the game, by contrast, are infinite and complex, although they usually involve the manipulation of people and situations to your advantage. (p. 4)

There are many symbols of power. As a vivid example, Korda describes the power symbols in the business world:

David Mahoney's enormous office, with a view of the midtown Manhattan skyline and both rivers, is a symbol of power and an obvious one, but so are his carefully cut blue suit, his Gucci loafers, his midwinter tan and his command of a limousine. (p. 212)

Here power is clearly connected to ascendancy and command. He emphasizes that even the smallest details reflect on an individual's ambitions and inclinations. "One thing is basic: power people like to have their shoes polished, or do it themselves," he writes. "In all shoe-wearing cultures, and in every age, a dirty shoe is a sign of weakness" (p. 209).

Power is accumulated. It is a scarce resource to be coveted, hoarded, and used in one's own interests. In interactions of power there are winners and losers, powerful and powerless. From this perspective we are basically alone and in constant competition with others. Korda puts it bluntly: "No matter who you are, the basic truth is that your interests are nobody else's concern, your gain is inevitably someone else's loss, your failure someone else's victory" (p. 4).

A special issue of *M: The Civilized Man* (1986) on "Real Power and How Men Use It" amplifies Korda's perspective:

It isn't only the heads of nations who have it and use it. In a world of global markets for virtually every commodity, including culture, it's possible to dominate territories and populations as much by controlling a corporate entity as by controlling a state. . . . The exercise of this new global power is more subtle and gradual than the political kind; a corporate chief, for example, usually cannot at a word have his enemies thrown into prison, though he may eventually be able to ruin them. But a company head can, with his decisions on production, pricing, and distribution of products, have as much impact on the lives of millions as any politician, short of one who declares war. These men control the food we eat, the clothes we wear, the drugs we're allowed when ill, and even the news, information and entertainment we receive. (p. 67)

What makes these men "civilized" is left unclear; what is clear is that relationships of control and domination are at the heart of the predominant notion of power in this culture and that these power relationships extend throughout the breadth of the institutions in which we live and work. A recent issue of the monthly magazine *Regardies,* which reaches primarily the Washington, D.C., local political and business community, captured this notion of power succinctly. They selected the "100 most powerful people in private Washington for 1988." The Editor's Note informs us, "The people who made our list are those who share one common trait: they're able to get other people to do what they want them to do" ("The Power Elite" 1988, 9)

In sum, not only are relationships of domination pervasive throughout our experiences of work, politics, education, and family, but these experiences of domination and submission create and at the same time limit our understanding of power. But I want to argue the opposite as well: *our particular conceptions of power also create and limit our experiences of relationship.* Thus we are caught in a conceptual and experiential straightjacket. Michel Foucault argues a similar point when he links power and knowledge. In fact, he presents them as one concept: 'power/knowledge'. He observes that "the exercise of power perpetually creates knowledge and, conversely, knowledge constantly induces effects of power" (Foucault 1980a, 52).

Foucault argues that it is in *discourse* that power/knowledge are joined together. He notes:

> in a society such as ours, but basically in any society, there are manifold relations of power which permeate, characterize and constitute the social body, and these relations of power cannot themselves be established, consolidated nor implemented without the production, accumulation, circulation and functioning of a discourse. There can be no possible exercise of power without a certain economy of discourses of truth which operates through and on the basis of this association. We are subjected to the production of truth through power and we cannot exercise power except through the production of truth. (p. 93)

Foucault uses *discourse* to refer to a "group of statements that belong to a single system of formation" (Foucault 1972, 107). That is, according to Foucault, a discourse exists whenever a pattern of regularity or a complex group of relations that function as a rule exist between statements, objects, or concepts (Foucault 1972, 39, 74). These patterns and rules determine what must be related, in a particular discourse, for particular statements to be made, for particular concepts to be used, and for particular strategies to be organized. For instance, what counts as a valid "medical statement" in this culture? In the dominant perspective in the field of medicine, known as allopathic medicine, there is a whole set of rules, patterns, and norms for making and justifying statements and forming interpretations that serves to legitimate some statements and interpretations and to invalidate others. These rules emerge, in part, from approaches to knowledge and truth that undergird experimental science. As a result, the statements, assumptions, interpretive methods, and healing practices of chiropractic, homeopathic, and a whole range of other "alternative" healing systems do not follow the rules of discourse that serve to legitimate statements about health and healing in this culture. In addition, practitioners of these alternative healing arts are limited by both law and custom in the manner in which they can practice and speak their knowledge. Thus, the defining characteristics of a discourse determine the underlying rules for both what and how things can be said as well as *"who can speak with authority and who must listen"* (emphasis in original text) (McLaren 1988, 180). Furthermore, the contours and limits of the dominant medical discourse in this country not only are intricately related to who has power in the field of medicine, but on the most fundamental levels they also are connected to nature of our medical institutions and the kinds of medical practices we experience each time we see a "doctor."

Sharon Welch (1985) points out that Foucault challenges the traditional distinctions between discursive practices (ideas, texts, theories, and the use of language) and nondiscursive practices (social systems, class divisions, economic needs, institutions), and that it is in the exploration of the relations between these practices that the links between domination and knowledge are illuminated. She observes that attention to how changes in discourse correlate with changes in institutional practices leads us to see, understand, and be "attentive to the power of language and ideas, to their imbeddedness in networks of social and political control" (Welch 1985, 16, 17). Indeed, Foucault argues that knowledge and control conspire in the production of "regimes of truth":

> Each society has a regime of truth, its "general politics" of truth: that is, the types of discourse which it accepts and makes function as true; the mechanisms and instances which enable one to distinguish true and false statements, the means by which each is sanctioned; the techniques and proce-

dures accorded value in the acquisition of truth; the status of those who are charged with saying what counts as true. (Foucault 1980a, 131)

It is my contention that there is, in fact, a dominant discourse of power in modern Western culture, which is reflected in our popular culture, in our institutions, throughout our social relationships, and within the social sciences. This dominant discourse is intricately enmeshed in and reflective of a wider "regime of truth" that has both constrained and produced modern societies.

Power Over: The Dominant Discourse in the Social Sciences

The social sciences are one important location of the dominant discourse on power in Western societies and key sites for the ongoing maintenance and production of the current "regime of truth" concerning power.[1] Bertrand Russell (1938) asserts that "the fundamental concept in social sciences is Power, in the same sense in which energy is the fundamental concept in physics" (p. 12). While Russell's argument for the primacy of power in explaining and understanding human interaction has been debated, it is undeniable that the concept of power—its nature, sources, and functions— has been and remains a central concern of social scientists, social activists, politicians, corporate leaders, and philosophers alike.[2]

Indeed, a survey of modern theories of power reveals wide disagreement as to the definition and boundaries of the concept. Different theorists find different dimensions of power interesting and worthy of study, and there seems to be no common terminology. David Nyberg (1981) describes the range of perspectives on power that have currency today:

Power has been regarded as an end in itself, and as a means to other ends. As a means it is sometimes seen as a subcategory of influence, but influence is sometimes seen as a subcategory of power. Persuasion is regarded as the opposite of power, though it can also be an example of it, while manipulation is taken to be an aspect of both, of neither, or of power alone. Some claim that force is the root of all forms of power; others drastically limit its role. Violence has been regarded as the opposite of power and as its very essence. It can be argued that power and authority are inextricably related or that the two are separate and categorically different.

Many maintain that power is an aspect of organization, of status, of position, and not characteristic of individuals. This can mean that class structure determines all forms of power, but some would insist that this is the work of hierarchy. Some believe that the traditional, economic, or legal bases for sanctioning social behavior are the deep clues to the nature of power. But to some people sanction means coercive intervention as a means of enforcement, while to others it means the exercise of moral authority, or "authorization."

Power is regarded as a controlled exchange of goods and services at all levels of social life, but can it not also be seen as the consequence of the breakdown of such an exchange system? It is spoken of as a possession and as an attribute of certain activities—thus one may or may not "have" it even while one "exercises" it.

In short, many patterns of relation have been proposed to define power, but none has succeeded in attracting consensus. (p. 35)

Nevertheless, despite this lack of agreement on a variety of important issues in theories of power in the social sciences, it is my contention that, among most prominent discourses of power, there *is* wide agreement as to the fundamental underlying nature and definition of power.

In fact, most prominent definitions of power share a common conception of power as a *relationship of domination,* as *power over.* Dominating relationships are characterized by inequality: situations in which one individual or group of individuals, in order to fulfill their own desires, have the ability to control the behavior, thoughts, and/or values of another individual or group of individuals. The relationship of domination is described through the *language of imposition.* Its vocabulary includes words such as *control, force, coercion, manipulation, sanctioning, obedience,* and *submission,* and phrases such as *overcoming resistance, getting others to do what you want,* and *gaining compliance.* While the debate among contemporary power theorists rages unabated, this common language reveals the shared conceptual base that undergirds most theories of power.

Three Foundations of Contemporary Power Theory

Most theories of power in the social sciences draw on similar foundations in their definitions of power. This tradition, actually going back to Plato, Aristotle, and Thucydides, is commonly grounded in Thomas Hobbes's definition of power. Hobbes was among the first theorists to attempt an explicit definition of power. His formulation grew out of the modern scientific revolution sparked by thinkers such as Kepler, Galileo, Bacon, and Descartes. Among the most important developments in the scientific revolution was the emergence of the mechanistic view of nature: the description of reality in terms of relations of linear cause and effect. Hobbes's contribution was to make among the earliest thorough attempts to use the mechanistic metaphor to describe human relations.

In *De Corpore* Hobbes presents his underlying conception of power:

> Correspondent to cause and effect are POWER and ACT; nay those and these are the same things. . . . For whenever any agent has all those accidents which are necessarily requisite for the production of some effect in the patient, then we say the agent has power to produce that effect, if it be applied to a patient. (Hobbes [1656] 1962, 126)

In human relationships, power is the accumulation, by the individual, of the means (e.g., wealth, reputation) by which she or he can obtain what she or he desires. Hobbes summarizes this conception in *Leviathan:* "The power of a man (to take it universally) is his present means to obtain some future apparent good" (Hobbes [1651] 1984, 150).

Hobbes's conception of power reveals his application of the mechanistic notions of the physical sciences to the social realm. Power is defined by relations of cause and effect: in fact, for Hobbes, "POWER = CAUSE." In human relations, power is the ability to fulfill one's desires; that is, to cause those effects that will allow for the fulfillment of individual desires. Hobbes argues that since individual desires inevitably conflict with the desires of others, power involves the ability to affect another, to cause another to act, think, or speak in a particular way. He notes: "And because the power of one man resisteth and hindereth the effects of the power of another: power simply is no more, but the excess of the power of one above that of another" (p. 35). There is no escaping the competition for power, for Hobbes claims "a general inclination of all mankind, a perpetual and restless desire for power after power, that ceaseth only in death" (p. 161).

Hobbes's discussion of power is better understood in the context of his notions of human nature and human society. For Hobbes, the "natural" human condition is "solitary, poor, brutish and short." That is, humans are ultimately separate and alienated. They are moved to fulfill totally self-centered desires that are in constant conflict with other people's desires for scarce resources. The natural human state is a state of war. Thus, in the struggle for survival the individual will, in all reasonableness, "by force or wiles," seek security by attempting to

> master the persons of all men he can, so long till he see no other power great enough to endanger him; and this is no more than his own conservation requires, and is generally allowed. (p. 184)

In the state of nature there is no alternative to either domination or submission. In seeking gain, safety, and reputation, men "naturally" and inevitably seek power over others.

Hobbes notes, however, that people gain "no pleasure, but on the contrary a great deal of grief, in keeping company where there is no power able to overawe them" (p. 184). It is out of this displeasure with the state of nature that the need and desire for the State, the Sovereign, the Leviathan, is born. Humans need a power greater than themselves to control their desires, for they cannot control themselves.

Thus, predominantly out of fear of one another and their rational evaluation of the raw state of nature, people submit to the Sovereign. The Sovereign enjoys virtually absolute power over his or her subjects. This is necessary to maintain order and is thus in the best interests of most people. As a result, Hobbes finds monarchy the best form of government, best able to contain human beings' natural passions and to assure order.

Hobbes's impact on contemporary theories of power has been significant. He argues that, whether power is exerted in its raw form in the chaotic state of nature or in its more ordered form in the workings of the State and the functioning of the Sovereign, it is fundamentally characterized by individuals controlling others, by relations of domination and submission. Power is conceived as power over others. This conceptualization of power, combined with Hobbes's application of the mechanistic notions of cause and effect to power relations and his view of human beings as essentially separate, in constant conflict for scarce resources, and in need of imposed order, was to have profound influence on most power theories that followed.

While Hobbes's contributions to most twentieth-century power theorists are usually implicit, the work of Max Weber is frequently referred to as an explicit starting point. For Weber (1946) power was

> the chance of a man or of a number of men to realize their own will in a communal action even against the resistance of others who are participating in the action. (p. 180)

Weber's definition points more directly to coercion as a central dimension of power. Power involves the confrontation of wills, where one will "even against resistance" imposes itself on others. Force, or the threat of force, is an essential, perhaps the critical, aspect of Weber's definition. As a result, Weber's conception of power is inextricably connected to violence and coercion.

In speaking about power within political institutions, Weber notes that all political associations, and the state in particular, are defined by control of the use of physical force. "If no social institutions existed which knew the use of violence, then the 'state' would be eliminated" (p. 78). The state has the sole legitimate use of force, and power resides in those who control the state.

Yet while force is the ultimate basis of political power, states do not maintain control through force alone. It is here that Weber develops his notions of legitimate domination. The success of the state, rooted in the monopoly of the legitimate use of force, relies on the fact that the dominated will "obey the authority claimed by the powers that be" (p. 78). This obedience is assured through traditional, charismatic, and rational authority. Individuals representing the state (or other political associations) maintain domination through the willing obedience of others.

Weber builds his analysis of politics on a conception of power as control over others. While power is ultimately based in the ability to coerce, it does not function through the use of physical coercion alone. Power, or at least "legitimate" power, functions within society through complex structures of domination that assure obedience by effectively making the dominated accept their domination.

Weber has much in common with Hobbes: he begins with the individual as his basic unit (p. 55) to which all analyses of social action must be reducible; he defines power in terms of relations of cause and effect (Weber 1968, 4; Clegg 1975, 58); and he sees the field of power relations as one of conflict and competition in which there are winners and losers and in which order is maintained through complex mechanisms of domination.

Bertrand Russell is another theorist frequently mentioned in the literature. In defining power as "the production of intended effects" he clearly follows Hobbes and Weber in describing power in terms of cause and effect. In and of itself Russell's definition is rather benign, if only because it is vague. But lest we be mistaken as to how he understands power, he clarifies his intentions:

> There are various ways of classifying the forms of power, each of which has its utility. In the first place there is power over other human beings and power over dead matter or non-human forms of life. I shall mainly be concerned with power over human beings. (Russell 1938, 36)

For Russell, then, power is manifest in relationships in which humans control the world around them. In social relations power involves individuals controlling others; it is defined by relationships of inequality and domination. Power relations among humans differ from human power relations to plants, animals, and rocks solely in terms of what is being controlled. That this is his perspective is made clear in the rest of his discussion of power, which consists of an exploration of the different "forms" through which people seek, gain, and exert power over others. He describes "leaders and followers," "priestly power," "kingly power," "naked power," "revolutionary power," "economic power," "power over opinion," "the taming of power."

Russell identifies three different ways an individual can exert power over another: by direct physical power over his or her body ("coercion"), by rewards and punishments as inducements ("inducement"), and by influence over opinion ("propaganda"). In each case power involves the "causing of intended effects" through the control or manipulation of others.

Contemporary Definitions of Power

Following Russell in the twentieth century, there has been a flourishing of theory and research on power in the social sciences. Virtually all of the most influential of these theories build on the basic notions introduced by Hobbes, Russell, and especially Weber. For instance, Lasswell and Kaplan's definition of power has been very influential. At the heart of this definition is the control of decision making through the ability to threaten and, if need be, apply severe sanctions:

> Power is a form of influence in which the effect on policy is enforced or expected to be enforced by relatively severe sanctions. Power is participation in the making of decisions: G has power over H with respect to the values K if G participates in the making of decisions affecting the K-policies of H.... A decision is a policy involving severe sanctions (deprivations).... The definition of power in terms of decision making adds an important element to "the production of intended effects on other persons"—namely, the availability of sanctions when the intended effects are not forthcoming." (Lasswell and Kaplan 1950, 74–84)

Following on Russell and Hobbes, Lasswell and Kaplan see power as the ability to create intended effects on other people. The notion of intentionality and linear cause and effect are central to their conception of power, as is the fundamental link between power and imposition. Underlying their definition is a model of community that is characterized by inherent conflict and competition for control of decision making.

Robert Bierstadt (1974), while agreeing with Lasswell and Kaplan's distinction between power and influence, makes a subtle distinction between the use of sanctions and the threat of sanctions:

> Influence is persuasive whereas power is coercive. We submit voluntarily to influence but power requires our submission.... Power is not force and power is not authority, but it is intimately related to both. 1) Power is latent force; 2) force is manifest power, and 3) authority is institutionalized power.... Force means the production of an effect, an alteration in movement or action that overcomes resistance.... In the sociological sense, where it is synonymous with coercion, it compels a change in the course of action of an individual or a group against the wishes of the individual or the group. It means the application of sanctions when they are not willingly received. Only groups that have power can threaten to use force, and the threat itself is power.... Without power there is no organization and without power there is no order. (p. 223–31)

While Bierstadt's distinction between having the potential to impose one's will and the actual use of force is provocative, his underlying belief in the coerciveness of power points even more directly than does Lasswell and Kaplan's definition to the link between power and relationships of domination.

C. Wright Mills made the relationship between power and domination, in particular the nature and functioning of the "power elite," central to his work. One of the most influential sociologists of his time, he defined power as having to do with "whatever decisions men make about the arrangements under which they live, and about the events which make up the history of their period" (Mills 1959, 40). While this definition is vague, it does echo Lasswell and Kaplan's focus on decision making. However, Mills's underlying conception emerges elsewhere and is clearly Weberian. He writes: "By the powerful we mean, of course, those who are able to realize their will, even if others resist" (Mills 1956, 9).

For Mills coercion through violence and the threat of violence represents the base form of power: "All politics is a struggle for power: the ultimate kind of power is violence" (Mills 1956, 171). Nevertheless, he recognizes the variety of mechanisms by which people maintain and exert power:

> Surely in our time we need not argue that, in the last resort, coercion is the final form of power. But we are by no means constantly at the last resort. Authority (power justified by the beliefs of the voluntarily obedient) and manipulation (power wielded unbeknown to the powerless) must also be considered, along with coercion. (Mills 1959, 40–41)

While Mills may disagree with Bierstadt's separation of power and force, his discussion does acknowledge, again in a Weberian vein, that power's most common expression is not through direct coercion, but rather, through more subtle mechanisms for obtaining compliance and obedience.

In contrast to Mills's work stands the work of Robert Dahl and the "pluralist" school of power theory, one of the most influential schools of power theory in contemporary political science. The pluralists challenged both the conceptualization of power and the methodologies for studying power in "power elite" theories such as Mills's.

In his earliest formulation Dahl (1957) produced a behaviorist definition of power: "A has power over B to the extent that he can get B to do something that he would not otherwise do" (p. 203). He offers this example of his definition in action:

> Suppose a policeman is standing in the middle of an intersection at which most of the traffic ordinarily moves ahead; he orders all traffic to turn right or left; the traffic moves as he orders it to do. Then it accords with what I conceive to be the bedrock idea of power to say that the policeman acting in this particular role evidently has the power to make automobile drivers turn right or left rather than go ahead. (pp. 202–3)

In his later, more developed conception of power Dahl (1976) uses the terms *power* and *influence* interchangeably. He explains this development in this way:

> One man's "influence" is another man's "power." For the time being I shall use these terms as if they were interchangeable. ... A influences B to the extent that he changes B's actions or predispositions in some way. (pp. 26, 29)

In this reconceptualization of power and influence, he somewhat ambiguously makes power a subform of influence/power:

> [power acts] when compliance is attained by creating the prospect of severe sanctions for noncompliance. Coercion is a form of power.... Power and coercion do not necessarily require the use or threat of physical force. However, physical force is often involved in power and coercion. (p. 47)

This new, narrow definition of power defines it as coercion; the ability to threaten and, if need be, apply sanctions. This reconceptualization is more in line with Lasswell and Kaplan's and even Mills's distinctions.

Throughout this somewhat confusing evolution of his definition, Dahl consistently defines power (or influence) causally:

> When we single out influence from all the other aspects of a human interaction ... what we focus attention on is that one or more persons in this interaction get what they want, by causing other people to act in some particular way. We want to call attention to a *causal relationship* between what A wants and what B does.... A controls B if A's desires cause a change in B's actions or predispositions. (pp. 30, 44)

Despite the pluralist critique of power elite theories, and whether we take Dahl's earlier or later constructions, Dahl is equally reliant on domination and the language of imposition and causality in his definitions of power. The main distinction between his earlier and later definitions is that in his second formulation power takes on a much narrower, more coercive character.

Responding to Dahl and the pluralist school, Bachrach and Baratz introduce the "second face" of power. They challenge certain parts of Dahl's operationalization of his concept of power and the methodology for studying power that grew out of it. Specifically, they argue that as a result of his behavioral approach Dahl fails to acknowledge that power can be wielded indirectly through the ability to limit what is brought into the public decision-making process.

However, despite their challenge to Dahl and the pluralists, Bachrach and Baratz (1970) accept Dahl's underlying definition of power: "As is perhaps self-evident, there are similarities in both faces of power. In each, A participates in decisions and thereby adversely affects B" (p.7). They then present their own definition:

A power relationship exists when (a) there is a conflict over values or course of action between A and B; (b) B complies with A's wishes; and (c) B does so because he is fearful that A will deprive him of a value or values which he regards more highly than those which would have been achieved by non-compliance. (p.24)

'Conflict,' 'compliance,' 'fear': these concepts remain at the heart of this conception of power.

Stephen Lukes directly takes on both the pluralists and Bachrach and Baratz. In attempting to articulate a "radical" view of power, Lukes presents what he describes as the "third face of power." He criticizes Dahl and Bachrach and Baratz on a variety of levels. Lukes's perspective is radical in that, unlike the first two "faces," it takes into account how social structures function to maintain the interests of certain groups over and against the expressed and latent interests of other groups in society.

Yet while leveling a sharp critique, Lukes (1974) states that he shares a fundamentally similar notion of power with Dahl and Bachrach and Baratz:

The three views we have been considering can be seen as alternative interpretations and applications of one and the same concept of power, according to which A exercises power over B when A affects B in a manner contrary to B's interests. (p. 26)

The "three faces" debate is *not* about the underlying conception of power. Rather, it represents disagreement over the way in which power presents itself and is expressed and maintained in social relationships. For Lukes, as with Dahl and Bachrach and Baratz, power is expressed in the ability of an individual or group to fulfill their interests when they conflict with the interests of others. Each seeks to discover and understand when, where, and how individuals and groups exert and maintain control over others.

Finally, Peter Blau's work reflects the perspective of exchange theory, a bold attempt to apply market theories to the understanding and explanation of power dynamics. Nevertheless, Blau's definition of power is strikingly similar to the ones cited above, if perhaps most stark in its use of the language of imposition. He leaves no doubt that he fundamentally sees power involving hierarchy, domination, and compliance in the face of real or potential threats:

> Power is the ability of persons as groups to impose their will on others despite resistance through deterrence either in the form of withholding regularly supplied rewards or in the form of punishment in as much as the former, as well as the latter, constitutes in effect negative sanction.... Physical coercion, or its threat, is the polar case of power, but other negative sanctions, or the threat of exercising them, are usually also effective means of imposing one's will on others.... Differentiation of power arises in the course of competition for scarce goods. (Blau 1964, 116, 117, 141)[3]

Power Over and Masculinity

As we have seen, the predominant images and interpretations of power in our culture embody a conception of power as the ability to impose one's will on others as the means toward fulfilling one's desired goals. It is the ability to direct and control and to manipulate and coerce if need be, sometimes for the good of all, most often for the good of the few. Power is embodied in images of the father, the teacher, the political leader, the policeman, the soldier, and the businessman. In a world of domination and submission, the ability to control others, for men in particular, is seen as an archetypical expression of identity, a confirmation of meaningful existence. It not only says "I am," but "I am on top," "I am special," "I have power."

It is difficult not to notice the link between men and *power over* in the images and conceptions of power that have been presented. Feminists have persistently pointed out that notions of "healthy" adult identity that focus on individuality, separation, autonomy, invulnerability, and control are much more characteristic of male development in this culture than of women's development.[4] They also point to the destructiveness of viewing these male patterns of development as models of health, for men and women alike. Nancy Hartsock (1983) explores the links between Western masculinity and Western manifestations and conceptions of power as domination:

> In the literature on power social scientists have frequently alluded to the links between virility and domination. For example, one scholar introduced a book on concepts of power, influence and authority with the statement that the first is linked with notions of potency, virility, and masculinity and "appears much sexier than the other two." Or consider philosopher Bertrand de Jouvenal's note that "a man feels himself more of a man when imposing himself and making others the instrument of his will." And what are we to make of Robert Penn Warren's statement that "masculinity is closely tied to every form of power in our society," or Henry Kissinger's telling but perhaps apocryphal remark, "Power is the ultimate aphrodisiac"? One must conclude that the associative links between manliness, virility, power and domination are very strong in Western culture. (p. 6)

Hartsock goes on to argue that in this society power carries a "masculine gender." Our conceptions of power have grown out of and reflected the experience of masculinity in this culture; particularly the experience of masculine sexuality.

Beneath the "polite language of sexual reciprocity," Hartsock uncovers "not only one-sided relations of domination and submission, but also dynamics of hostility, revenge, and fascination with death" (p. 176). Her thesis is that these masculine sexual dynamics are rooted in the male fear of intimacy and "fusion" with others, male denial of the body and fears of death, and male fears of women's powers of generativity and reproduction. She argues that these fears and their manifestations in the male experience of sexuality play a central role in shaping the nature of relationships in human communities in this society. Thus they profoundly influence the material dynamics of power relations, and our conceptions of power as well. She concludes that the

> masculine gender carried by power intensifies the tensions of community and leads to the construction of an even more conflictual and false community than that formed by means of exchange. It is a community both in theory and in fact obsessed with revenge and structured by conquest and domination. (p. 177)

Adrienne Rich (1976) links men and *power over* directly, drawing connections to relationships of domination that run across society:

> It would seem therefore that from very ancient times the identity, the very personality, of the man depends on power, and on power in a certain, specific sense: that of *power over others,* beginning with a woman and her children. The ownership of human beings proliferates: from primitive or arranged marriage through contractual marriage-with-dowry through more recent marriage "for love" but involving the economic dependency of the wife, through the feudal system, through slavery and serfdom. The powerful (mostly male) make decisions for the powerless: the well for the sick, the middle-aged for the aging, the "sane" for the "mad," the educated for the illiterate, the influential for the marginal. (p. 49)

Rich goes on to make an important observation: those who hold power over others can "take a short-cut through the complexity of human personality." That is, they can remain separate from the powerless, closed to their feelings, experiences, to their "souls." They do not have to hear or try to understand the voices of the powerless, "their many languages, including the language of silence" (p.49). Thus the *power over* relationship cuts off human communication and creates barriers to human empathy and understanding. This separation from and deafness to the experiences of the powerless creates the space in which domination is exerted and thrives.

The link between *power over,* masculinity, and everyday relationships in schools and classrooms is not remote. Joe Clark, the
baseball-bat-wielding Patterson, New Jersey, high school principal
who has been canonized by William Bennett and Ronald Reagan,
has said, "Don't give me male administrators.... They turn on you.
But women unhappy at home—in their forties and fifties, after
menopause, when they're more consistent—can give untiringly to
me of their services" (Kirp 1989, 39). A recent advertisement
appeals for new recruits to teaching in bold black print: "REACH
FOR THE POWER: TEACH." The text of the ad is somewhat ambigu-
ous; it calls on people to "wake up young minds, wake up the
world" (there are many ways to "wake people up"), but the picture
in the ad leaves no confusion as to the nature of the power appeal.
A white male in shirt and tie, arm raised to the blackboard,
"Odyssey" and "Iliad" written on the backboard (calling up images
of Greek warrior heroes), stands over blurred and barely visible
students —masculinity, the hero, control, and status are all
entwined in this representation of power. The advertisers' recruitment strategy is clear, and their use of the predominant notion of
power in this culture to appeal to potential teachers is revealing.

Power Over and the Scarcity Paradigm

Western views of power reflect and grow out of a particular
way of explaining reality. In this construction, which shaped and
was shaped by the scientific revolution and the mechanistic
metaphor, reality is perceived as composed of "discrete and separate entities, be they rocks, plants, atoms, people" (Macy 1982, 30).
The physical and social world is like a machine, made up of individual intricately ordered parts working together. Carolyn Merchant
(1980) observes:

> The mechanical view of nature now taught in most Western
> schools is accepted without question as our everyday, common
> sense reality—matter is made up of atoms, colors occur by
> the reflection of light waves of differing lengths, bodies obey
> laws of inertia, the sun is in the center of our solar system.
> None of this was common sense to our seventeenth century
> counterparts. (p. 193)

At the heart of this view is the belief in an objective reality that
functions through relations of linear cause and effect. Joanna

Macy (1983) calls this paradigm "patriarchal," seeing its roots in male domination. Don Oliver and Kathleen Gershman (1989) see this view of reality as representative of what they call the age of "modernity," the rational scientific culture, which is characterized by unlimited functional specialization, industrialization, and a notion of progress built on a faith in the ability of technical knowledge to solve problems. Mustafe Asante (1987) calls this "Eurolinear thinking," pointing to its roots in European culture.[5]

Merchant (1980) argues that this world view emerged out of what she calls the "fundamental social and intellectual problem of the seventeenth century . . . the problem of order" (p. 193). She observes:

> The new mechanical philosophy of the mid-seventeenth century achieved a reunification of the cosmos, society, and the self in terms of a new metaphor—the machine. New forms of order and power provided a remedy for the disorder perceived to be spreading throughout the culture. . . . In the mechanical world, order was redefined to mean the predictable behavior of each part within a rationally determined system of laws, while power derived from active and immediate intervention in a secularized world. Order and power together constituted control. Rational control over nature, society, and self was achieved by redefining reality itself through the new machine metaphor. (pp. 192–93)

Thus the desire for power—human control over nature and people—fundamentally influenced the emergence of the machine metaphor and modern science. Out of a web of churning social and intellectual forces that transformed society in the West—the problem of "disorder," the emergence of capitalism, the maturing of patriarchy, the need for order and control, and the development of new approaches in science and philosophy—grew a view of reality that profoundly shaped the subsequent development of theories of power and the nature of social relations in modern society.

Hobbes and others applied the mechanistic metaphor to the social world as well as to the physical world. For Hobbes the "body politic was composed of equal atomistic beings united by contract out of fear and governed by a powerful sovereign" (Merchant 1980, 209). As a result, a new view of the synthesis of the cosmos, society, and human beings emerged, and a "new concept of the self as a rational master of the passions housed in a machinelike body began to replace the concept of the self as an integral part of a close-knit harmony of organic parts united to the cosmos and society" (Merchant 1980, 214).

The machine metaphor is in stark evidence in our nation's schools. Enter almost any classroom anywhere in the country, and chances are you will see rows of student desks, all facing the front of the room and the teacher's desk. In their linear and hierarchal organization, these classrooms are the physical embodiment of the logic of the mechanistic world view. The organization of time in schools into neat and equal blocks is another manifestation of this world view. The methodical ringing of school bells informs teachers and students of the boundaries of these time blocks and their relationships. Their endless and regular ringing regulates the rhythm of physical movement within the building as well as the steady progression of virtually unvarying school days. Theodore Sizer (1984) has described life in schools as "a systemized conveyer belt" (p. 83) process where the "clock is king" (p. 79). And the structure and norms of schooling have been consistently linked to those of the factory and the assembly line.

Oliver and Gershman (1989) point to the effects of the machine metaphor on curriculum selection and planning. As an example they offer an April 1984 document published by the National Council for the Social Studies called a "Preliminary position statement on scope and sequence for the social studies," which is a long list of goals, knowledges, values, beliefs, and skills aligned with specific grade levels. Under skills, they note, an exhaustive chart lists more than a hundred items, each rated according to how much instructional emphasis is recommended and cross-indexed with grade level. They point out that

> this highly specific mode of curriculum making, we would argue, provides an example of the technical fallacy that is embedded in the fundamental nature of the global culture we have called modernity. We come to see the world as bits of information relating to discrete problems, which can be understood through rational analysis. We presume that when problems are broken down into their various minute parts we can deal successfully with one small, solvable part at a time. (p. 18)

Richard Katz explores how this paradigm has influenced our understanding of human society and the nature of Western societies. He calls the dominant Western paradigm the "scarcity" paradigm. Katz also argues that the Western social sciences, reflecting and reinforcing wider social perspectives, are based on a view of society as consisting of separate and separating selves. This is evident in the Western obsession with autonomy, the individual, and individualism. Within this perspective it is assumed that there are constant and inevitable tensions between individuals and their communities. Katz argues that this paradigm "assumes that resources are scarce, their presumed scarcity largely determines their value," and that within the paradigm "individuals or communities must compete with each other to gain access to these resources" (Katz 1983/1984, 1). According to Katz, there is an inherent resistance to sharing, inherent pressure for accumulation at the expense of others.

Macy argues that within this paradigm power is seen as a property of separate entities, reflected in the way they push one another around. Thus, she argues, power is identified with domination; for power, like the rest of reality, is viewed as a "zero-sum game in which the more you have the less I have" (Macy 1976, 30). In order for there to be "winners," there must be "losers." The view of reality as made up of separate and competing entities reinforces, or perhaps creates, the view that power means strong defenses, invulnerability, inflexibility—in short, domination. Power consists of separate entities struggling amongst one another for strength, control, superiority, and their *separate* interests.

It is precisely this paradigm of reality that we have seen undergirding the work of Thomas Hobbes and the other *power over* theorists who followed him. Fundamentally, each theorist has described power in terms of linear causality. Running through each definition is a fundamental view of social relations as consisting of separate, discrete entities competing with one another, struggling against one another, imposing on one another, applying force to one another, and threatening one another with sanctions. In all the definitions of *power over* there has been the implicit or explicit assumption of inevitable tensions between individual fulfillment and the needs and desires of other individuals and the community as a whole. In each, power has been seen as a dynamic in the competition for scarce resources and as a scarce resource itself.

Oliver and Gershman (1989) describe how thoroughly this conception of power and reality permeates modern educational practice:

Modern education constructs the classroom in Hobbesian terms. The classroom is composed of objects in motion—the teacher and the students. The teacher controls information (in the form of small packages—books, tapes, films) which has the 'force' to influence and move the students. Educators have developed schema by which to describe the 'interacts' between teacher and student. In such a model we have solid objects (people), force and motion (the act and interact), and assume causal relationships between the motion of the objects and the power of the acts. Effective teaching occurs when the student object is affected (influenced) by the teacher object. We see these settings occurring in physical time counted on clocks and have expressions which embody this idea, such as 'time on task.' Within this model, we see what is "learned" as repeatable acts (such as doing items on a test or reading a passage from a book). So the concept of power within the framework of Hobbesian politics is force driven by one unit of mass (a person or teacher) over another. The purpose is to control the nature of the force over another mass (a student) so that one can produce predictable and controlled behavior on the part of the object being influenced. (pp. 177–78)

Beyond the Limits of the Dominant Discourse

Foucault observes that "discourse transmits and produces power, it reinforces it, but also undermines and exposes it, renders it fragile and makes it possible to thwart" (Foucault 1980b, 101). His point is an important one. Regimes of truth are not omnipotent and eternal, rather they are always changing, inherently unstable, as shifting as the ongoing interplay of knowledge and power, in which new formations, new correspondences, new techniques, practices, and strategies are always emerging and re-forming in what he describes as a "multiple and mobile field of force relations." He warns against oversimplifying and rigidifying the complex relations between and among multiple discourses: "We must make allowance for the complex and unstable process whereby discourse can be both an instrument and an effect of power, but also a hindrance, a stumbling block, a point of resistance and a starting point for an opposing strategy" (p. 101).

It is somewhat ironic, then, that even in Foucault's own discussion of power, which in so many ways turns traditional power theory on its head, he ultimately, if reluctantly, accepts an underlying conception of power as *power over*. He writes in an essay toward the end of his life: "For let us not deceive ourselves, if we speak of the structures or the mechanisms of power, it is only in so far as we suppose that certain persons exercise power over others" (Foucault 1982, 786).

It is precisely at the level of this underlying dominant conception of power underpinning the discourses on power discussed in this chapter, that I seek to engage, challenge, and extend the discourse on power. The view of power as restricted to relationships of domination is constricting. It limits our sense of possibility. In the chapters that follow I uncover, describe, build on, and explore alternative conceptions of power that do not take the relationship of domination as the starting point for understanding the power relationship. These formulations point to the limits of the present regime of truth in discourses on power. My interest is to open up a new terrain for more fully understanding and exploring the meaning, the experiences and the mechanisms of power. My hope is that such an exploration, will, perhaps, present not only some starting points for a strategy in opposition to domination, but also begin to uncover dimensions of power and possibilities of human relations that may help us conceptualize, describe, identify and create alternatives to relationships of domination both inside and outside of our schools.

Notes

1. Foucault's analysis of discourse is very complex, and one that was continually evolving in his own work. The analysis that follows does not attempt to be a "discourse analysis" in Foucauldian sense of the term. In particular, I do not attempt to identify the rules of formation of the dominant discourse of power in the social sciences. And, while I do at times suggest some of the nondiscursive influences on the discourse of power (a key theme for Foucault), such as the influence of patriarchy and the extensiveness of relationships of domination discussed in chapter 1, my analysis here tends to focus on theories of power and their essential ideas—seeking to identify a common underlying theme that runs throughout the diverse contours of the dominant discourse of power in the social sciences. I believe this analysis has value in relation to my overall project of exploring the meaning *and* experience of power in the process of empowerment.

2. Interestingly, power has not, traditionally, been a central concern of educators (see Nyberg 1981). Recent works in critical and feminist pedagogy are exceptions to this pattern.

3. Nancy Hartsock (1983) offers a superb analysis of Blau and of exchange theory's conceptions of power. Among the revealing observations she makes is that Blau's theory leads him to argue that "relations of domination and submission must be understood as not only beneficial for the community as a whole (increasing collective output and efficiency) but also as making a positive contribution to the equality of members of the community" (p. 32). She points out that "the Panglossian nature of this reasoning cannot be overemphasized. No matter the apparent inequality and harm occasioned by relations of domination and hierarchy, in reality all is for the best" (p. 32).

4. Among the feminist psychologists who have challenged male constructions of human development are Carol Gilligan (1982), Jean Baker Miller (1976), and Dorothy Dinnerstein, (1976).

5. See Merchant 1980, Macy 1982, French 1985, Starhawk 1982 and 1987, Asante 1987, and Oliver and Gershman 1989.

3

Power With: Toward an Alternative Conception of Power

The master's tools will never dismantle the master's house.

Audre Lorde (1981, 99)

The conditions of human life have changed drastically over the past few centuries, largely because of the potency of the idea of power. We continue to worship the principle that has brought this pass, without considering the nature of the pass. We seek solutions in the very mode of thinking/acting that has caused the problems.... The bomb could become a symbol of the insanity and impossibility of life conceived as a power struggle, of continuing delusive, sacrificial power seeking. It may force us—all of us, the human race—to stand still for a moment and think: If we can no longer channel our energies and miseries in aggressive action, what shall we do with ourselves?

Marilyn French (1985, 511)

Does power fundamentally involve relationships of domination? Are power and *power over* synonymous? Have empowerment theorists made a wise decision in avoiding power as a central concept in their work? Jean Baker Miller (1976) has argued that power's meaning has been "distorted" or "skewed" by the fact that it implies behaviors and attitudes that are more associated with men than with women; that, in fact, because of its association with men, the meaning of power may have acquired connotations that may not be necessary or even essential. She urges an exploration of the intrapsychic and interpersonal dynamics of power not based on patriarchal needs for control over others. Thus Miller points to the importance of investigating the limits of power based on *power over* and the possibilities of power not based on relationships of domination. She calls not for the rejection of power, but for its reclamation and reconstruction.

In seeking to understand power, most theorists have looked to its most pervasive, obvious, and dominant expressions in our society. In seeking to reconceptualize power it is useful to return to the root meanings of the word and to explore those images, experiences, and expressions that may be excluded from the dominant conception. It is also important to seek out those theorists, working outside of the mainstream discourses of power, who have explored alternative notions of power.

Etymology and the Reexamination of Power

The English word *power* derives from the Latin *posse:* "to be able." It is significant that the notion that one is "able," while implying the ability to assert oneself in the world, to be able to fulfill one's desires, does *not* necessarily imply that effectiveness can only occur as a result of controlling or dominating others. The ability to impose one's will, to control others, is only one possible dimension of "being able." Significantly, the multidimensional meaning of being able, of having power, has been lost in much power theory and research.

In fact, the first meaning of *power* in the *Oxford English Dictionary* is the "ability to do or effect something or anything, or to act upon a person or thing." While there is clearly an imposing dimension to the second part of this definition, the first part is quite free from domination (while domination is certainly possible within the definition, it does not limit power to dominating action and relationships). It is not until the fourth definition of power that the full connection to relationships of domination is made: "Possession of control or command over others; dominion, rule; government, domination, sway, command, control, influence, authority, often followed by -of, -on, -over." *Webster's New World Dictionary* presents the same progression of meanings. Notably, however, in *Webster's* discussion of power and its synonyms, it is squarely described as *power over:* "Power denotes the inherent ability or the admitted right to rule, govern, determine, etc."

Let us look again at how the term *power* is used in our culture. When I asked the group of tenth graders referred to in chapter 2 their immediate thoughts about and images of power, *power over* words predominated. But there were also some terms and images that were not so easily categorized as *power over,* terms such as *life* and *happiness* and images such as *sun* and *earth.*

What is the link between power and life? Between power and

happiness? On the one hand, it may mean that life is a constant battle for power over others and that happiness is found in achieving such power. But is *power over* adequate to describe the power of life and happiness? What is the power of the earth and the sun?

I have conducted similar exercises with other groups, and I have discovered that peppered in among the images of domination and selfishness are terms such as *community, friendship,* and *giving of oneself.* In one group, *Martin Luther King, Jr.* and *Mahatma Gandhi* were squeezed in among the many negative terms and images. I asked the group: *is* the power of King and Gandhi the same power as that captured in the other images of domination and control the group has shared? This question began to chip at the edges of the predominant conception of power as *power over.* No, a member of the group replied, their power was "good" power (someone disagreed, arguing that it was all the same). What is the difference between good power and bad power, I asked. Is good power merely power exerted by those with whom you agree? No, someone replied. Well, then what is the difference? This question sparked a discussion of the power of nonviolence and love and a boundary-crossing exploration of the meaning of power. Challenging questions were raised as to the nature of King's and Gandhi's power and the adequacy of *power over* for fully understanding and describing their ability and their movements' ability to effect change.

Love is said to be powerful. Is the power of love the same as the power of the threat of violence? What is the difference between these two conceptions, and what do they have in common? What is the power we experience when we listen to a captivating concert or watch a riveting play? Do we mean we have had an experience of dominating or controlling others? Has the music or the drama dominated or imposed upon us? Nonviolent disobedience is said to be powerful. Yet does nonviolence derive its effectiveness from its ability to impose and dominate? What is the nature of the power manifest in dialogue? In friendship? In a powerful learning experience? What does it mean to have a "powerful experience"? While it may mean that we have imposed our will on others, more often it seems to mean that we have received something; not that we have dominated or been dominated, but rather that we have achieved or experienced effectiveness with others. Dorothy Emmet (1954) partially describes this type of power when she observes:

> Here power is effectiveness in some form of original activity, so that it is possible to speak of a powerful writer or thinker

with reference to his style or the content of what he writes, and without implying that he is seeking to influence and still less to dominate other people. We know that contact with such people or with their work may have the effect of heightening vitality, will-power or morale. I should maintain that the kind of stimulus which comes to a person A from contact with someone B who is a person of creative powers is distinguishable from the attempt on the part of A to direct and control B's actions. (pp.89–90)

In her book *Truth or Dare* (1987), Starhawk describes a confrontation between a group of women who had been arrested for a peace action at Lawrence Livermore Laboratories and some of their prison guards who had chased a woman into the large gymnasium in which they were all being held:

And then the woman runs in. She bursts through the open doorway that leads to the concrete exercise yard outside. Six guards are after her. 'Grab her! Grab her!' they yell. The woman dives into our cluster, and we instinctively surround her, gripping her arms and legs and shielding her with our bodies. The guards grab her legs and pull; we resist, holding on. The guards and the women are shouting and in a moment, I know, the nightsticks will descend on kidneys and heads, but in that suspended interval before the violence starts we hold our ground.

And then someone begins to chant.

The chant is wordless, a low hum that swells and grows with open vowels as if we had become the collective voice of some ancient beast that growls and sings, the voice of something that knows nothing of guns, walls, nightsticks, mace, or barbed wire fencing, yet gives protection, a voice outside surveillance or calculation but not outside knowledge, a voice that is recognized by our bodies if not our minds and is known also to the guards whose human bodies, like ours, have been animal for a million years before control was invented.

The guards back away. (1987, 5)

How do we understand the power at work in the interaction between the women and the guards? Did the women dominate the guards?

Did they impose themselves? What was the source of their power? What was its nature and how did it work? Starhawk observes:

> what had taken place is an act that could teach us something deep about power. In that moment in the jail, the power of domination and control met something outside its comprehension, a power rooted in another source. To know that power, to create the situations that bring it forth, is magic. (p. 5)

Keith Grove teaches mathematics at Dover-Sherborn High School in Massachusetts. For the past two years he has been working to make his classes more empowering and democratic for his students. He has included students in decision making with regard to a wide range of issues, including grading, homework assignments, pacing of material, and classroom rules. Through small and large cooperative group learning experiences he has also involved them to a high degree in the learning *and* teaching process. Students play major roles in "teaching" one another the material. I interviewed Keith's tenth-grade geometry class during June 1988. This is an excerpt from the interview transcript on the nature of power in their class:

Q: Does Keith use power over you in this class?
S1: No, No. No.
Q: Not at all?
S2: Well, a little bit.
S3: Well if you get out of hand he has a right to do that.
S4: He never raises his voice. He just gives you a look like 'Shut up.'
S5: He just says stop.
S6: He will just wait for you to stop talking and you feel kind of dumb, but you don't feel humiliated that he stood up in class and started yelling at you.
Q: And you feel as though he is using power over you at that point.
S3: Yeah...
S4: Well it's not really power...
S1: It's not a negative power... he's just reminding you.
S7: Instead of saying you oh you remember our rule he is like...
S8: Sometimes he sat there for five or ten minutes of class just sitting there doing nothing until we quieted down.
Q: Do you feel as though you have power in this class?
S2: Yeah.

S5:   Everyone does.
S6:   If someone said in the middle of class, 'Wait a minute, this is
      really dumb,' he'd say, 'Why (chuckle) lets talk about it.'
Q: Would you describe this class as democratic?
MANY VOICES: Yeah.
S3:   Everyone gets their say.
S6:   Everyone is heard.
S2:   If we don't feel like having a quiz tomorrow we can vote on it.

How do we understand the nature of power in Keith's classroom? What does it mean that "everyone" has power? What is the
nature of Keith's power? What is the nature of his students'
power? Keith reflects on his teaching and talks about power:

> I just think that working together and that way of being con-
> nected to each other is something that doesn't take place when
> the teacher is in charge, when the teachers have the answers,
> when it is up to the teacher to help each individual student to
> understand. . . . There is something lacking that is important,
> the word that can be used is community, but it goes deeper. It
> gets into human connectedness. I think the structure of the
> class like this where the teacher isn't in charge and has all of
> the power allows more power to take place between students
> and students and between teacher and students because the
> issues that come up are so much more real. They are the
> issues human beings deal with all the time, issues of trust and
> respect and support. (personal interview, June 1987)

Keith argues that by giving up his power as a teacher he actually allows there to be more power among students and between
students and teachers. If we take *power* to simply mean *power over*
as characterized by command, control, and competition for scarce
goods, this makes little sense. Keith seems to be describing a broader concept of power. He seems to be arguing that if he as a teacher
gives up *power over,* another kind of power emerges in the group—a
kind of power to which everyone in the class has access. It is an
expanding resource created through human interconnections.

Power With: An Emerging Concept in the Social Sciences

Upon closer examination of the meaning, uses, and experiences of power in our culture, it becomes clearer that conceiving

power as solely *power over* is inadequate. The definition of power as domination and control is limited; it is incomplete. There is another dimension, or form, or experience of power that is distinctly different from pervasive conceptions.The ignored dimension is characterized by collaboration, sharing, and mutuality.We can call this alternative concept *power with* to distinguish it from *power over*.[1]

Beginning in the early twentieth century a few social scientists and psychologists, most of them women, have challenged dominant discourses of power that are based on relationships of domination. These theorists present the outlines of an alternative discourse on power that is emerging in theory and research. It is no accident that women and feminist theorists have taken the lead in developing alternative conceptions of power. Women's experiences are a form of subjugated knowledge that has been silenced and excluded by the dominant patriarchal discourses. Miller (1982) notes "the undeniable truth that the world has been explained so far without the close observation of women's experience" (p. 5). She argues that women's experiences with power "bring new understanding to the whole concept of power" (p. 2). Indeed, she points out that "what we find when we study women are parts of the total human potential that have not been fully seen, recognized, or valued. These are parts that have not therefore flourished, and perhaps they are precisely the ingredients that we must bring into action in the conduct of human affairs" (p. 5).

While the theories discussed below present a variety of perspectives for understanding power, it is my contention that the concept of *power with* synthesizes their alternatives to *power over* and offers a clear theoretical counterpoint to *power over*. Grounded in different sensitivities, experiences, and frameworks of critique and analysis, the exposition and development of theories of *power with* emerge from a different set of imperatives concerning how to study and understand power. What we see, I believe, is a different discourse on power—with different rules and different frameworks for conceptualization and articulation. It is important to keep this in mind as we explore the nature of *power with;* that in fact we are being challenged on fundamental levels to reexamine our taken-for-granted assumptions about how we should think about and analyze power. *Power with,* this suggests, is not a concept that can or should simply be incorporated into existing theories of power and domination—rather it challenges us to rethink our categories, our frameworks, our underlying assumptions, and ultimately our grand analyses of how power functions—both for domination and for liberation.

Erich Fromm is one theorist who saw the limitations of conceiving power as *power over*. Although he did not explicitly articulate a definition of *power with*, his discussion of power does offer some essential distinctions for rethinking its nature. In speaking of the "human ability to use his powers and to realize the potentialities inherent in him," he notes that "if we say *he* must use *his* powers we imply that he must be free and not dependent on someone who controls his powers" (Fromm 1947, 91). Fromm's psychology demands that people be free of domination in order to realize their potentialities.

Fromm states that power denotes two contradictory concepts, "power of = capacity" and "power over = domination." He argues that "power = domination" results from the paralysis of "power = capacity." *Power over* is "the perversion of power to." When the human capacity to act in the world is perverted, it takes the form of domination. While domination is one form of power, for Fromm it is the perverted form. For him the more basic and life-affirming form of power is the capacity to act in the world to fulfill one's potential *with* other human beings, not *over* and *against* other human beings. It is being able, or what he calls "productiveness."

Fromm envisions human power relationships in which individuals work together for their mutual self-actualization and fulfillment through productive activity. His faith is that if the more basic form of power as "action together" were to flourish, then power as domination would diminish and eventually disappear. His practical suggestion is "humanistic communitarianism"—the creation of "human-size" communities for work and politics, where people share in decision making, resources, and work. On the quality of relationship that would predominate in these small communities, he writes:

> Love is the productive form of relatedness to others and oneself. It implies responsibility, care, respect and knowledge, and the wish for the other person to grow and develop. It is the expression of intimacy between two human beings under the condition of the preservation of each other's integrity. (Fromm 1947, 116)

For Fromm the positive form of power manifest in productive relationships is captured in the dynamics of love. His analysis brings the concepts and experiences of intimacy, caring, responsibility, and mutual respect into the discourse of power.

Throughout the 1980s an important discourse on power, *power with,* and empowerment has emerged from the work of a group of psychologists at the Stone Center for Developmental Services and Studies at Wellesley College, whose research has focused on understanding the development of women. In her book *Toward a New Psychology of Women* (1976), Jean Baker Miller identifies the pervasive notion of power in our culture as *power over.* She observes:

> Power has generally meant the ability to advance oneself and simultaneously to control, limit and if possible destroy the power of others. Power so far has at least two components: power for oneself and power over others. . . . The history of power struggles as we have known them has been on these grounds. The power of another person, or group of people, was generally seen as dangerous. You had to control them or they would control you. (p. 116)

Miller rejects the inevitability of this notion of power. She states that to control or be controlled

> in the realm of human development is not a valid formulation. Quite the reverse. In a basic sense, the greater the development of each individual, the more able, more effective and less needy of limiting or restricting others she or he will be. (p. 116)

In this she is in agreement with Fromm. The ability to act in the world to achieve fulfillment does not derive from our ability to control others. Rather, as we act for ourselves and with others, our need to control others diminishes. This suggests that the more one is capable of *power with,* the less one will seek *power over.*

Miller offers a useful definition of power as the "capacity to implement."[2] In this definition the notion of "being able" is paramount, as it is in Fromm's sense of "capacity." Miller's definition has within it the possibility of dominating power, but it also allows for co-agency. She writes that "women need the power to advance their own development, but they do not 'need' the power to limit the development of others" (p. 117). She describes ways of being powerful "that enhance the power of other people while simultaneously increasing our own power" (Miller 1982, 2). Power, then, is not by definition a win-lose situation. Power can be an expanding, renewable resource available through shared endeavor, dialogue, and cooperation.

Miller ties the need to assert power over others to models of human development based on patterns of male development, with their focus on separation, individuation, and autonomy and the corresponding developmental process of severing relationships of nurturance, vulnerability, and interdependence. She is critical of models of development that denigrate the latter supportive relationships and points to the contradictions in expecting the individual to be able "to be intimate with another person(s) having spent all of his prior development geared to something very different" (Gordon 1985, 44). It is precisely these kinds of supportive and generative relationships that allow for another kind of assertiveness in the world, one that is not based on the need to impose oneself on others. She describes a central theme in human development as "agency-in-community." In its healthiest expression agency-in-community is manifest when individuals support and enhance one another's empathic, generative, *and* assertive qualities. The power manifest in agency-in-community is quite different from the *power over* exerted in the more common perception of "self-separate-from-community."

Janet Surrey (1987) describes this form of power as *power with*. She also uses the terms *power together, power emerging from interaction, power in connection, relational power,* and *mutual power* (pp. 2, 4). She links *power with* and empowerment, arguing that empowerment is nurtured through *power with* relationships. At the heart of these empowering power relationships is "response /ability," the capacity to "act in relationship." Response/ability involves "the capacity to engage in an open, mutually empathic relational process" (p. 6). In relationships such as these, individuals have the capacity to be responsive to, indeed to be "moved" by, the other person's thoughts, perceptions and feelings: "both people feel able to have an impact on each other and on the movement or 'flow' of the interaction" (p. 7).

> This process creates a relational context in which there is increasing awareness and knowledge of self and other through sustained affective connection, and a kind of unencumbered movement of interaction. This is truly a creative process, as each person is changed through the interaction. The movement of relationship creates an energy, momentum, or power that is experienced as beyond the individual, yet

available to the individual. Both participants gain new energy and new awareness as each has risked change and growth
through the encounter. Neither person is in control. (Surrey
1987, 7)

Miller and Surrey stress the importance of connection—of ongoing
relationship—in the dynamics of *power with*. Surrey suggests that
power with transcends the dichotomy of actor and acted upon that
exists in *power over*, saying that "all participants in the relationship interact in ways that build connection and enhance everyone's
personal power" (Surrey 1987, 4). Indeed, response/ability implies
the ongoing capacity to consider in one's own actions the interests,
thoughts, feelings, and experiences of others, what Judith Jordan
calls "mutual intersubjectivity" (1984, 7).

Miller and her colleagues' discussion introduces to the discourses of power the themes of connection, nurturance, mutuality,
community, openness to change and growth, and "maintaining the
relationship." Indeed, addressing these themes in the context of
discussions of power jars our taken-for-granted meanings and
presses us to reconsider our categories and experiences. As such,
they represent major contributions to our understanding of the
limits of *power over* and the nature of *power with*.

Rollo May (1972) is another psychologist who directly
addresses the distinction between *power over* and *power with*. He
outlines five types of power: exploitative, manipulative, ccompeti-
tive, nutrient and integrative. He describes exploitative and
manipulative power as *power over*, competitive power as *power
against*, nutrient power as *power for*, and integrative power as
power with. For him, the key distinction is between "constructive"
and "destructive" power. Exploitative and manipulative power are
destructive, and his analysis of them is very similar to my previous discussion of *power over*. Competitive power has both destructive and constructive dimensions. He says:

In its negative form, [power against] consists of one person
going up not because of anything he does but because his
opponent goes down. (p. 108)

This is the destructive side of competitive power. "It continuously
shrinks the area of human community in which one lives" (p. 108).
However, he also argues that competition can enhance both com-
petitors' abilities; it "can give zest and vitality to life . . . to have

someone *against* you is not necessarily a bad thing; at least he is not *over* you or *under* you, and accepting his rivalry may bring out dormant capacities in you"(p. 109).

Nutrient and integrative power are constructive, and May's discussion of them offers insight into the nature of *power with*. Nutrient power is power for the other. It is relationships between parents and children, between teachers and students, and among friends and loved ones. He describes it as "power that is given by one's care for another"(p. 109). It involves exerting ourselves for the sake of another. He says that teaching is a good example of *power for:* "Nutrient power comes out of a concern for the welfare of the group" (p.109). May's discussion of nutrient power is brief, and he fails to discuss how easily *power for* can become *power over*, as depicted in the relationship between the woman and her husband in "The Yellow Wall-Paper." This would seem to be the great danger of *power for;* it is easy to distort one's responsibility for another, to insist on exerting control rather than sharing it.

However, what distinguishes *power for* from the conception of power as manifest in relationships of domination is that while *power over* is characterized by rigid boundaries between self and other, by force and the confrontation of wills, nutrient power is characterized by openness to others; by inclusion, care, connection, and nurturance; by giving as well as receiving. These are important elements in alternative conceptions of power.

In the case of integrative power, which May explicitly describes as *power with*, one's own power "abets my neighbor's power" (p. 109). Integrative power is characterized by a continuing dialectical process: that is, by thesis, antithesis, and synthesis. When integrative power emerges within a group of individuals committed to the process of dialogue and group problem-solving, there is a dynamic, dialectical interaction involving connection, synthesis, and mutual growth—co-developing power.

May also addresses the issue of how integrative power functions when one party in a conflict is unwilling to take an open and dialogical stance. May points out that the power of Martin Luther King and Mahatma Gandhi's nonviolence is integrative. It is based on human connection, memory, and morality.

May argues that the source of the power of nonviolence comes from the individual's "authentic innocence." The individual does not cut off awareness, renounce responsibility, or have individual gain as his or her ultimate aim. Rather, the force of innocence comes from the individual's openness and awareness. It is shaped by one's willingness to take responsibility and the desire to achieve something for the good of the community. Through integrative power, individuals and groups can create dynamic situations in which synthesis, change, and growth are possible, even among individuals and groups with apparently irreconcilable desires or interests.

May believes, however, that in a particular situation where there is a conflict of interests and where one of the actors in the interaction is an "unwilling partner," then the unwilling actor must be "coerced" into cooperation.If this is in fact a correct analysis, then integrative power would be based on the initial use of *power over*. Here May fails to carry his own analysis far enough.The dynamics of the power of nonviolence as he describes them are fundamentally different from the dynamics of *power over*. *Power over* depends on the ability to close oneself off from others, to create defenses and engage with others only from a position of strength.The effective power of nonviolence is different.It is based on the power of self-assertion, openness, and human connection rather than self-imposition, invulnerability, and human separateness.

The effectiveness of nonviolent action as a mode of social change is the result of two equally important aspects. First, nonviolent action represents a withdrawal of willingness to participate in an oppressive situation. This refusal to participate is assertion, not imposition. It breaks the oppressive bond, but at the same time affirms fundamental human bonds. Second, nonviolent resistance does not seek to compel others into dialogue and change, but rather it seeks to create situations that impel people toward dialogue and change. Thus, those who utilize nonviolent action gain access to others *not through the use of force, but rather through the use of mechanisms of human encounter that activate in others the openness to fellow humans that can never be fully closed off*. This is a fundamental distinction between *power over* and *power with*.

May's power typology challenges us to consider the positive and creative sides of power as well as its restrictive and destructive aspects. His discussion of integration focuses our attention on themes of openness, authenticity, dialogue, synthesis, and cooperation.

Starhawk, a peace activist and a prominent figure in the feminist spirituality movement, makes the analysis of power a central component in her development of a "psychology of liberation." Starhawk (1987) distinguishes between "power-over," "power-from-within," and "power-with." Her discussion of power-over is very similar to my discussion and critique in chapter 2. She links power-over to domination and control and to a form of consciousness she terms "estrangement." She points out that in the atomized and mechanical perspective of power-over, individuals are not valued, inherently, for who they are, but rather in relation to "some outside standard" (p. 9). She links this form of consciousness to the conception of God "who stands outside the word, outside nature, who must be appeased, placated, feared, and above all, obeyed" (p. 9). She sees power-over as pervasive in our culture, so much so that

> we are so accustomed to power-over, so steeped in its language and its implicit threats, that we often become aware of its functioning only when we see its extreme manifestations. For we have been shaped in its institutions, so that the insides of our minds resemble the battlefield and the jail. (p. 9)

In contrast to power-over, Starhawk defines the concepts of power-from-within and power-with and the experiences they represent. Power-from-within derives from power's etymological roots in *being able*. It is an attitude and spirit with which an individual engages the world, "akin to the sense of mastery we develop as young children with each new unfolding ability: the exhilaration of standing erect, of walking, of speaking the magic words that convey our needs and thoughts" (p. 10). Thus power-from-within is linked to a sense of competence and joy at one's unfolding capacities. Power-from-within rises from our sense of connection, "our bonding with other human beings, and with the environment" (p. 10). She argues that we experience power-from-within frequently:

> Although power-over rules the systems we live in, power-from-within sustains our lives. We can feel that power in acts of creation and connection, in planting, building, writing, cleaning, healing, soothing, playing, singing, making love. (p. 10)

While power-over describes relationships between people, power-from-within is less defined by the dynamics of relationships than by one's sense of self and sense of connection to the world. In this, Starhawk's concept of power-from-within is very similar to Fromm's and Miller's focus on "power-to" and capacity. Her conception of power-from-within is distinctive in her focus on its rootedness in "spirit," on a perspective of the world and life and matter as sacred and as imbued with immanent value. Within this perspective, no one, nothing, has more value than another, "for we are, ourselves, the living body of the sacred" (p. 15). As we come into connection with spirit, we experience our own and others' inherent value. Our power-from-within rises out of experiences of "spirit, mystery, bonding, community and love" (p. 18).

Starhawk presents a third concept of power, power-with, which she argues bridges the value systems of power-from-within and power-over. Similar to power-over, power-with describes a particular way in which people can relate to one another. Starhawk calls power-with "influence," distinguishing it from "authority," which she links to power-over. Power-with is manifest in groups in which each member is seen as an equal by each other member of the group. It is the power of an individual not to command, "but to suggest and be listened to, to begin something and see it happen" (p. 10).

The source of power-with comes from the willingness of others to listen to our ideas. It is manifest in groups in which there is mutual respect; that is, respect not for one's role, but for "each unique person." She observes that power-with relies on the ability to hold back. "It affirms, shapes, and guides a collective decision —but it cannot enforce its will on the group or push it in a direction contrary to community desires" (p. 13). She uses the example, cited earlier, of the woman who began to chant in the gymnasium. When this chant was joined by the other women in the group, the results were dramatic. The woman was exerting influence within the group, but she did not impose the chant on anyone. Rather, her role was accepted and extended on its merits at that moment. Unlike power-over, through which the powerful person has the ability to impose his or her ideas, power-with is "always revokable." Group members consider ideas, but they may accept or reject them as they see fit.

Starhawk seeks to divide power into three symmetrical concepts, and this suffices when she focuses on each as a form of consciousness. However, when she turns to discussing the *social* nature of power and its manifestation in relationship, her conceptual framework (much like Fromm's power-over, power-to distinction) turns out to be asymmetrical. Her conceptions of power-over and power-with are social. They are described and defined by relationship. In contrast, her conception of power-from-within describes a dynamic of individual psychology. It appears, in fact, that power-over and power-with stand as conceptually opposite but parallel concepts, while power-from-within doesn't quite fit into the conceptual map. While she argues that power-with is the bridge between power-over and power-from-within, it appears more likely that power-from-within reflects the personal psychological dynamics that propel and allow individuals to engage in power-with. While she attempts to develop each concept separately, arguing that each represents a particular mode of consciousness and world view, her distinctions between power-from-within and power-with are not clearly delineated. She herself tends to lump them together. She observes that "power-from-within and power-with are grounded in another source, akin not to violence but to spirit" (p. 16). And she argues that community is essential to both power-from-within and power-with. Community counters the estrangement of power-over, it reconnects. "In community we have the power to heal each other and to help each other, power that goes beyond the individual self" (Starhawk 1982, 96). It seems that power-from-within and power-with represent two sides of the same concept of power (what I am calling *power with*), one that stands in contrast to power-over.

Fromm, Miller and her colleagues, May, and Starhawk, all offer important insights into the nature of alternative conceptions and experiences of *power over*. However, in each case, the theorist's predominant focus on the intrapsychic psychology of power, while eloquently revealing the inadequacies of *power over* and presenting valuable new perspectives on power, limits the scope of the discussion. While it is important to understand the personal psychology of power (and certainly these accounts are not limited to personal psychology), such a focus can also distract us from the fundamental fact that power has to do with relationships among people.

Power also involves access and control of valued resources, but this too can be a distracting formulation. It is *people and the institutions and communities created by people* that determine the division of resources. Power involves the dynamics of the relationships among people *with regard* to access to and control of valued resources. Thus it is essential that we maintain a clear focus on the interpersonal dynamics of *power with*.

Mary Parker Follett (1918, 1924, 1942), writing in the first third of the century about industrial organization and administrative management, makes the earliest and clearest distinction between *power over* and *power with* that I have uncovered. Writing long before the theorists cited above, she goes further than they do in providing a description of the specific types of relationships and modes of organization that are characterized by *power with*.

Follett describes *power over* as "coercive" and *power with* as "co-active." She associates *power over* with domination, where one person or side achieves victory over another. She describes *power with*, on the other hand, as "jointly developed power," where people fulfill their desires and develop their capacities through acting together. Through this simple distinction Follett frees the term *power* from the idea of domination and clearly articulates an obscured and neglected dimension of its meaning.

Ultimately, like Fromm, Follett defines power as "capacity" developed by the individual through interaction with other individuals. Power is the ability to do. Like Fromm and Miller, she sees *power over* as a destructive form of power: "Genuine power is not coercive control but co-active control. Coercive power is the curse of the universe; co-active power, the enrichment and advancement of every human soul" (Follett 1924, xii). *Power over* is not genuine power because it is ultimately dysfunctional. It stifles the development of capacity.

Pivotal to Follett's conception of power in its positive form of *power with* is that:

> Power is not a pre-existing thing that can be handed to someone. We have seen again and again the failure of power "conferred." The division of power is not the thing to be considered, but the method of organization which will generate power. (Follett 1942, 110)

Power with is not a zero-sum proposition where one person gains the capacity to achieve his or her desires at the expense of others. Rather, *power with* is a developing capacity of people to act and do together. Follett offers a description of the types of human relationships and social organization that cultivate *power with*.

Follett (1942) does not deny that conflict exists. Rather she begins with the reality of conflicts of interest. She describes the process of "integration." Integration is the process by which all parties in a given situation, even those with initially conflicting interests, get what they want, with neither side being forced to sacrifice anything. Through integration people transcend their conflicts and discover their capacities to fulfill their desires together. Integration represents a particular mode of relationship that differs sharply from relationships of domination.

There are two key concepts in Follett's description of the process of integration: "reciprocal influence" and "emergence." She describes the interactions in this process as reciprocal influence. Rather than offering a description of the functioning and development of power in linear cause and effect terms, she offers a "circular" description:

> A good example of circular response is a game of tennis. A serves. The way B returns the ball depends partly on the way it was served to him. A's next play will depend on his own original serve plus the return of B, and so on and so on. (p.44)

> The key to our problem lies in what we mean by reciprocally influencing. Do we mean all the ways in which A influences B, and all the ways in which B influences A? Reciprocal influencing means more than this. It means that A influences B, and that B, made different by A's influence, influences A, which means that A's own activity enters into the stimulus which is causing his activity. (p. 194)

In her conception of causality, multiple actors in a group are connected through webs of relationship where influence flows dynamically.

In the integrative process, reciprocal influence occurs simultaneously with emergence. Emergence is the aspect of integration in which individuals and groups create new solutions, new values, new capacities, and more power:

> Each calls out something from the other, releases something, frees something, opens the way for the expression of latent capacities and possibilities. (p. 197)

Emergence represents the most dynamic dimension of the process of integration. It is synthesis and creation achieved in the process of circular influencing:

> We see that the functional relating has always a value beyond the mere addition of the parts. A genuine interweaving and interpenetrating by changing both sides creates new situations. . . . Functional relating is the continuing process of self-creating coherence. . . . If you have the right kind of functional relating, you will have a process which will create a unity which will lead to further unities—a self creating progression. (pp. 200–202)

The process of integration takes place within a particular kind of organization—the integrative unity—where ideally

> all parts [are] so coordinated, so moving together in their closely knit and adjusting activities, so linking, interlocking, interrelating, that they make a working unit—that is, not a congeries of separate pieces, but what I have called a functional whole or integrative unity. (p. 196)

Obviously, few organizations ever reach this ideal state of unity but "the more highly integrated unity you have, the more self-direction you get" (p. 205).

Within this context *power with* is the expanding capacity of each member of the organization to achieve his or her goals within the evolving goals of the larger organization. She writes that "in a functional unity each has his function—and that should correspond as exactly as possible with his capacity" (p. 107). Within the integrative unity *power with* is cultivated: "Power-with is a jointly developing power, the aim, a unifying which, while allowing for infinite differing, does away with fighting" (p. 115).

Follett does not adequately discuss the relationship *between* *power over* and *power with* and how the two forms of power both may be manifest in any group or organization. This leaves an important gap in her theory, for she fails to discuss the obstacles to creating integrative unities in any depth. In part this is because her work lacks a critical analysis of domination and the complex ways domination permeates this culture's social and organizational structures and class, race, and gender relations. Such an understanding would have provided her with a critical overlay for her discussion of power and sharpened her sometimes naive and idealistic discussion of integrative unity. Nevertheless, I find Follett's discussion of power and the dynamics of *power with* quite profound. Her work is an important (and unfortunately obscure) contribution to our understanding of power.

Follett summarizes her conception of power poetically:

> Power is the blossoming of experience. (p. 111)

A New Paradigm for Power

In chapter 2 I explored the connection between *power over* and the mechanistic world view, suggesting a link between our conceptions of power and our underlying view of the nature of reality. Reconceptualizing the nature of power calls for addressing not only the limitations of *power over* but the adequacy of the world view or paradigm of reality that underlies it as well. The following observation by Oliver and Gershman (1989) helps us to understand this task:

> Paradigmatic differences ferment and boil up from unconsciously grounded world views. Ideological differences are much less profound in that they share similar feeling and conceptions about metaphysical categories (time, space, causation, force, power, humanhood, etc.) but place different weights on their relative importance or how they would have them structured. We would consider welfare capitalism and Marxism, for example as both within the paradigm of modernity. (p. 7)

Such an inquiry calls on us to question the very roots of the current regime of truth.

The machine metaphor or the scarcity paradigm, as we have seen, is linked to the rise of modern science, patriarchy, the market economy, and the modern state. It is interesting that modern science itself is moving beyond the machine metaphor and beginning to offer new perspectives on the nature of reality. These perspectives offer alternatives to the dominant view of reality as reducible to discrete and separate entities relating in objectively observable patterns of linear cause and effect. They offer insight into the outline of a world view that may help us to develop a fuller understanding of power.

Systems theory developed as an alternative model of inquiry and understanding to the mechanistic model and offers important insights into the limits of the mechanistic world view. The biologist Ludwig von Bertalanffy was an early systems thinker:

> Von Bertalanffy found that the behavior of phenomena could best be understood in terms of wholes, not parts, and that wholes, be they animal or vegetable, cell, organ or organism could best be described as "systems." A system is less a thing than a pattern. It is a pattern of events, its existence and character deriving less from the nature of its components than from their organization. As such it consists of the dynamic flow of interactions that cannot themselves be

weighed or measured. It is "non-summative" and irreducible; that is, the character of a system as a pattern of organization is altered with the addition, subtraction or modification of any component. Hence it is more than the sum of its parts. This "more" is not something extra, like a vitalist principle or *élan vital*, but a new level of operation which the interdependence of its parts permits. It is lost from view when a system's composite units are investigated independently of each other. (Macy 1978, 61)[3]

Von Bertalanffy also saw that the dynamics that occur in the internal functioning of a living system "also [typify] its relations with its environment. Whether it is an organism, a cell, or organelle, it functions and evolves within a larger system—in regard to whose character it is both dependent and indispensable" (Macy 1978, 62). His crucial insight here is that "systems enclose and are enclosed by other systems with which they are in constant communication, in a natural hierarchical order. The organized whole found in nature is not only a system but an *open* system. It maintains and organizes itself by exchanging matter, energy and information with its environment" (Macy 1978, 61).

Systems theory fundamentally challenged the atomistic assumptions of modern science and suggested a more holistic conception of reality. However, despite this break from the mechanistic metaphor, many systems theorists are still drawn back to the mechanistic metaphor. This drift is seen in the tendencies of many systems thinkers to stand outside the system and to seek to break it down to its separate parts so that it can be "controlled" in the sense that one can predict and thereby make predictable changes (Stamps 1980). Merchant (1980) notes:

Systems theorists claim for themselves a holistic outlook, because they believe that they are taking into account the ways in which all the parts in a given system affect the whole. Yet the formalism of the calculus of probabilities excludes the possibility mathematizing the gestalt—that is, the ways in which each part at any given instant takes its meaning from the whole. The more open, adaptive, organic, and complex the system, the less successful is the formalism. It is most successful when applied to closed, artificial, precisely defined, relatively simple systems. Mechanistic assumptions about nature push us increasingly in the direction of artificial environments, mechanized control over more and more aspects of human life, and a loss of the quality of life itself. (p. 291)

Evelyn Fox Keller (1985), in her discussion of the work of Nobel Laureate Barbara McClintock, describes how a new paradigm is emerging in the biological sciences. She quotes McClintock as saying that we are in the middle of a revolution that "will reorganize the way we look at things, the way we do research" (p. 172). Keller describes how McClintock's work in genetics has contributed to this revolution, and in her discussion we clearly see how an older view of an atomistic and hierarchically ordered universe is being challenged by another reality.

Until recently the "central dogma" in genetic theory and research has been what Keller calls the "master molecule theory," which emerged in the discovery of the structure of DNA by Watson and Crick: "The DNA is posited as the central actor in the cell, the executive governor of cellular organization, itself remaining impervious to influence from subordinate agents to which it dictates" (p. 169). Keller explains:

> In locating the seat of genetic control in a single molecule, [the central dogma] posits a structure of genetic organization that is essentially hierarchical. . . . In this model, genetic stability is ensured by unidirectionality of information flow, much as political stability is assumed in many quarters to require the unidirectional exercise of authority. (p. 171)

This central model for the understanding of genetics has been profoundly influenced by the mechanistic metaphor, the atomistic view of reality and linear conceptions of cause and effect.

Keller notes that McClintock's work on transposition suggests an alternative model based on the recognition that

> genetic organization is necessarily more complex, and in fact more globally interdependent, than such a model assumes. It show[s] that the DNA itself is subject to rearrangement and, by implication, to reprogramming. Although she did not make the suggestion explicit, the hidden heresy of her argument lay in the inference that such reorganization could be induced by signals external to the DNA—from the cell of the organism, even from the environment. (p. 171)

McClintock's work challenges the basic assumptions of the scarcity paradigm in suggesting that open, interdependent, and mutually influencing systems are the most fundamental building blocks of life.

Fritjof Capra (1975) describes equally radical developments in physics:

> Quantum theory has thus demolished the classical concepts of solid objects and of strictly deterministic laws of nature. At the subatomic level, the solid material objects of classical physics dissolve into wavelike patterns of probabilities, and these patterns, ultimately, do not represent probabilities of things, but rather probabilities of interconnections. A careful analysis of the process of observation in atomic physics has shown that the subatomic particles have no meaning as isolated entities, but can only be understood as interconnection between the preparation of an experiment and the subsequent measurement. Quantum theory thus reveals a basic oneness of the universe. It shows that we cannot decompose the world into independently existing smallest units. As we penetrate into matter, nature does not show us any isolated "building blocks," but rather appears as a complicated web of relations between various parts of the whole. (p. 57)

Keller and Capra note that the old paradigm's premise of objectively observable discrete and separate entities relating in hierarchies of linear cause and effect is being challenged by the reality of fundamental interconnections, webs of relationships, and the dynamic and creative flowing of energy. These interconnections also exist between the observer and the observed, so that our conceptions of objectivity are being challenged as well. Capra observes that

> in contrast to the mechanistic Cartesian view of the world, the world view emerging from modern physics can be characterized by words like organic, holistic, and ecological. . . . The universe is no longer seen as a machine, made up of a multitude of objects, but has to be pictured as one indivisible, dynamic whole whose parts are essentially interrelated and can be understood only as patterns of a cosmic process. (Capra 1975, 78)

The emergence of this new paradigm in systems theory and the biological and physical sciences is particularly significant in view of the fact that, beginning with Hobbes, the conception of *power over* in the social sciences has corresponded to the very notions of reality that Keller and Capra tell us are being shattered in the physical and biological sciences.[4]

Beyond Linear Causality

At the center of the cracking of the old paradigm and the emergence of a new paradigm is the notion of causality. In the West the concept of linear and unidirectional causality has been a driving force in the development of Western science and technology and the scarcity paradigm. It is central to the way we make sense of our world. But it is not the only way to understand the nature of life and matter and how life and matter function and relate. In fact other cultures have made sense of their world in different ways that might be described as "holistic" or "integrative." For instance, in the "Afro-circular" world view of African cultures, "there was no separation, dichotomy, or division between matters, materials, forces, and entities within the universe. There was not a view of strife, odds, or conflict between good/evil, man/nature, cause/ effect, mind/body, and others." (Burgest 1982, 49).[5] The Buddhist concept of *paticca samuppada* or "dependent co-arising" is central to the teachings of Gautama the Buddha given 2,500 years ago and to the Buddhist way of life. Reality is seen as an interdependent and reciprocal process in which no one factor is solely determinative: "All factors, psychic or physical, subsist in a web of mutual causal interaction, with no element or essence held to be immutable or autonomous" (Macy 1978, viii).

Richard Katz has made the concept of "synergy" central to his research on healing and community. Synergistic interactions stand in contrast to interactions of linear cause and effect. Katz describes synergy in this way:

The term *synergy* describes a pattern, a particular way in which phenomena relate to each other, including how people relate to each other and phenomena. . . . A synergistic pattern brings phenomena together, interrelating them, creating a new and greater whole from the disparate parts. In that pattern phenomena exist in harmony with each other maximizing each other's potential. Two phrases capture this quality: "The whole is greater than the sum of the parts," and "What is good for one is good for all." (Katz 1982, 197)

Katz's definition of synergy suggests two key aspects of synergistic interaction: the dynamics of interactions among parts of the whole and the corresponding phenomena of the maximization of potential and the expansion of the "whole." These two central dimensions of synergy are effectively described by Mary Parker Follett in her descriptions of reciprocal influence and emergence, which were outlined in some depth earlier.

Follett's description of reciprocal influence captures the dynamics of synergistic interaction:

> A good example of circular response is a game of tennis. A serves. The way B returns the ball depends partly on the way it was served to him. A's next play will depend on his own original serve plus the return of B, and so on and so on. (Follett 1942, 44)

Reciprocal influence involves the complex interactions and interdependent relationships among parts of a whole. It points to the severe limitations of describing social interactions in terms of linear cause and effect by identifying and describing the ways in which social interactions are complex and mutually influencing.

Second, Follett's description of emergence captures the synergistic dynamic in which, in Katz's words, a "new and greater whole" is created "from the disparate parts" so that "phenomena exist in harmony with each other maximizing each other's potential":

> We see that [reciprocal influencing] has always a value beyond the mere addition of the parts. A genuine interweaving and interpenetrating by changing both sides creates new situations. . . . Functional relating is the continuing process of self-creating coherence. . . . If you have the right kind of functional relating, you will have a process which will create a unity which will lead to further unities—a self creating progression. (Follett 1942, 200–202)

Joanna Macy (1978) also makes valuable contributions to our understanding of synergistic interactions. Macy's conception of "mutual causality" is described within the framework of systems theory. She notes that "the activity of the open system . . . as a transformer of energy and information in interaction with its environment, indicates a causal process that, in contrast to classical linear notions, is reciprocal or mutual" (p. 88).

The key to Macy's discussion of causality is the dynamics of feedback in open systems:

> Feedback represents the process by which a system receives information about its own performance. Data about previous actions, as part of the input it receives, is fed back so that the system can "watch" itself and direct its behavior. . . . Just as the performance of a motor or heating coil is monitored back to a radar screen or a photo electric cell, so is that of a muscle or sense organ. . . . The feedback concept then is circular and self-referential by nature. "Cause" and "effect" cannot be categorically isolated, but modify each other in a continuous process whereby input and output . . . interact. This interaction between perception and action is basic to an organism's capacity to adapt and organize itself; it is evident in exploratory and learning behaviors, as it is in self stabilization. (p. 89)

Macy notes that the same processes of feedback that operate within systems operate between and among different systems. Macy's description of these reciprocally influencing dynamics below is strikingly similar to Follett's, except that Macy's language is more mechanistic (perhaps indicative of the "mechanistic drift" of systems thinkers):

> The output from A modifies B, whose response becomes part of A's input. The way B responds to A is an aspect of A's self-monitoring; hence B's response informs A about itself and its progress towards its goals. In this information-processing exchange A functions for B in the same way. Though they may perceive a given datum in very different ways, depending on their internal codes, both are altered by their perceptions of their effect on each other. (p. 89)

Synergy, Community, and Power

Katz offers us insight into the quality of synergistic interactions among people in human communities. He has developed the concept of "synergistic community," a community in which a significant number of human interactions in relation to valued resources are synergistic (Katz 1983/84). In synergistic communities certain valued resources are experienced as accessible, expanding, and renewable, rather than as scarce. Katz posits that "resources created by *human activity and intentions,* such as helping and healing, are intrinsically expanding and renewable, and need not be subsumed under a scarcity paradigm"(p. 1, emphasis in original). In addition, within synergistic communities, mechanisms and attitudes exist that guarantee the equitable distribution of valued resources. Katz notes:

> Within the synergy paradigm, a resource is activated by individuals and communities who function as its guardian and not its possessor, and who, often guided by the motivation of service to others, allow the resource to be shared by all members of the community. Increasing amounts of the resource become increasingly available to all, so that collaboration rather than competition is encouraged. Paradoxically, the more the resource is utilized, the more there is to be utilized. (p. 2)

Rather than seeing themselves in inevitable conflict with other individuals and the community, members of synergistic communities see themselves as defined by their interconnections with others. They experience "self-embedded-in-community." In synergistic community, "self and community work toward the common good while seeking to fulfill their own perceived needs" (Katz 1986, 22). The dynamism of the experience of synergistic community is captured in the phrases *the whole is greater than the sum of the parts* and *what is good for one is good for all.* In contrast to the zero-sum, win-lose dynamics inherent in the scarcity paradigm and *power over,* synergistic community represents an expanding whole in which win-win relationships are real possibilities (winning in this case involves having access to valued resources such as healing, learning, power, etc.).

Macy (1982) describes the nature of power within a synergistic system. She agrees with Miller, Follett and Fromm in arguing that the old notion of power as domination is both "dysfunctional and inaccurate." Viewing power from the synergistic perspective, it becomes clear that "life processes change and growth evolves through dynamic and symbiotic interaction of open systems. Power is not power over but 'power with'"(p. 30). She calls this "power with" synergistic power.

To illustrate the qualities of synergistic power, she describes the nature of the power of neurons in a neural net:

The power of open systems is not a property one can own, but a process one opens to. It arises in interaction, as systems (be they people, plants, molecules . . .) engage and enhance their own and each other's capacities. Efficacy is transactional. Take the neuron in a neural net. If a nerve cell were to suppose that its power were a personal property to be preserved and protected from other nerve cells, and increased at their expense, it would erect defenses and isolate itself behind them. It would become dysfunctional as, indeed, a blocked neuron is. Its efficacy lies in opening itself to the charge, letting the currents of knowing and feeling flow through it. Only then can the larger system of which it is a part learn to respond and think. The body politic is much like a neural net. (p. 31)

She points out that life systems evolve not through closing themselves off and creating barriers to the environment but by opening themselves up to ever wider "currents of matter-energy and information" (p. 31). Power in this situation requires openness, vulnerability, and readiness to change. Power is not something one can accumulate but a "process one opens up to." It arises in interaction, as "systems engage and enhance their own and each other's capacities." This is synergistic interaction. In Katz's terms, power is a "resource produced through human activity and intentions" that is expandable and renewable and need not be seen in terms of the scarcity paradigm—that is, in terms of competition and domination.

At times Macy gets somewhat carried away in the progression of her thesis, equating power with *power with* and apparently ignoring the reality of domination and *power over* in our experience and our world. Nevertheless, her discussion of *power with* is important. She notes that synergistic power summons us to develop "our own capacities for nurturance and empathy, for participation and self-assertion" (pp. 31–32). The dynamic interrelationship between self-assertion and openness is crucial. *Power with* does not mean the subsuming of one by the other, but rather it involves identity within relationship, mutual assertiveness, and openness within community.

Katz and Seth note that "synergy is an inevitable aspect or phase of community, existing in a dialectical, but non-dualistic relationship with scarcity" (Katz and Seth 1986, 8). Even communities that primarily function within the scarcity paradigm seem to require "at least brief moments of synergy to hold them together." The important point to emphasize here is this:

> When we speak of synergistic community, we are talking about both a phase of synergy that is intrinsic to community, and those particular communities in which the balance is toward synergy, where, relatively speaking, there is more sharing and connectedness and the valued resources are renewable and equitably distributed. But, also, it seems that a community cannot always function synergistically. (Katz 1983/84, 9)

If, indeed, synergy and scarcity are fundamental to the functioning of communities, then it is very possible that *power over* and *power with* are fundamental as well.

If the concept of synergy seems somewhat elusive, it is because synergy defies full definition. Synergy is one of those concepts that is difficult to define, but one knows it when one experiences it. Katz and Seth (1986) address this difficulty with definition:

> The concepts of synergy and synergistic community may seem elusive. They describe a special quality, something in the "atmosphere" or "climate" of a group when it is resonating, functioning beyond words. Yet the actual *experience* of synergy and synergistic community, which is the important focus is palpable, concrete, and easily recognized by those who experience it. (pp. 3–4)

Using the synergistic paradigm as an organizing framework, we can see interconnections among the various theorists discussed in this chapter, and their challenges to conventional notions of power come into better focus. These theorists have remarkably similar critiques of the nature and limits of *power over* and strikingly congruent insights into the possibilities of human relationship, human community, and effective action. Key themes common to these theorists include agency-in-community, mutual enhancement of capacities, openness and connection to others, and the expandable and extendable nature of power.

The possibility of effective action within communities stands at the center of all these discussions of power. Macy and Katz make synergistic community the focus of their work. Fromm focuses on humanistic communitarianism, Miller on agency-in-community,

May and Follett on integration, and Starhawk on immanence, interconnections, and community. In each case each theorist speaks to the possibility of liberatory community—communities character- ized by mutuality, dialogue, respect, and equality. They describe communities in which individuals can fulfill their needs and devel- op their capacities not at the expense of others but by acting in con- cert with others. They describe empowering communities.

Fromm's conception of power as capacity for fulfillment of potential is synergistic. His notion that people acting in the world together can, and by definition must, reach their potential through modes of activity that do not involve domination, expresses the idea that what is good for one is good for all. Miller and her col- leagues describe this synergistic concept when they argue that the greater the development of individuals' capacities, the less people will need to limit one another.

Fromm, May, Follett, Miller and her colleagues, and Starhawk all argue for the possibility of individuals mutually enhancing one another's growth, fulfillment, and power. That is, what is good for one can be good for all. Power can be an accessi- ble, renewable, expandable and expanding resource, through the dynamic interaction of human beings acting and implementing together in nondominating ways. In this way all challenge the notion of scarcity, of a zero-sum system in which it is inevitable that there be will losers in order to have winners.

Power with, for Follett, is co-action, the development of indi- vidual capacities within a greater integrative unity. Integration, the process by which *power with* is generated within an integrative unity, is strikingly similar to synergistic interaction. Follett notes that power is generated and emerges out of interactions of recipro- cal influence among members of an organization or community. The more people act and interact together in an "integrating man- ner," the more their common and individual power increases. Thus power is clearly conceived as expanding and renewable. Follett notes that the dynamic interaction of individuals within an inte- grative unity always has "a value beyond the mere addition of the parts. A genuine interweaving and interpenetrating by changing both sides creates new situations" (Follett 1942, 200). This corre- sponds to Katz's description of the interrelating of parts that cre- ates new patterns and new wholes, and where the whole is greater than the sum of the parts. Follett notes that within an integrative unity, "individualism is not an apartness from the whole, but a contribution to the whole"(Follett 1942, 301). This is precisely the relationship between self and community within synergistic communities.

Starhawk (1987) also challenges the underlying view of causality undergirding *power over* and posits another perspective with notable similarity to the discussions of causality above:

> When we see spirit as immanent, we recognize that everything is interconnected. All the beings of the world are in constant communication on many levels and dimensions. There is no such thing as a single cause or effect, but instead a complex intertwined feedback system of changes that shape other things. (p. 22)

May's conceptualization of constructive power, or nutrient and integrative power, also fits within the synergistic paradigm. Nutrient power is characterized by connection, openness, sharing, nurturance, and receiving through giving. These are all qualities of synergistic systems and incompatible with *power over* within the scarcity paradigm. May's description of integrative power shares with the synergistic paradigm an emphasis on the qualities of openness (authentic innocence) and vulnerability. His description of integrative power as "my power abets my neighbor's power" captures the essence of the synergistic interaction. In one phrase it illuminates the two central concepts in synergistic community: that the whole is greater than the sum of the parts and that what is good for one is good for all. His notion of integrative power as being action for the community rather than solely for the individual corresponds to the synergistic notion of self-embedded-in-community.

A Conceptual Framework for *Power With*

It would appear that the pervasive notion of power as domination is a limited perspective. An increasingly clear conception of *power with* emerges from the multiple discourses on power cited above. Combined, these discussions of power provide the beginnings of a counterdiscourse to the discourse of *power over* and present a challenge to the current regime of truth.

Power with is manifest in *relationships of co-agency*. These relationships are characterized by people finding ways to satisfy their desires and to fulfill their interests without imposing on one another. The relationship of co-agency is one in which there is equality: situations in which individuals and groups fulfill their desires by acting together. It is jointly developing capacity. The possibility for *power with* lies in the reality of human interconnections within communities.

The relationship of co-agency is described through the *language of assertive mutuality*. This language, while generally familiar to us, is unfamiliar within the context of discussions of power. The vocabulary of assertive mutuality includes such words as *coaction, interconnection, sharing, mutuality, integration, collaboration, cooperation, synthesis, vulnerability,* and *interdependence,* and such phrases as *agency-in-community, giving and openness to others, self-assertion as opposed to self-imposition,* and *the capacity to act and implement as opposed to the ability to control others.*

"Synergistic interaction" and "synergistic community" provide a conceptual context within which *power with* can be described and understood. The concept of synergy helps us to go beyond the limitations of seeing all human interactions in terms of scarcity, linear cause and effect, and domination. It allows for the complexity and dynamism of relationships among individuals within social groups. By presenting the possibility of an expanding whole and expanding resources within this whole, it allows for us to conceptualize an expanding power in which access to valued resources and the actualization of individual and group capacities can be maximized within community.

Power With, Empowerment Theory, and Education

This discussion suggests that any general conception of power must be wide and deep enough to encompass *power with* as a dimension of power in human relationships. The reality of power seems to be that both domination and co-agency exist, both coercion and coaction are manifest in human relationships. Our understanding of power must include both kinds of relationships and both qualities of experience.

This discussion of *power over* and *power with* does not seek to denigrate the valuable insights that theorists (including many of those discussed in chapters 1 and 2) have contributed through their critical examination of *power over* and the micro- and macromechanisms of domination. Many of these critiques, in particular the work of Gramsci and Foucault, are essential for any serious attempt to understand modern society and the nature of the struggle for justice and democracy. My point, however, is that these perspectives are not enough, that most discussions of power are grounded in a limited and distorted definition of the concept. As a result we have been handicapped in our attempts to understand and describe alternatives to relationships of domination. In particular, this limited conception of power has constrained our ability to understand and describe the process of empowerment and the dynamics that empower. Miller's notion of power as the "capacity to implement" may be a more inclusive definition of power. Unencumbered by the language of imposition, her definition captures the most basic sense of power as capacity, or being able, but goes further in focusing on implementation, which stresses power's fundamental connection to *action*.

Fromm, Follett, May, and Miller and her colleagues all argue that *power over* is a distortion of *power with*. They argue that *power over* is a manifestation of sickness, oppression, and alienation, while *power with* is the expression of health, liberation, and community. If this is so, which I tend to believe, then *power over* and *power with* are not merely analytic terms in our understanding of power, but each carries an ethical dimension with important implications for ethical action.

The outline of a conception of *power with* and the potential for a "liberated" conception of power presented here raises many questions with regard to our general understanding of power and the nature of power in theories of empowerment. We need to build on our current understanding of *power with*. On a broad theoretical level, the concept of *power with* challenges us to reexamine our understanding of power as it relates to culture, domination, hegemony, ideology, resistance, and liberation. In particular, the relationship between *power over* and *power with* needs to be explored in more depth, for the interrelationship between the two has been insufficiently addressed in the literature.

Foucault (1980a) warns, however, against the temptation to develop all-encompassing theories of power. He observes:

> The role of theory today seems to me to be just this: not to formulate the global systematic theory which holds everything in place, but to analyze the specificity of mechanisms of power, to locate the connections and extensions, to build little by little a strategic knowledge (*savoir*). (p. 145)

It seems enough, then, to hope that the concept of *power with* can help us to better understand some of the ways in which power operates in our culture and that it might in some small way contribute to our emerging "strategic knowledge" of how we can improve education and work for the empowerment of people.

In this spirit, the positioning of the concept of *power with* beside the concept of *power over* points us back to the central question laid out in chapter 1: What are the dynamics of power in the experience of empowerment? While *power with* seems to offer a conception of power more consistent with contemporary discussion of empowerment, this should not be taken for granted. We must explore in more depth the power dynamics that empower people as well as the power manifest in empowered persons' engagement with the world and struggles for change. What role does *power with* play in these processes? And exactly what role does *power over* play in the process of empowerment?

Power with appears to have the potential for offering empowerment theory in general, and pedagogies of empowerment in particular, a dimension of power that is more compatible with notions of empowering human relationships and empowering settings. *Power with* offers a conception of power that is not based on domination, imposition, and control of others. Nevertheless, theories of empowerment must deal with the realities of power in our culture, which means that they must come to terms with *power over* and the reality of domination as well. Perhaps theories of empowerment must acknowledge the need to develop skills in the exercise of *power over*, perhaps resistance and struggle inherently include forms of control and domination, but this remains to be seen.

For educators who are attempting to develop pedagogies of empowerment, the emerging understanding of the nature of *power with* offers an additional critical concept for investigating the ways in which schools and predominant pedagogies perpetuate and cultivate patterns of domination. Critical and feminist pedagogies have taken us a long way in understanding the cultural contexts and ongoing dynamics of domination in U.S. education. What the concept of *power with* offers these educational discourses, as a key building block in a theory of empowerment, is a conceptual matrix for more fully understanding and more effectively creating *alternatives* to structures and relationships of domination that traverse our educational system and our society. Thus *power with* can help us conceive alternatives to conventional patterns of relationship in the organizational structure of schools (in the power relationships among administrators and teachers). It can help us create new approaches to curriculum development (transforming the power relationships between curriculum developers and teachers and between teachers and students in the choice and development of classroom materials) and classroom relationships (transforming the power relationships among teachers and students and between student and student). It forces us to rethink how the content of school curricula contributes to the reproduction of predominant notions of power as *power over*, and it challenges us to more closely consider what it means to cultivate students' abilities to control their lives. However, as exciting and inviting as such critical inquiry is, I believe that the temptation to do this kind of analysis should be tempered by another approach, one that emphasizes the experiences of teachers and students, one that is more dialectical and dialogical. Put simply, in order to explore the nature of *power with* and its place in the process of empowerment, we should listen to the voices of teachers and students. Do people truly experience *power with?* In describing the process of empowerment, do teachers experience power in terms of *power over, power with,* or both (what is the nature of power that empowers)? What are the dynamics of *power with* in relationships and groups? What is the relationship between *power with* and *power over* in the experience of empowerment?What are the dynamics of power in empowering student–teacher relationships? In this process, theory will be more closely tied to experience, and a much clearer understanding of *power over, power with,* synergistic community, and the process of empowerment will emerge. The second section of this book is an attempt to listen carefully to some of these voices.

Notes

1. The earliest reference to the term *power with* that I have uncovered is in Follett (1924).

2. In a later formulation Miller (1982) offers a slightly different definition of power as the "capacity to produce a change" (p. 2), but I prefer her earlier formulation.

3. Upon reflecting on this quote Don Oliver (personal communication, June 1986) comments, "I am not sure that the thing is not something extra, like the *élan vital.* If the sum is greater than the parts (as in any living organism), how can one escape the conclusion that there is a new and different quality of being?"

4. Related insights are to be found in the work of Lewis Thomas (1974), Gregory Bateson (1972), Gary Zukov (1979), Alfred North Whitehead (see Oliver and Gershman 1989), and Donald Oliver (Oliver and Ger-

shman 1989). It is also ironic and telling that this "new" paradigm bears strong resemblance to the world views of preindustrial cultures, in particular those of Native American and African cultures (Oliver and Gershman 1989, Katz 1982, Asante 1987, and Burgest 1982).

5. Burgest (1982) seems to have coined the term as *Afro-circolor;* Asante (1987), borrowing from Burgest, changed the spelling to *Afro-circular.* I have chosen to use Asante's spelling.

4

Six Teachers' Experiences of Empowerment in Educators for Social Responsibility

I've felt that I mattered. That I made a difference.... It's changed the way I think about things and the way I act.

Lally

The second section of this book revolves around a series of interviews with six educators conducted in late 1985 and early 1986. In the chapters that follow I explore the experience of empowerment and empowering and the nature and dynamics of power in these experiences. These interviews provide an opportunity to examine a range of questions raised by the theoretical discussions in the first section of this book: Are *power over* and *power with* effective tools for expanding our understanding of empowerment? How can our understanding of these concepts be deepened by the insights and reflections shared in the interviews? What are the dynamics of empowering groups and empowering pedagogy? What kinds of group dynamics and individual experiences did these teachers consider to have been central to their empowerment? What approaches to teaching and what kinds of teacher–student relationships foster the empowerment of students? Finally, pushing beyond the language of critique *and* the language of possibility, what is the *experience* of possibility?

The six educators whose reflections and experiences are the focus of these chapters were active members of the steering committee of the Boston Area Educators for Social Responsibility (BAESR) between 1984 and 1986 or longer. Educators for Social Responsibility (ESR) was founded in the spring of 1982 by educators seeking ways to address their own and their students' concerns about the possibility of nuclear war. By 1986 ESR had emerged as a national grassroots organization of teachers and other educators who believed that schools can help students develop the values, insight, skills, and commitment to address contemporary problems and to shape a more peaceful and just world. Committed to educational approaches that promote cooperation, nurture dialogue, present divergent viewpoints, stimulate critical thinking, and encourage students and teachers to act on their convictions, ESR has been a persistent voice, on both the national and the local level, for pedagogical approaches that address pressing social issues in our nation's schools in critical and empowering ways.

The Boston area chapter is one of the oldest and largest chapters in ESR, achieving a peak membership in the mid 1980s of over 600 educators. Between 1982 and 1986 the steering committee of the BAESR was responsible for guiding the chapter's growth and direction. The chapter's activities included curriculum development, teacher workshops, summer institutes and conferences. Participants in the steering committee were the most committed members of the organization. Empowerment had become a guiding concept not only in how steering committee members described their teaching goals, but in the way they described their participation and experiences in the organization as well. Given the centrality of empowerment in the culture of Boston ESR and the willingness of members to participate in the study, the experiences of these six educators provide a unique opportunity to explore the nature and dynamics of power in the experience of empowerment.

My own involvement in ESR has been extensive and complicated. From 1982 until 1986 I was deeply involved in the growth and development of the Boston area chapter. I served on the steering committee and participated in writing curricula. I wrote funding proposals, conducted workshops in area schools, and licked envelopes for bulk mailings. For the last two years of my active participation in the Boston chapter I also conducted the in-depth interview study and supplementary participant observation upon which the following chapters are based. This multifaceted activity in the organization presented me with a range of research challenges that needed to be worked through in the development of the research project. For a more in-depth discussion of my research model please refer to my doctoral dissertation, *Transforming Power: Toward an Understanding of the Nature of Power in the Experience of Empowerment* (Harvard University, 1986).

It is important to emphasize that the chapters that follow do not present a case study of Boston Area Educators for Social Responsibility; rather the focus is on six educators' reflections on their experiences in BAESR, on their teaching, and on their lives. The history, development and functioning of ESR as an organization is discussed only in relation to the reflections of the teachers as it helps to provide a context for understanding their experiences. ESR is the context and the focus of many of their reflections on their personal empowerment as teachers and as educational and social activists. The focus, and intent, is not so much to understand or present ESR as to explore these six educators' experiences of empowerment and power.

My goal in the following chapters is not to obscure or subsume the reflections of the six people I interviewed with a thick layer of interpretation and theory. Rather, it is to permit their voices to speak as clearly as possible, while simultaneously seeking to identify and explore patterns and common themes. Thus I include long excerpts from interviews, longer than are usual in interview studies. It is a delicate balance to maintain the uniqueness and integrity of individuals' responses and at the same time identify and discuss patterns and theoretical implications of their words and experiences. I have tried to strike a respectful and reasonable balance.[1] In this chapter I introduce the six teachers and I explore the reasons for their participation in ESR and the processes of their personal empowerment through their involvement in the organization. This discussion offers valuable insights into the process of empowerment and provides a context within which to situate my discussion of the dynamics of power in their experiences of empowerment and in their attempts to develop an empowering pedagogy.

Six Educators

Gene: Why did I become a teacher? I guess for two reasons. When I was in high school, I decided to go to a school that had an education department because I was coaching basketball and I liked watching people learn. I liked having something to do with young people learning, and how that made me feel; to be able to help them, knowing that it was making them feel good.... It does have to do with empowerment.... I would be as excited as Judy was when she could dribble the length of the court. I liked the group part of it, too, when I was coaching, to feel that we were a team and we were all in it together and helping each other and were more than just the sum of the parts. I was also really motivated in school. I did well in school. I thought a lot about my teachers and what

they were doing and what I liked and what I didn't like. . . .
Finally, I was a female and I think that was a big reason in
choosing that over some other kind of work. I was the valedic-
torian of my class and nobody talked to me about what I
wanted to do except go to college. I'm sure it would have been
different if I had been a man. So, that's how I ended up going
to college and studying to be a teacher . . . and then when I got
into it . . . when I actually got into the middle of it, I think my
reasons changed and became more political . . . although I
didn't drop my initial reasons. . . . My perception of the teaching I had experienced in the education system, the way I had
experienced it, was that nobody wanted to turn out anybody
who was a little different. It was basically like a factory, and
they wanted to turn out people who knew their place and
where to go and how to act and how to be. It was like a big
machine, and we were just preparing cogs for the machine. I
knew I wanted my students to go out and evaluate the
machine and ask questions about the world, but even beyond
that, to be able to do something after they had asked the
right questions and done the organization; to be able to make
a difference and to make the world a better place.

Gene's commitment to helping students "make the world a
better place" has continued to drive her work as a teacher, teacher
educator, and activist. For four years she taught English and social
studies in an alternative program at Watertown High School, a
public high school in a mixed working-class and middle-class sub-
urb of Boston. After leaving Watertown she taught at the Fayerweather School, a progressive, predominantly middle-class, private
school in Cambridge. There she team-taught in a sixth, seventh,
and eighth grade combined classroom. An active member of ESR
since 1982, she serves on ESR's national board, and participated in
the writing of the Boston chapter's curriculum guides *Dialogue,*
Perspectives, and *Making History.* From 1985 until 1988, she was
the full-time paid coordinator of the Boston area chapter of ESR.

Rachel: I grew up in a very small town and was aware of
very few options. Everybody in my family was a lawyer, so
actually the question was always whether or not to be a
lawyer. There was no other question. It wasn't whether to be
a lawyer *or* something else. It was just whether or not to be a

lawyer. It was only during college that I decided I just didn't like dealing with people from an adversarial perspective, and I didn't think things changed from the top down. That was why I started looking at education, because better changes tend to come about from the bottom up. And, believe it or not, I read Jonathan Kozol's book [*Death at an Early Age*], and that was one of the first things that made me realize that there was another field that I was much more interested in. I didn't decide I wanted to be a teacher 'til near the end of [college]. What interested me while I was at Tufts was sitting around my sociology classes . . . and hearing everybody talk about wanting to change the world and do justice and all that stuff, when I could look around and I knew full well that these people were all going to be accountants and stock brokers. I kept thinking 'What's the difference? What is it that makes someone really believe what they say?' . . . So, that was how I started in education. I started working at the United Way—the Voluntary Action Center—working on a project that promoted high school and college students to do more community action kinds of stuff and thereby improve their academic experiences. Then after college I enrolled in the University of Massachusetts teacher certification program.

Rachel taught for a year at Cambridge's Rindge and Latin High School. While there she taught in a comprehensive alternative program and in an alternative English/social studies program that was originally guided by Lawrence Kohlberg's work on the "just community." She also taught in the general high school. She then went to the University of Michigan for two years to earn a master's degree. After returning to Boston, she worked with a large nonprofit organization that provides volunteers and educational support for the Boston public schools. One of her major projects was to collaborate with students from Boston English High School on a fund-raising event to help end world hunger. Before leaving for Michigan she was an early participant in ESR. Since her return to Boston in 1983 she has been an active member of Boston ESR's steering committee. She was also the coordinator and collaborator in the social studies, math, and science sections of the Boston chapter's *Participation* curriculum series. In July 1986, just after this research project concluded, she became co-coordinator of the Boston area chapter of ESR.

Vera: I became a teacher somewhat by accident. Although I think in many ways it was probably something that I should have known I would like to do because I always, I guess, had a streak of the crusader in me and wanted to do something that would make the world better . . . I also always felt that my own upbringing hadn't been fully satisfactory and that I wanted to do something better for other kids. But I also enjoyed school and enjoyed being a student, and I enjoyed being a good student. Anyway, I found that it was really very hard to get a job in international relations when I got out of college. I read this book, *I Learn From Children,* by Caroline Pratt, quite by accident, the summer after I graduated from college. I thought, 'This is really so exciting, such an exciting way to think about teaching, about experiential learning, about active and involved learning.' It was such a new way for me to think about teaching as something that made it possible for kids to learn rather than as a process of pouring information into people, even though you might do that in a very creative and interesting way. So I went to Bank Street the fall after I graduated from college and became a teacher.

Vera's desire to find alternatives to "pouring information" into students has led her to a varied and rich teaching career. After several years' teaching elementary school on Long Island, New York, she taught in Paris and Norway. The bulk of her experience comes from more than fifteen years of teaching at the Shady Hill School, an elite K–9 private school in Cambridge. It was here that she began teaching ninth graders both English and social studies, eventually focusing entirely on social studies. Although a member of ESR since its early days, Vera's active involvement began in the summer of 1984 when she worked on the *Making History* curriculum guide. In July of 1986 she became the head of the Anglo-American School in Moscow.

Lally: When I first became a teacher . . . I became a Headstart teacher because the program in New Haven, where I had just moved, was looking for someone who could do music with young kids, and that appealed to me. I hadn't even thought about teaching before that . . . and I loved it. . . . I liked the kids, I was fascinated by all these different teaching approaches I was seeing. And when an opening came up, I was asked if I wanted to take the head teaching position, and

I was able to do so if I went to Southern Connecticut State College and took so many credits per year.... So that's how I got into it... no forethought, it's not something I wanted to do from the time I was ten.... I loved when the kids got excited about stuff themselves, whatever it was. If it was a mud pie, or some puzzle they solved, or a block building, whatever. I love seeing kids struggle with something and go like that when they did something that's important to them.... That's what really excited me.... When I moved up [to Boston] I actually didn't want to do any more social service work.... I just felt burned out and wanted to try something that wasn't so demanding. So I ended up being a secretary at the Upward Bound program at MIT, which felt okay for about three or four months.... So right at the same time that I was thinking about changing jobs, I went on staff at the Upward Bound program and started an adjunct for girls... it was all boys at that point... and so they made it coed, and so I recruited and started a program for girls at Wellesley.... I did that for about a year, ... so that was my first real work with high school students... and the same kinds of interactions excited me with high school kids as with young kids.... It wasn't 'til I came to Watertown that I actually taught a course, and that was by accident also.... I had job resumes in a variety of places at that point.... Watertown got funding for the child development program, and the assistant superintendent saw my resume somewhere. A friend of his gave it to him, and my experience with preschool and inner-city high school kids was the combination he liked. So I got that job. That was fifteen years ago.

Lally's delight in people characterizes all her work. At Watertown High School she ran an innovative child development program that includes an experiential component in which high school students are placed in elementary classrooms to tutor and to assist classroom teachers. She has also taught health courses at Watertown High's alternative program. Active in ESR since 1982, Lally has been closely involved in the writing of ESR's curricula *Dialogue, Perspectives,* and *Making History.* She has also been very active in the Central American Network of Educators, which has helped local teachers develop curricula about Central America and U.S. involvement in those countries. In June 1988, she left teaching at Watertown High School after eighteen years.

Shelley: I really became a teacher because . . . I guess that the motivating factor for me was that I'd been very politically involved all through college, very concerned about Vietnam and very concerned about civil rights and concerned about all sorts of issues, peace and justice, including nuclear weapons. I worked in Washington for a year afterward and found that I hated the political scene. There were so many egos involved. So little seemed to change that I felt that I needed to do something different. I went up to Maine and lived there for a year doing actually nothing. During that time not only did I fall in love with Maine, but I found that in thinking about what I could do, I felt that educating people would be the greatest way that I could make a difference in the world in terms of communicating that people could be socially conscious and caring and compassionate to each other and that we could really create a better world. I was pretty idealistic. I guess I still am. I was even more idealistic then, and I did a lot of reading about teaching before I even went into school . . . not a real lot, but *How Children Learn, How Children Fail.* When I was in Washington I was friends with some people who went up to direct a free school. I had read *Summerhill,* and I thought it would be a way to create change.

Shelley's continuing idealism, combined with hard-headed realism, has made him a driving force in the creation of ESR nationally and in the growth of the Boston chapter. Having moved to Boston in the late seventies, Shelley taught at the alternative School Within a School at Brookline High School. One of the founders of ESR, Shelley was the Boston chapter's first coordinator. In this role he organized ESR's professional development team and coordinated the *Dialogue, Perspectives,* and *Participation* curriculum writing projects. He has also served on the national board of ESR since its inception in 1982. In the summer of 1985 he left his position as Boston chapter coordinator to work on his doctorate at the Harvard Graduate School of Education. In 1987 he was elected president of the national organization of Educators for Social Responsibility.

Lucile: I never wanted to be a teacher. I went to college because everybody went to college. I was an English major because it was most interesting to me. I never thought about what I was going to do. I attribute it partly to growing up female, nobody really talked to me about work. Somehow I got to my senior year, and I had no clue as to what I was going to do. My father had said to me to take some education courses in case you want to be a teacher. I said it was the last thing I was going to be. But I didn't see what I could be with an English major, so I decided, well, okay, I better be a teacher. So I went to Boston College Graduate School for an M.A.T., and in the first summer I happened to get two incredible people to work with me in the courses I had to take. They were just incredible. I remember one of the teachers practically had us engrave on our arms the sentence *Kids learn by what they do and say, not by what you do and say.* So I didn't go into teaching because I always wanted to, I just fell into it, then I loved it. I feel like it was this serendipitous discovery on my part, that it was something that I like and that I could do well. . . . I always loved the literature, and I loved reading what kids wrote, and I loved the interactions with kids and the discussions.

Lucile's "serendipitous discovery" has led to a challenging and fulfilling career in teaching. After receiving her master's degree she taught for a year at Girl's Latin School in Boston. The following year she taught seventh graders grammar and writing in Everett, Massachusetts. For the past fifteen years she has taught primarily English, and some social studies, at Arlington High School.

Having been drawn to ESR in 1982 by the *Dialogue* curriculum writing project, Lucile was fully involved in the organization for three years. In addition to being a member of the Boston area steering committee, she was a member of the national board of ESR and Boston ESR's professional development team. During the 1984–85 school year she took a sabbatical to devote herself full-time to ESR. In the fall of 1985 she began to cut back on her involvement in ESR in order to devote more time to teaching and writing. By the summer of 1986 her participation in ESR had become minimal.

Joining ESR: Toward a Community of Shared Purpose

Between 1981 and 1984 each of these six educators was drawn to Educators for Social Responsibility and quickly became committed and active members of the organization. What motivat-

ed these individuals to join ESR? What attracted them to the organization? What needs and interests did ESR address? What role
did their initial reasons for being attracted to the organization
play in their subsequent experiences? Exploring the answers to
these questions offers insights into the experiences of teachers in
this culture and the personal, organizational, and political factors
that interact in the process of empowerment.

For Shelley, perhaps more than any other individual, the initial impetus behind his involvement in ESR was anger and frustration at political events occurring in the United States:

> My initial involvement in ESR was pretty political. What real-
> ly moved me was hearing Reagan's statements and feeling
> that I wanted to do something. I wanted to stop this insanity.
> There was a war mentality. There was a ... not only a waste
> of money ... but it was a serious waste of human and natural
> resources, and also a very, very dangerous situation. The first
> statements about a winnable nuclear war ... all those initial
> Haig statements and Reagan statements were reminiscent of
> some of Nixon's lies during Vietnam, and I just, for some rea-
> son, I got incredibly angry.... I was saying that you could be
> political in the classroom.... But what got me involved was,
> wanting a group to be able to work to make a difference, ... to
> change the situation and get Reagan out of office, ... to build
> a strategy for the next four years, ... to build a strategy for
> disarmament.

Shelley was reacting to the political realities of the early
1980s, which were characterized by the Reagan administration's
aggressive anti-Soviet stance and an accelerated arms race. He felt
a strong need to do something to counteract these policies, and as
he watched other professional organizations emerging in the peace
movement, he was excited about the possibilities of a teacher's
organization working on these issues.

Others responded to the same events in different ways. For
Gene, fear and despair were the dominant feelings, and in her
reflections one sees how the personal fears created by political
realities were interwoven with her commitment to teaching and
her responsibilities to her students:

> I went to see the Helen Caldicott movie, "If You Love This
> Planet." I remember walking out absolutely devastated, and

all I could think of was . . . I guess I was teaching for about
four years, and I was doing a women's career course, and I
thought, what does it matter? What does it matter? If I teach
women's studies . . . kids are talking about sex roles and obstacles and barriers and thinking about their futures and talking with women who had overcome obstacles, and it could all
be blown up. . . . What does any of it matter? And it really
threw me for a loop. I didn't expect to have that reaction, and
at that point I started searching for something.

The heightened political debate over the arms race and its
accompanying media coverage also affected the students with
whom the six were working. The recognition that their students
had fears and questions concerning the possibility of nuclear war
was another impetus for involvement in ESR. Shelley shares his
experience: "Hearing some of my kids talk about nuclear war was
scary. Hearing their reactions and their anxiety and what they
were thinking about was concerning me."ESR Another factor that
led individuals to ESR was that ESR was committed to educational
change. Gene states:

[ESR was] the first organization that I could see or that I had
found that if you played out the philosophy . . . you radically
change education.

Each of the study participants maintained a long-standing commitment to exploring alternatives to mainstream pedagogical practice. In fact, five of the six had spent significant portions of their
teaching careers involved in innovative educational experiments
that challenged the status quo. They were, even before they joined
ESR, educational activists. But their activism was individualis-
tic—centered on their work in their classrooms with their students. One is struck in the interviews by the depth of their concern
for their students, by their commitment to listening to them and
responding to their needs. They have an intuitive understanding of
the link between the culture of the classroom and the larger culture. Each was searching for ways of teaching that would help students to better comprehend the world around them. The belief that
it was essential for schools to respond to students' fears and questions concerning the possibility of nuclear war is but one example
of this search. And each intuitively understood the political nature
of teaching and its interconnections with larger political and social

realities, although their abilities to articulate these connections varied.

Of the range of interconnected factors that led each individual to ESR, perhaps the most important was that each person was experiencing professional and often personal isolation as he or she confronted social realities and struggled to understand how to respond professionally. This was true despite the fact that most of them were involved in alternative programs where, presumably, they were working with other teachers with similar concerns and commitments. This isolation is powerfully communicated in the interviews and is testimony to the disempowerment of teachers and the failure of our educational system to provide teachers with a sense of support, purpose, and community. Vera describes her feelings:

> I think so often when you're teaching, you get so isolated. It's you and your little cell there and your kids, and maybe it's you and your school, but it's really very important to see yourself as part of a broader mass of people and to meet people who are not part of your school but who teach in different schools and who have different problems but still have the same kind of ideals and who have to find different solutions because their situations are different. . . . When you're all alone you sort of feel like a tadpole in a big pond wiggling your legs, they're just emerging, but you don't know quite where you're going with it.

Shelley describes the kind of frustration that this isolation can engender:

> [I was] feeling isolated and feeling alone and feeling crazy. If at some point ESR had not come along, I would have probably left teaching or found something else, another way to work within education.

And Gene echoes similar feelings:

> I didn't know what to do. . . . I wanted to talk to people, I wanted to talk to other teachers. I wanted to know whether other people felt the same way. . . . I didn't know anything about nuclear weapons, and I had worked some in the anti–nuclear power movement, and nobody would talk about

weapons. . . . So I wanted to talk with some people who had done some thinking about it. I wanted a bigger group than was in my school. And also you just don't go up to people and say, 'I just saw this movie, and I'm really devastated, and I'm morbid about nuclear war.' I mean it is a hard thing. You have to really trust someone to do that.

ESR provided the opportunity to meet colleagues with similar commitments and work on the political and educational issues they felt were important. ESR offered connection, community, and a context for meaningful action. Lally expresses these sentiments well:

You know, I think I got involved because what excites me about what happens to the kids is what happened to me or began to happen for me at the Waging Peace Conference. . . . I just remember a lot of dedicated teachers talking in a real excited way about things they were doing. I don't remember the content that much, but just having that sense that I was around a really lively interesting group of people.

Although initially unsure of her interest in ESR, "something caught fire at the Waging Peace Conference," and within months Lally was very involved in a curriculum writing project. The project was intimidating and challenging, but this made the work all the more exciting:

None of us really knew what we were undertaking in writing this curriculum, and I felt maybe like I was doing something that was more than I could handle. But that challenge was exciting as well, and I just remembered the group that we were in was incredible. The ideas that would come boom, boom, boom, at any of our meetings. How to get something going or how to look at something. It was just electric. . . . It was just one meeting after another. To me, it wasn't a real commitment to the nuclear issue at that point, that became important, it was really the dynamics of this group that kept me going.

What excited Lally most, initially, was something she was not experiencing in her school: a unique opportunity to learn, grow, organize, and collaborate with other teachers on issues that were central to her commitment to teaching.

Learning those skills, being around people who really wanted to talk about that and talk about what it means to help kids feel like they're doing something worthwhile, that they can make a difference. I didn't do that in Watertown at all. I think that opportunity was really exciting to me. The nuclear issue was not something I had been particularly involved in at that time. It was more these interactions and talking about new ways of teaching that hooked me into it. And then the nuclear issue came into context.

Vera describes very similar feelings:

First I just joined because I had heard of the organization and I believed in what they were doing. . . . I really didn't become active until the summer of '84 when I got the notice that people were needed or that at least people were welcome to come and try to write another curriculum, and I wanted to be part of that. . . . I think the experience of writing the curriculum was very positive and very exciting and a lot of fun and challenging. I think that most of all the people who were there were people with whom I felt I had things in common and who had interests that I had and who saw things the way I did. That was very nice to find, that there were people to whom you didn't have to explain yourself or defend yourself and who right away sort of saw what you were after and where your ideas sort of fit in complementarily with their ideas. You could gain from them and you could give back to them, and that's always a very positive, exhilarating kind of feeling, when you're with a group of people with whom you feel comfortable very quickly.

The entire group shared a concern for the nuclear issue, combined with a broader commitment to peace and justice, which in turn was intricately connected to their commitment to teaching and their students. Lucile's account of her introduction to ESR reveals how the dynamics of personal change were interwoven with her desire to be an effective teacher. She described a web of personal, social, and professional issues that together combined to stimulate her to become involved in the kind of educational advocacy that is uniquely the mission of ESR.

As the 1980s began, Lucile was politically and personally alienated. Although she had been involved in various student movements in the 1960s, since Watergate she had withdrawn from politics. "I just paid no attention, didn't read the paper, didn't know what was going on, didn't care." She felt powerless to make any difference in current social conditions.

In January 1982, she was drawn to a weekend workshop entitled "Beginner's Guide to Ending Hunger." This experience reconnected her to long-submerged social ideals. She remembers carrying two key ideas away from that weekend, which sparked an interest in "working in the world again." The first idea was "just the sense that little things make a difference, that you don't have to be Mother Teresa." She began to give money to Oxfam, "and I felt good, I mean it was a little piece, there was work going on, and I was making a contribution to it." The second idea involved the tension we experience between our vision of the world and its reality.

> They did this great demonstration of stretching a rubber band and saying one end of the rubber band is reality, the real world the way it is, and the other end is the ideal world, the way we would like it, and that the tension between those two is hard to live with, so you either get rid of it by forgetting reality and living in this visionary world or forgetting the visionary world and living with reality. It's painful to hang on to the reality and the vision, but basically the work that's involved in making a difference is learning to live with this tension between what's real and ideal so that kind of helped me think about it in a new way, that the tension is just inherent in the work ... in that our job is to learn how to live with that tension.

Just as she was beginning to move beyond the barriers that had kept her away from social action, professional and political events began to "fall into place at the same time":

> My students at school started talking about the Soviet Union and nuclear weapons, and I realized I didn't know anything about it, and they didn't, and I thought it was really criminal that they were high school seniors and were so ignorant about the world and also that I was.

At precisely this time Roberta Snow, who had developed the curriculum *Decision Making in a Nuclear Age* (1983), was conducting her first five-day workshop in Boston. Lucile enrolled and "in the middle of it, I said, 'What organization can I join to do work on this?'" Roberta told her about ESR. She called Shelley. "Shelley said, 'We're working on a book. There's a meeting at Cambridge Rindge and Latin. Why don't you go?' So I went."

Lucile's account reveals how personal change, professional interests, and social forces combine and interact to move people to a particular set of actions. Evident also are some of the intrapersonal dynamics at work in the rise of social movements. Lucile's personal transformation coincided with larger political events that also were manifest in her classroom, in particular in her students' concerns about nuclear issues. These events, forces, and personal processes were not occurring in isolation. As mentioned earlier, other educators, moved by similar concerns, were asking similar questions and gathering in a nascent educational movement that was part of a larger movement for social change. Lucile was not alone, and in ESR she found an organization that could meet and respond to a variety of her emerging interests and needs.

The discussion above reveals a common web of feelings and commitments that led each individual to ESR. Each was feeling a sense of *personal despair and feelings of powerlessness* in the face of the nuclear threat and other pressing social problems, combined with a *desire to act meaningfully to respond to these issues*. Each teacher was *distressed at hearing students express their fears and concerns about nuclear war*, their futures, and the possibility of creating a more peaceful and just world. Each of the six educators felt a strong *need for connection with other educators* with similar concerns and commitments. And finally, each person was *committed to working for educational change* as a vehicle for social change and desired to develop and understand educational approaches that could better meet the needs of their students and the need for positive social change. While there were definite differences in the degree of influence various factors had in leading each individual to ESR, all five factors provided the rationale for their involvement.

Finally, all of these educators saw their teaching as the main vehicle for their political work. Not one was a long-term social activist. They did not join ESR with well-formulated agendas for political and educational change (although this did vary). Rather, they were drawn to the work of ESR by conscience, professional commitments, and contemporary events. In ESR they created a community of shared purpose. Gene put it this way:

It's given me hope to make changes happen. I mean, I think

it's much better to work with people on something. It's a more hopeful, optimistic way to work. Less frustrating. More energizing. And that's empowering.

Empowerment: "Making a Difference"

Rachel: When I feel empowered, I feel all at the same time more energetic and enthusiastic about something as well as calmer, sort of calmer in the sense of being more centered ... or stronger about my ability to work on an issue, and therefore having the energy to work on it.

Shelley: My sense of empowerment is that it's a feeling, at some level it's feeling a confidence to be able to act in the world.... Real empowerment comes for me in terms of being able to have my vision, in however limited a way, begin to grow in the social environment.

Lucile: Well, I guess that I define [empowerment] more loosely the longer I work on ESR work. First it was about nuclear weapons, which is not a small thing to be trying to make a difference about, and then it was United States foreign policy. But the more I work with it, the more I think that in order to be able to do those things, we need to see empowerment as being part of day-to-day life, that is, ways in which we as teachers and citizens and our students as students and citizens can affect our environments: our communities, our schools, wherever we are in our lives, we feel like we can and ought to interact in a way that will change it.

Gene: Empowerment works two ways ... you can empower somebody, you can be empowered ... the end is the individual having both the skills and the confidence to make change ... or to make a difference or have an affect on something.

Vera: I guess you might describe or define [empowerment] as a state in which a person feels that he or she has some control over his or her life, over the decisions that he or she has to make, and that those are not capricious or decided by fate or the person has no control at all ... and that if you find yourself in a situation which is difficult for you or not to your liking, you have some skills and some strategies for trying to better the situation.

Lally: [For me, empowerment means] to feel like I make a difference, that I have something to say that matters to other people, that confidence that I can think critically about something, that I can look at something and have a reaction or response, that makes a difference to me and to other people and that stimulates other people to care and feel about something... and that what I do out of that makes a difference... whatever action I take out of that is going to matter, just having that faith that it's going to matter ... whether it's the right decision to take or not.

In these responses a simple yet powerful notion of empowerment is expressed: to be empowered means to be able to effect change. Empowerment is the process by which individuals and groups become able to "make a difference." In these definitions empowerment is both the knowledge that one can make a difference and the actual ability to act. Empowerment, they indicate, involves the development of feelings of confidence, centeredness, and efficacy and the development of skills in self-expression, organization, decision making, and communication—what Kieffer has called "participatory competence" (Kieffer 1981). These teachers all believed that their experiences in ESR had been empowering. Involvement in ESR had enhanced their ability to make a difference.

Praxis: Reflection and Action

Lally observed:

Empowerment has to do with the combination of feeling strongly about something and caring about it—thinking about it and acting. All that is combined and never any one happens in isolation. So I can't just think strongly about something and feel empowered, usually, unless there is an action piece of it too... nor do I feel comfortable just acting on something without continuing to think about it, and I get into that sometimes—I get involved in doing, and I kind of stop thinking about the issues.

Lally's observations were echoed in all the interviews. It was consistently stressed that ESR provided a context in which each person felt that her or his understanding of teaching, social issues, and social and educational change was deepened and extended as a result of the dialogue between reflection and action in the organization.

Lally describes ESR as an "intellectually exciting" environment, and Rachel captures the group's sentiments very well:

> What's very different about being involved with ESR . . . is having built-in time to reflect pretty consistently. Whether it's in steering committee meetings or other kinds of meetings or the kinds of topics that we talk about. . . . It's built-in reflection. And so it hasn't necessarily changed what I believe about the world, but it's built into my routine the time and the process to really think through and really believe those things, [for instance] that changing the world *is* better bottom-up rather than top-down and that people really do have to change things for themselves, in themselves.

Everybody stated that their understanding of teaching and their actual teaching has changed as a result of their ESR involvement. Lucile noted that ESR had been empowering for her because it was "a place to think about educational issues and to work to implement a different kind of teaching in my own classroom and to a certain extent to take that to other teachers in workshops." Shelley describes how ESR provided a context in which he could grapple intellectually and practically with pedagogical issues:

> I've changed my educational philosophy a great deal. I believe that I came in with a certain sense of . . . a question about how to be political in the classroom—how to create change—what's the most effective way to create change, and I struggled through a lot of different ways of doing that. One way was to support and build the self-worth of students and the second through academic stuff . . . just keep on giving them positive feedback. . . . And then I began struggling with how do you help educate for real social consciousness. And I think when I went into ESR I was struggling with whether you present many sides. Do you present one side? What do you do with the politics of it? And how political can you be? And I had tested out in Brookline, actually this is before I left

teaching, I had tested out being very, very political, and it didn't work. So what I was trying to struggle with was how do you teach what's at the core of the issue and what's the core of what we need to change without making it a politically biased and a propagandistic mode of teaching. And so I think in the last three years what I've been able to do is struggle with that question over and over again and come to a place where I feel like I understand what can be done. Teaching the Harvard [MA] course was sort of a culmination of that.... Where I had to test it out ... and it worked.

Shelley describes a process in which he regularly tests his ideas through teaching. His experiences inform his thinking; they offer feedback and new information for the crystallization of new insights, which can again be tried out in the classroom. He indicates how crucial critical understanding is to empowerment and how the interaction of reflection and action spurs greater insight, clarity, and change. This is the dynamic interaction Lally referred to above.

Steering committee members are involved in ESR not only to become more effective teachers, but because they feel it is important to spread the organization's message; in Vera's words, to do "something that is beyond your classroom.... It is my political stance, in a sense, as well as my professional stance." ESR offered concrete opportunities to work for change outside the classroom. Shelley commented, "ESR is a forum for me to act with other teachers to create changes." Lucile notes that ESR has empowered her

to lead teacher education workshops, to make speeches, to write curricula, to write articles.... ESR offered me an opportunity to do those things in the context of goals that I cared about and with people who encouraged me and helped me do them.

Much of the work in ESR involves the development and maintenance of a grassroots social change organization. As such it involves reflection, decision making, and action around a variety of issues ranging from the educational philosophy of the organization to fund-raising, from workplace management issues to budgeting.

A related theme throughout the interviews was that members of ESR work hard to create organizational structures and strategies for working for change that are consistent with the pedagogical and social values the organization espouses. Lucile observes, "We spend time thinking about the questions of what we are doing and how we are doing it." Gene echoes this when she emphasizes that ESR

> respects the process, it respects the means to the end. And I don't think many groups do. Many groups talk about making social changes, making a better world, but when you look at their organizations, nobody can talk to each other.

The dynamic praxis that occurs in the discussion of pedagogical issues continues in the ongoing dialogue about the mission and purpose of ESR. This dialogue has affected each individual and played an important role in her or his empowerment. Shelley observes:

> The other thing that helped create the change, the changes in me, were the discussions . . . the dialogue that we've maintained for the last three years about whether. . . . Do we endorse a particular organization? How do we fund-raise? Or the essential guts of it. What are we trying to do? What's the message we're trying to communicate? How do we educate for a peaceful world?

Thus ESR is a laboratory for educational and social change. The ongoing praxis of espoused goals and daily implementation of programs contributes to each individual's developing understanding of the dynamics and possibilities of change.

Positive Self-Image and the Development of Participatory Competence

The study participants all indicated that their involvement in ESR had enhanced their sense of competence and self-confidence. Their belief in their ability to "make a difference" was reinforced by a more positive self-image. This came as a result of interactions within the organization, as in Lally's experience:

> Before I came to ESR I really didn't have a whole lot of confidence in the way I thought of things. I saw myself as a doer . . . but . . . in ESR . . . I can really feel inside myself that I have something to say, that I have a way of thinking about something or looking at an issue that's laid out in front of me that's

valuable. That gives me a lot more confidence in my ability to think about things.

It also emerged as a result of a changed perception of each individual by colleagues in the wider educational community, as was Gene's experience: "I feel respected as an educator by being part of this organization."

Rachel describes the impact of this enhanced sense of self:

> I am more confident and comfortable with what I believe on a very deep level... and underneath it all I feel very centered... centeredness is first of all feeling stronger, meaning more power, more stability, and more committed to something.

This improved self-image, which grew out of small triumphs, made possible the tackling of larger challenges and risks.

Shelley's comment below illustrates the links between the development of self-confidence, the experience of connection with other people, and the feeling that one can make a difference:

> I feel a lot more confident. I don't feel crazy in what I believe. I feel there are other teachers that care about what teaching is about and that all of us can make a difference.

This feeling of confidence, in their values and in their ability to teach and act effectively for change, grew in tandem with the development of concrete skills. These skills included the cultivation of a variety of teaching skills, from conceptualizing courses to developing ways of relating to students and promoting dialogue in the classroom, as well as skills in organizing, speaking, fund-raising, and conducting workshops.

Perhaps more fundamentally, individuals described the enhancement of their ability to interact with people in a way that promotes change in both parties. That is, they developed their skills of dialogue: the ability to say what they believe *and* to listen carefully; to be able to hold on to what seems true *and* to let go of outdated or outmoded ideas. This ability to be both assertive and open in relation to others was an important skill for all participants. Rachel describes these changes:

> It is communicating more sensitively. That's a whole area that I think I have learned through ESR. I was a much more

argumentative person a couple of years ago, and I was much more defensive a couple of years ago. . . . I'm confident and comfortable with what I think on a very deep level.

Rachel's capacity to identify and articulate her vision and needs developed concurrently with the ability to listen, to be open to new ideas, to growth, and to change:

It's much more confidence about changing my mind. Normally you'd be confident about keeping your opinion, but in this case, I've gotten more comfortable being able to change my mind about something and feeling more comfortable not having to stick to an opinion and not having to defend something so much as question it.

Both asserting one's convictions *and* being open to personal change were seen as two sides of the dialogic dynamics of working for change.

Empowerment:
A "Marriage of the Internal and the External"

Of the six participants in this study, Lucile is the one who, during the course of the interview process, made the decision to significantly cut back on her involvement in ESR. Since 1986, Lucile has been only minimally involved, although she has remained a member of the organization and maintains strong relationships with many people she met through ESR. Close examination of her decision to pull back from her involvement offers valuable insights into the dynamics of empowerment.

In reflecting on her retreat from ESR, Lucile observed that empowerment "has something to do with some marriage of external situations and your own internal state of being." After three years of intensive involvement in ESR, Lucile began to feel a separation of her internal state of being and the external goals and roles available to her in ESR. She experienced this disconnection in three important areas.

First, she began to have doubts about whether ESR was in fact "making a difference":

The people who manage to stick with it do believe and continue to believe that it makes a difference, and I go in and out of

feeling that. A lot of times I feel, okay, it does not make a difference what we do, and I see the people who continue to be
able to do the work still pretty much thinking that they make
a difference. And they are willing to recognize the slowness of
the change and be patient with it and trust it and I get impa-
tient. You know what? We still have nuclear weapons.... I've
gone through a stage where it is not clear to me that individuals do make a difference or how they make a difference.

Clearly, the sense that one's work is having an effect is crucial to
keeping an individual engaged in any attempt to effect change.
The ability of an organization to help its members maintain perspective on the pace of change and the effectiveness of its strategy
is vital to both the health of the organization and the empowerment of its members. A sense of efficacy, as we have seen, was crucial to the process of empowerment. Lucile was losing her patience
and doubting her effectiveness. Her doubts led her to reconsider
her commitment to the organization.

Second, as the organization and Lucile grew and changed
over the years, the avenues of action provided by the organization
began to diverge from Lucile's evolving needs. As any organization
matures, maintenance activities increase, reducing the time allot-
ted to creative activities. Lucile describes this evolution and its
effects on her:

The work we ended up doing on the steering committee, at
least for me at that point, seemed pretty removed from the
original connection that I came to ESR with, which was working with teachers and writing *Dialogue*. And I guess too distant from whatever might be the hoped for outcome. I mean
there is a lot of time spent on figuring out how to make a budget work, and then for me, to make the leap from what the
budget means and what this budget will enable us to do is a
long way.... Maybe it was the wearing off of the initial enthusiasm, partly.

The movement from the initial infusion of creative energy in an
organization in its genesis to an increasing need to balance creative,
administrative, and maintenance functions may inevitably produce
tensions. Organizations provide different rewards and have different needs at various times in their histories. Thus their ability to
provide empowering opportunities for their members varies as well.

Finally, Lucile was feeling tension between different commitments and interests. She felt the time she was devoting to ESR was affecting the quality of her teaching negatively:

> I found it exhausting. The year that I did both teaching and ESR work I never felt very good about teaching. I did like the work I was doing in ESR but felt I was, in a way, neglecting my classroom.

Moreover, she had neglected to continue other activities that gave her great personal satisfaction. "I have gone back to writing poetry, which I love and missed. I read."

Organizations such as ESR, created to respond to specific needs and issues, cannot meet all of the needs, goals, or ambitions of their members. They are not all-encompassing communities.

Lucile's observation about the importance of a match between an external situation and internal needs is significant. It relates to Richard Katz's argument that empowerment involves access to valued resources. As long as ESR allowed Lucile to have access to opportunities that were important to her—working for change, being part of community of shared purpose, improving her teaching, writing curricula—it was an empowering environment. But as Lucile's personal needs and the work of the organization changed, ESR no longer provided access to what was important to her, it no longer provided access to her valued resources, which increasingly included time for teaching and writing poetry.

The combination of these three factors—doubts as to effectiveness, shifting organizational tasks, and changing personal priorities—meant that active participation in the organization was no longer empowering for Lucile. This occurred even as the match between the internal and the external continued for others. They continued to see participation in ESR as providing access to resources they valued, and thereby providing access to empowering experiences.

Empowerment: The Emergence of Voice

The underlying theme that emerges from these six accounts is that empowerment in ESR meant that each individual was able to *cultivate and express her or his own unique voice*. The authors of *Women's Ways of Knowing* (Belenky, Clinchy, Goldenberger, and Tarule 1986) note that "voice" is more than just developing a point of view. The theme of voice stands in contrast to its opposite, silence. It is a metaphor for how people describe their identity, self-worth, and feelings of isolation from or connection to others:

> describing their lives women commonly talked about voice and silence: 'speaking up,' 'speaking out,' 'being silenced,' 'being not heard,' 'really listening,' 'really talking,' 'words as weapons,' 'feeling deaf and dumb,' 'having no words,' 'saying what you mean,' 'listening to be heard,' and so on. (p. 18)

In developing their own voices, individuals begin to become authors of their lives, thus voice and action are intimately linked.

Through their involvement in ESR each of the six teachers encountered her or his own voice within and found support for its development and expression. They felt better about themselves and more capable of expressing their values and beliefs and acting in accordance with them. They developed their abilities to think critically, to speak forthrightly, to listen carefully, and thereby to act more effectively. ESR represented for each of them a movement out of silence and isolation into self-assertion and community.

Lally's comments below echo the themes of the metaphor of voice:

> When I say something I really feel it is heard, and by the way that other people react to it, I feel like, yeah, I said something that made a difference.... I feel it happening, and I can really feel inside myself that I have something to say, that I have a way of thinking about something or looking at an issue that's laid out in front of me that is valuable.

Voice emerges as one develops a sense of self in relation to others. It is an internal process—tied to feelings of self-confidence and self-worth and to the feeling that one has something to say. And it is also an external process—cultivated in a context in which being listened to by others reinforces the internal belief that one has something worthwhile to say. Rachel captures these dynamics when she comments, "I feel more confident about my skills and my views, and I feel more able to offer those to other people."

The cultivation and expression of voice occurred both within the organizational dynamics of ESR and as individuals carried ESR's work to their classrooms, schools, and communities. Shelley describes how interaction with the wider educational community contributes to the development of voice:

> What I have been trying to do is find a way to express what I feel about the way the world could be. In that way it's made me feel like I can . . . I keep coming back to simplistic terms like 'I can make a difference,' or 'I can have my point of view or my insights heard in the larger world,' that I can create change in the larger world.

Too often our political system silences its citizens. Too often the structure of schools silences teachers. Too frequently teachers are drained of their idealism. Isolated and alone, teachers become defensive and teach defensively. They stifle their own and their students' voices. Too few schools tap teachers' sense of idealism, too few cultivate a sense of hope, too few nurture teachers' voices. Schools rarely are true communities. They fail to build teachers' sense of self-esteem and competence and to promote teachers' intellectual growth. All too rarely do administrators create cultures of creativity and change, rarely do they provide adequate mechanisms for change.

I hear these criticisms and frustrations every day from many of the teachers with whom I work. Daily, I listen to the fears of my students—teachers in training—who, after observing and speaking with veteran teachers, dread that their idealism, their hope, and their creativity will be destroyed when they enter the profession.

Kathleen Weiler (1988) states that

> the empowerment of students must entail the empowerment of teachers. Teachers need to have their work as intellectuals respected and recognized. Teaching is valuable and highly political work and both teachers and those outside the schools need to recognize the value of that work. But teaching as political work entails more than simply what goes on in isolated classrooms. . . . Classroom teachers need to break out of the isolation of their own classrooms. . . . For their own empowerment and in order to organize against increasing bureaucratization of schools, progressive teachers and administrators must seek out ways of working collectively and collaboratively. (p. 152)

Boston Area Educators for Social Responsibility, a volunteer group of educators working for a shared set of goals outside of regular school structures, provided a context in which teachers could find opportunities for solidarity and collective action. Within a community of shared purpose, these six educators felt their own sense of competence enhanced as the barriers of isolation were broken. They felt they were making a difference in changing the direction of important educational and social issues. Through ESR they discovered and expressed their voices while simultaneously becoming better able to help others develop their voices as well.

Notes

1. For a more extensive, technical discussion of the methodology used in this study, please see Kreisberg 1986.

5

Power in the Experience
of Empowerment

In terms of our action as an organization, the places where I did feel empowered, I think, definitely were *power with*.

Lucile

So many of my experiences have fallen into categories of *power over* and *power with*. . . . I was talking about *power over* and *power with* throughout. Sometimes in so many words, and sometimes in the words of authority versus trust; sometimes in the words of hierarchy versus democracy. . . . I see my [experience of empowerment] as being very much tied to *power with*. I don't know if I feel confident enough, anymore, to never associate it with *power over*, but, certainly, I rarely associate it with *power over*.

Rachel

What is the nature of power in the experience of empowerment? This is the central question anchoring this book. And it is to this question that I now turn, examining the interpersonal dynamics that nurtured and sparked the empowerment of these six educators and exploring their approaches to educational change.

Co-agency in Community:
The Relational Matrix for Empowerment

[ESR is] a forum for me to act with other teachers to create changes that need to be made. So it's a very positive and powerful group. It feels like a group of similar thinkers who are energized and active and caring and sort of working together to do something. The collective energy is so much greater than my own ability to do something as an isolated individual.

Shelley's comment emphasizes that whereas empowerment enhances the individual's ability to act effectively in the world, it is not the ability to act alone. Rather, empowerment facilitates the ability to act with others to fulfill individual and group needs and goals. Indeed, as members recounted the various actions they have taken within Boston ESR, they all emphasized their collective nature. They saw themselves acting with others for their own good and the good of the community (both their ESR community and the wider communities of which they were members).

The experience of egalitarianism was stressed as an integral aspect of their empowerment. In working with other people to achieve shared goals, relationships were horizontal rather than vertical. Shelley reflects on this:

> I sense that no one feels superior to anybody else. . . . There are collegial, collaborative relationships.

Vera notes:

> There is no hierarchy or status climbing on other people's shoulders to get to the top within the organization.

Co-action. Collaboration. Equality. These are key characteristics of relationships of co-agency. What distinguishes co-agency from domination is that one's experience of effectiveness does not come from the ability to impose one's will on others. Rather, a sense of efficacy evolves from accomplishing tasks through cooperation and mutually supported action.

In chapter 4 we saw how a range of common factors combined to draw individuals to create a community of shared purpose. Every individual emphasized the vital role her or his relationships with other ESR members played in her or his experiences of empowerment. Each person stressed how important it was for her or him to connect with others with similar concerns and commitments. Enhanced self-image came in large part from receiving the respect and support of fellow ESR members. Reflection was not practiced in isolation. Rather, each person described a reflective community in which a dynamic dialogue sparked individual critical reflection and action. Finally, action was not solitary, but always felt to be connected to the work of a larger community, which was, in turn connected to a larger social reality. This web of interpersonal affinity and support formed the matrix for empowerment.

Lally describes her feeling of connection in this way:

It really makes me feel like part of a community; kind of centered in myself and part of this community that is larger than myself.

She goes on to emphasize that she not only feels connected to the community but takes part in its ongoing creation. For her, ESR is an open and accepting place:

I just feel like there's a place for everybody.... I find that really warm and kind of inclusive. I also find that just very exciting. Intellectually I find it exciting, emotionally I find it's kind of a warm and accepting place for everybody and I don't have to like everybody all the time, but it's still O.K. for everybody to be where they are, at that particular [moment].

For Rachel, the sense of community reminds her of the acceptance and challenge of family relationships:

The organization feels sort of like a family, in being accepting, yet challenging and argumentative, but you still like them afterwards in the way that a family [can be].... It was how the interaction with other people worked, it was so unique and made learning about educational issues and political issues so much more supported.

Lucile emphasizes the importance of being valued and trusted in the group and the feeling of support that this engenders:

There's an incredible amount of trust there for people who take on work. That it will happen, that they will be able to do it. I mean I feel that about other people on that steering committee, ... and I also feel that when I take on work, that in back of me is this trust, that how I decide to do it and what I do will be right.

Shelley describes the support and closeness of his relationships with steering committee members:

The steering committee has actually been the best support, or the key support for me.... I always walk away from steering committee meetings feeling high. I mean I just feel it is a great group and we work so well together. For me it's a psychological and emotional support in terms of the work I've done; but also they're my friends. It's really a friendship relationship. I really like the people, and I think that one of the things that I cherish about it is the people in the steering committee and the relationships I've had and the support I've had and been able to give to others to do good work and to grow.

Gene emphasizes how the sense of community in ESR reinforces her commitment to its work:

People feel responsible and committed to the continuance of the community. It is hard to feel committed if you think you are the only one. But my commitment is continually renewed by watching other people renew their commitment.

I have argued that to understand power we must look at the quality of relationships among people in relation to valued resources. In fact, virtually all the transformative processes described in the preceding pages were made possible by the exceptional quality of personal interaction within the organization. This particular quality of community within ESR provided the conditions, the opportunities, and the types of relationships that promoted and supported empowerment. Community was the social matrix from which empowerment was nurtured and provided a base out of which each person acted in the world.

Undergirding the creation and maintenance of this sense of community was a common set of values. Below Vera identifies these values:

some of the values we share are respect for people and for their opinions and for their feelings, and another value we probably share is the importance of hearing people out and giving them a chance to explain themselves. Another value that's shared, I think, is a real liking for kids, and another one is probably a real desire to improve the world in some way and to be active in doing that, not just think about it, or spout about it, but be active. I think we also believe in the importance of including kids in concerns of adults in an appropriate way and in teaching them how to think . . . and what else. . . . I think most of us enjoy our life as teachers even though we may have disagreements here and there with the system that we work in. [We] think that it's an important profession to be in. I don't know how much we share this, I feel strongly that it's very important to work toward improving the status of teachers, at least the way teachers are perceived by the rest of society, and I think groups like ESR help to do that. And most of all, of course, we all share the view that we have to do something about the dangerous political situation that we live in, and that's not just nuclear stockpiles of weapons and money being spent on further development, but this kind of confrontational policy that certainly Mr. Reagan has pursued, and that as adults, we need to make a statement. That's something we can't always do in the classroom, so it's important to have a place where we can share that commitment. We share a lot of beliefs of what a good teacher is like, not that we all necessarily need to be the same, but that we all believe in respecting children and involving children, and in making children's learning active and responsive. We all believe in listening to children and hearing what they have to say and responding to their concerns and interests. We probably all believe in some form of experiential, hands-on education at whatever is an appropriate age level. I think we all believe in the importance of community, democracy.

The importance of shared values cannot be underestimated. While individuals may have disagreed on a variety of issues over the years, their common values (and, I would argue, this *particular* set of common values) have allowed them to discuss, to listen to one another, and ultimately to agree on a plan of action. Without some degree of shared values, it is doubtful whether an organization or community can maintain the strength of interconnections and the quality of dialogue necessary for effective action and empowerment.

Just as importantly, these shared values were anchored by a common commitment to educational and social change—to transforming relationships of domination in schools and society. Thus personal and collective empowerment were situated within a wider context of struggle for peace and social justice.

Consensus, Synergistic Community, and the Emergence of Voice

The steering committee of the Boston area chapter was the consistent center and ground for the empowering experiences of each of study participants. In 1986, as well as in the previous four years, Boston Area ESR was run by a steering committee whose membership fluctuated between ten and fifteen individuals who met every other Tuesday throughout the year. The steering committee had responsibility for approving programs and finances, hiring staff, and making virtually all important decisions. While ESR staffing evolved in the four years leading up to the period of this study, in 1986 paid staff in the Boston area chapter consisted of an overall coordinator and two coordinators of membership services and fund-raising. Steering committee membership was open to all chapter members; staff were full participants in the committee. During the four years prior to the end of this study, all steering committee decisions were made by consensus.

For these six individuals, the process of consensus decision making within ESR—in the steering committee and in all other committees and action groups—was a critical factor in cultivating relationships of co-agency and empowerment. The model of consensus used in ESR seems quite simple. Gene puts it this way:

> We talk a lot. We're a very verbal group. We talk and talk and talk and we talk and we keep talking until we're saying the same thing.

Anyone present at a meeting could block consensus; everyone's voice was equally valued. In Shelley's words, "No one feels left out, everybody's listened to." No decision on the steering committee had ever been made without consensus. In fact, rarely, if ever, was there a formal vote.

This can be misleading, however. The history of consensual decision making in organizations is littered with power struggles, dissension, endless meetings, and dissatisfaction. While consensus may create a structure in which *power with* can be achieved, it by no means guarantees success. Yet despite these potential pitfalls, steering committee meetings ended within a reasonable time period, and there was genuine agreement with policies. People expressed great satisfaction with the process of decision making, and there appeared to be few if any power struggles. In general, consensus seems to have worked. People reached agreement and felt good about it. The homogeneity of the group probably played a role in this success, but even homogeneity is no guarantee of agreement.

It is impossible to know exactly how and why consensus worked so well for the steering committee. It has, in fact, proven difficult to reproduce the same results within ESR's national organization. However, by investigating the quality and nature of interactions among members of the steering committee, we can better understand how people experienced power within this empowering group and suggest ways in which power, consensus, and empowerment are linked.

As noted earlier, Mary Parker Follett (1942) has observed that the process of reciprocal influence occurs simultaneously with emergence. She describes reciprocal influence in this way:

> Do we mean all the ways in which A influences B, and all the ways B influences A? Reciprocal influencing means more than this. It means that A influences B, and that B, made different by A's influence, influences A, which means that A's own activity enters into the stimulus which is causing his activity. (p. 194)

She argues that as people open themselves to mutually affecting interactions, new solutions, new capacities, better ideas, and clearer insights are generated. This is the expanding dimension of synergy:

> We see that the functional relating has always a value beyond the sum of the parts. A genuine interweaving and interpenetrating, by changing both sides creates new situations. . . . Functional relating is the continuing process of self-creating coherence. (pp. 200–202)

The dynamics of reciprocal influence and emergence are vividly described in the interviews. Lally makes the most striking statement describing these processes:

> When I say something that I wonder about, or react to somebody, it doesn't stop there, somebody really hears it and it moves along. It just keeps going. So it's a combination of feeling like I've been heard and then having this machine start or being part of this kind of machine where ideas just keep bouncing, and I keep looking at things, and where we arrive at together is sort of a combination of everybody who has chosen to engage at that moment. It's not always everybody in the room. It's whoever has chosen to engage in that particular issue. It really makes me feel like part of the community and

kind of centered in myself and part of this community that's
larger than myself.

She goes on to describe "a kind of an energy in the group," a
"kind of sharpness and aliveness" that people "tap into." The
metaphor of the energy source is striking; it is a kind of communal
electric outlet into which individuals can plug themselves. The
result, she says, is "a kind of ripple effect. I can bounce off someone's else's enthusiasm, I can create and contribute that to the
group at that time." This energy helps "move ahead whatever the
task is":

> When all of us are doing that, it shapes the decisions that we
> make. Without that kind of energy, without that kind of
> thinking and that kind of hearing, we would reach very dif-
> ferent decisions.

These reflections correspond to Follett's description of emergence:

> Each calls out something from the other, releases something,
> frees something, opens the way for the expression of latent
> capacities and possibilities. (Follett 1942, 197)

Shelley responded to this quote from Follett:

> That echoes with my experience. I felt that we did such cre-
> ative work because we worked with each other, we thought
> together, and we moved far beyond what any of us could have
> done individually. It was like an emergence of something that
> we could all feel.

Gene is describing this feeling of emergence when she says, "I
feel like everybody walks away knowing a little bit more." Rachel
is also talking about reciprocal influence and emergence when she
describes dynamics in which people's ideas are altered, expanded,
and built upon with the result being that the group comes up "with
something better because we're all involved." Lucile describes it
this way:

> whenever we had an intense discussion, we never ended up
> [with] the initial choices we had. We always came up with

new solutions to fit together the pieces and the concerns that come out of the discussion.

The relationships described here are neither limiting nor controlling, nor are there clear lines of interpersonal cause and effect. Rather, the dominant image is of an expanding whole: individuals and the group forging new possibilities together.

Listening is a central element in these synergistic interactions. Consensus works because people listen and are listened to. Really listening means creating space for people to share their concerns. More importantly it means being willing to change one's opinions, to integrate the concerns of others into an evolving decision. Vera describes how this occurs:

> Most of the time we seem to reach decisions by consensus. . . . How does that happen? I think it happens by taking enough time to really hear everybody and trying to accommodate what seem to be important reservations that people have and make compromises so that in the end you come up with something everyone can live with.

Lally describes a very similar dynamic:

> It feels like we really listen to everybody's angle on the issue, whoever's willing to contribute, and really take it seriously and find a way to incorporate that into a decision we're going to make. And somehow when one or two people disagree, it's taken seriously, and we don't kind of reach a decision without folding it in. I can't remember a time where someone felt really strongly and they just kind of got knocked aside, you know like we can't deal with that because everybody else feels differently.

Vera's description of accommodating ideas, and Lally's idea of incorporation and her use of the metaphor of folding in, pinpoint the key indicators of true listening: individuals' ideas are integrated into decisions. This is the theme of inclusion. One sees oneself have an impact on the group. This experience is vital to feeling that one is making a difference and that one has the ability to participate in decision making.

In order to maximize listening and make synergistic interactions possible, each person must be willing to express his or her opinions *and* be willing to listen to the perspectives of others. Each must be assertive yet open, capable of speaking with conviction while simultaneously remaining open to change. This is not an easy way to be with others. The dynamics of reciprocity and mutuality are described by Shelley:

> I don't think anyone's had any really strong investment in their opinion or in dictating opinions. People have been flexible and willing to say, 'Here's what I think. I may be wrong, but my mind can be changed.' In that way it's been a more flexible, less rigid organization where it's not a fight against, but it's working with, so it's all of us working with particular questions.

Vera describes how she balances assertiveness and openness:

> It means that being really clear doesn't mean really stuck in what you're doing. It means that whatever you believe is open to revision or to addition, more to modification in some way, so that you have to say to yourself, 'Hmm, I never thought about it that way before,' or 'I hadn't considered this,' or 'maybe I'm wrong about that,' or whatever. And revise what it is you believe and say what you believe in a new way—test it out and see how it feels. I think that's what happens, inevitably. You can be real clear, but that doesn't mean you have to be fixed, and therefore you're never absolutely clear. You never really know.

The flexibility that allows for collaboration is nurtured by trust. This is illustrated by Gene:

> I trust the people in the organization so I can talk about something I didn't know and say I don't think I would have done it this same way, and I trust that somebody would then help me explore that, and I don't have to feel defensive about it.

Within a context of trust and mutual respect one can feel less defensive. One can be more open to learning, growth, and change. Such openness means making oneself vulnerable and taking risks. But as Rachel notes, "It's because it's such a supportive atmosphere that I'm willing to take risks." Shelley describes how listening and vulnerability create empowering dynamics:

Not only do you listen to the other person struggling, and support them, and that feels good, and it feels like you have contributed to somebody else's struggle, but you can feel vulnerable and allow that vulnerability to show and to be supported, and so it allows you to grow more, and it allows you to feel strength even in your vulnerability. That's something people usually defend against. They don't want to be vulnerable. But I think vulnerability in the situation of community is incredibly empowering, to share something, and then have it supported, makes you feel more whole. It makes you feel like you'll grow, and there's a greater sense of confidence in dealing with the things you are more sensitive about.

In many groups "consensus" is reached because people submit to the will of a leader. They avoid asking the hard questions and bury their own strong beliefs. The problem with this approach is that it inevitably leads to alienation, resentment, and domination. It is based on *power over* rather than *power with*. However, for these six members of the Boston area ESR steering committee consensus was reached in a very different manner. Rachel describes the steering committee as a "committee of leaders":

We're not a couple of leaders and a lot of followers.... Everybody has their own views. No one tries to push their views on everybody else and there's no expectation that we will all have the same view on any given topic.

For instance, as chapter coordinator, Shelley was a central actor in the organization. As a full-time employee, he was a key initiator and implementor of programs and policies. His position contained opportunities to exert *power over* and in fact, Gene notes, the group never outvoted him or overruled him:

but we never acquiesced to him because he was the coordinator and we were just the steering committee. That was never the feeling. We never acquiesced and said, 'Well you know more, okay, you are the expert.' We did say things like, 'Tell us more, because you're the one who has the most information on that,' but we never just were submissive to him.

Gene feels that the reason the group could do this was because each person felt competent and had a sense of ownership of the organization.

In Boston Area ESR it appears that consensus was not built by avoiding difficult questions. Rather, questions were asked in a challenging yet supportive, critical yet trusting, environment. Rachel observed:

> Someone at a given meeting will always ask the hard questions and make you think about your own life and being consistent and all that, but at the same time you are supported, because everybody is trying to answer those hard questions.

Lally described it this way:

> In ESR I find that even when we disagree about stuff that's close to home for a lot of us, for the most part we really hear each other, and it's very hard to do sometimes, but I feel we really do that. I feel there's a kind of full feeling I have after coming out of conversations like that.

Lally contrasts this feeling to feelings she has had when she seeks to address difficult issues with other friends and family:

> I don't know quite how to describe it because my experience in the past, with friends and with family as well as in groups, is that to challenge is to threaten someone's position, to threaten kind of who they are, and that I lose the closeness with them or at least it feels like that. In my own family, people kind of back off if you challenge too much, and I find that a lot of people do, rather than engage and allow a friendship to build out of that, that it's something that pulls people apart.

Lally stresses that in her experience with the steering committee, people did not bury their strong beliefs. Rather, they listened carefully and determined whether their concern was really important. The goal was not to have one's own idea adopted, but for the organization to reach the best and most effective decisions possible. Gene described the process well:

> But why do we end up talking about the same things? I think people change their minds. I listen to the direction of the conversation, and I think, 'Okay, sounds like lots of people agree with this, so maybe we should concentrate on that.' I can let go of a piece of it. And I focus more on what I agree with, and if I still have a real problem, I still keep bringing it up, but I

pretty much respect that people only keep raising something as an issue or problem if it's really an issue or problem for them. It's just a real stickler, and you can't let go of it; it's real important. I think people do believe that about everybody in the group. And so then the upshot of it is the person saying 'Yea, but' gets a whole lot of attention and thought. I want to know, 'Why are you saying that?' and implied in that question is, 'Maybe I should change my mind? I really want to know what you're saying.' So I think there's a lot of asking of questions of each other.

The synergistic dynamics of listening and being heard; of cultivating one's own and others' voices simultaneously; of developing new insights, new solutions; this is the process of *dialogue*, and it is characterized by *power with*. For these six individuals, these experiences cultivated their voices, sparked their empowerment, *and* made ESR an effective organization.

Follett observes that in groups in which reciprocal influencing and emergence—what I have called "synergy"—are functioning, "Each [person] has his function—and that should correspond as exactly as possible with his capacity" (1942, p. 107). This is the same process that Shelley describes as occurring within ESR:

Different people have different talents and can help out in different areas, at different times. We can all contribute in little ways in different ways to those projects. It's collaborative and mutually supportive. It's people sensing what other people can contribute and accepting that is a contribution and seeing that there is a larger task to be done and that each person could put in, you know that there's room for everybody to put in what talents they have and what they want to offer. That's the larger perspective of it. In the smaller perspective, in terms of the day-to-day workings, it means that we work as a team. There's a level of equality among the people. There's a level of acceptance of what other people have to offer. There's a sense that each person has that I'm helping other people do the best work that they can do. I want other people to do the best work that they can do, so I'm going to be supportive of that.

But Follett also emphasizes that one's capacities are always emerging, developing, expanding. This is the synergistic growth of mutually enhanced capacities, and precisely what Shelley describes as happening in ESR:

> Empowerment becomes sort of a spiral where it's continual and it grows rather than diminishes. The level of empowerment, the sense that you can make a difference in the world, grows because you see your capacity, you see other people's capacities, [grow] in spite of all the adversity and all the problems that come up.

In Katz's terms, empowerment—the capacity to make a difference, to participate in decision making, and to take action for change—is a renewable resource to which individual access is assured through specific mechanisms and attitudes. As a result, competition is minimized. Shelley explains:

> It is not a zero-sum [situation], we can grow infinitely, so to speak. Where if I support your effort, it only adds to mine, and it only adds to my interests. For you to do the best you can do will help me to do the best I can do, and that's true of everybody. If we are doing the best we can, then we're all getting more of what we want than we thought possible, and definitely more than we thought would be individually possible.

In this comment we see three of the four elements in Katz's (1982) conception of synergistic community: valued resources are expanding and renewable, what is good for one is good for all, and the whole is greater than the sum of the parts.

Gene and Lucile echo these sentiments. Lucile argues that people are not empowered at the expense of others. Empowerment involves "mutuality and connection" with other people, "where they're getting something, and you're getting something, and the more they get, the more you get." Gene argues that

> somebody who is empowered uses power to strengthen connections, to strengthen other people's efficacy, to create community. In the end that's all in your self-interest. When you have a relationship with somebody, if you really want to get something out of the relationship, in the end it's to your advantage to have the other person feeling good about [her or himself].

Shelley also describes the reciprocity and generativity of empowerment and *power with:* "Being empowered feels generative, it feels like a communal, cooperative, collaborative thing. It feels like if I'm empowered, I reach out and empower others." Interestingly, Gene describes her feeling not as Katz's "what is good for one is good for all" but as "what is good for all is good for one":

Somehow you work it out so that you have something that is good for everyone. You know it is good for the whole group, and because you have worked it out together, it's good for each individual. It may not be what each individual would have wanted alone, but they're willing to buy into it because it's more important to have a community; its more important to feel connected—that fills a need that is really important, and it means that you're more than the sum of your parts.

Co-agency: Power, Voice, Equality

During the initial interviews, I asked each person whether she or he felt she or he held power on the steering committee. The answers were revealing. Vera responded,

I feel that any comments I want to make will be listened to and heard, and that is really all the power I want.

Gene observed,

I think that you have power when, when you speak, people listen and consider it; and I always felt I had that kind of power.

Shelley said,

I feel that I have a lot of power, and that power is that when I say something, people will listen.

Lucile said,

Yes I did [have power. It was] a kind of mutual respect that I had with other members of the steering committee, whereby I felt that they had so much respect for me and for what I was saying that they would listen to my perspective and, therefore, that I could be heard.

And Lally explained,

> Yeah, I do [have power on the steering committee.] I'm just
> not sure that anything I do is different from anything anyone
> else does. I think we all do this: listen to a bunch of ideas and
> then piece them together.

These descriptions of power are revealing. When asked what
it meant to have power on the steering committee, the group
responded consistently. For them, having power meant being listened to. These responses stand in stark contrast to those I elicit
when I ask diverse groups to list their first and dominant notions
of power. The power described by steering committee members is
not *power over*. The comments cited above do not describe the ability to compel other people to do things, nor the ability to have one's
will become the way for the group. They do not refer to an individual's status or position within the organization, nor to the number
of committees upon which individuals serve. Rather, power is
being able to participate in dialogue and decision making.

These descriptions correspond to the dynamics of decision
making described earlier. Within an empowering setting, power
means being heard, having your ideas taken seriously and "folded
into" decisions. Power is conceived as participation rather than
imposition, as collaboration rather than control. Rachel observes,

> [Where I work], if I were to feel power at a staff meeting, it
> would mean that I would have power to run something. But
> feeling power in the steering committee means not feeling
> suppressed, and feeling valuable in that my ideas will be lis-
> tened to and I don't have to be afraid to bring them up. ... I
> feel powerful in the steering committee not because I have
> power over anybody but because no one has power over me,
> and because I feel so equal to everybody and feel like there is
> such give and take.

In contrast to feeling suppressed or exerting control over others,
she describes the power of participation in a context where she
feels equal, valued, and heard.

As each person discussed power in the steering committee,
they took time to qualify their answers. Shelley noted," I don't feel
that I have any more power than anyone else." Vera commented, "I
feel I have as much power as anybody else." And Gene echoed these

same sentiments, saying "I'm not sure that I had any more power than anyone else." This pattern of response indicates a common experience of equality within the group. The feelings of equality grow out of the shared feeling that, in Lucile's words, "there is room in the steering committee for anybody's point of view." Apparently, to a very high degree people respect and listen to one another.

In light of these strong feelings of equality, it was surprising, then, that when asked to name the most powerful members of the committee, each person had ready answers (which usually included about half of the steering committee). What makes one person more powerful than another?

Powerful people are those who are listened to more attentively by the group. Lally says, "I listen to them a little more carefully." Gene describes it this way:

> I think people listen to everybody, but they take more seriously what those people say [the more powerful people], consider it more carefully, have more of a tendency to think they might be right or that they have something very important to say that will change the course of a decision or a discussion.

It appears there are a range of skills and personal qualities people exhibit that lead others to listen to them more carefully than to others.

Although more powerful people generally speak more often, amount of participation is not directly proportional to degree of power. Rather, people listen because of the integrity of an individual's words. Lucile links power in the group to the depth of conviction and feeling that moves an individual to speak. She feels people listen to these voices more attentively. Lally emphasizes that more powerful people are those who wrestle with ideas and issues and can synthesize what other people are saying in new or interesting ways. Power here is the ability to make connections and to express not only one's own voice but a collective voice as well.

Gene emphasizes the link between communication skills and the willingness to act on ideas. She says people are powerful

> by being more than just words, by being willing to put some muscle behind words and do some work. I think that makes one powerful in the group.

Rachel points out that the power of individuals' voices in the group is connected to the respect those individuals receive from the group:

Power on the steering committee means having the respect of
other steering committee members and having interesting
things to say or unusual things to say that are adding to the
conversation. If you have more power, you get more respect,
because you have creative and original things to say. You
don't automatically get power just because you have something to say.

Another factor that determines how powerful people are is
how an individual's commitment to the organization is perceived.
Gene emphasizes that one gains and maintains respect if one's
ideas and actions are seen as growing out of a commitment to the
goals and success of the organization rather than to individual
ambitions:

I think that makes people powerful. I think that if there's a
sense that it's just for you alone, that people tend to listen
less, take the comments less seriously.

Thus one becomes powerful through being perceived as acting in
the best interests of the entire group. Power comes not through
selfishness but through connectedness.

A final factor in being "more powerful" is personal experience
and the expertise it engenders. People recognize other people's wisdom. Gene describes how this works in relationship to one particular member of the steering committee:

[He] reminds me of a wiser, older person who struggles with
the questions, and lets people in on the struggle, and comes
up with some directions, and tries to get people to think
about those directions.... The upshot of that is that when he
speaks, we listen. He is one of those people who is wise. After
a while you get recognized as someone who's wise, who sees
things in that way. So when you speak, people listen.

These differences in quality of participation, ability to communicate, commitment, length of experience, depth of analytic skills,
and the respect one engenders from others would seem to create
the potential for domination, where the more eloquent speaker, the
more committed person, or the "wise" individual could impose her
or his will on the group. But the six reject the idea that these qualities create the dynamics of *power over* in this group. It would be

necessary to survey many more past members of the steering committee in order to establish the accuracy of this assessment; but the fact that all meetings are open and that everyone present at a meeting has veto power on decisions may be a crucial factor. Moreover, the way in which "powerful" people relate to others is essential as well. Lally describes the role these people play in the group:

> What those powerful people do is provide an exciting place for people to be and an opportunity to draw out of people whatever is in them at that moment. I think it is okay. I don't think everybody needs to be equally powerful.

Gene also describes how these "more powerful" people function in the group. She begins by stating that their power is not the ability to persuade, which she sees as manipulative. She argues that when individuals set out to persuade others, they see themselves as right. From this stance, the challenge of social interaction is to find out how to convince others of their rightness. She argues that a different dynamic is at work in steering committee dialogue:

> I think it's different when, say, an issue comes up or a lot of ideas have been presented, and you say, 'Hey, wait a second. Looks like these ideas all connect. What if we did X and we did, you know, put these three ideas together and the committee works on those?' and people say, 'Hey great idea,' and you've got some power because you were able to see the big picture and to present that idea and people went with it, but people made the choice. It's more honest.

What makes this *power with* is its inclusive quality. It helps the group to achieve its goals. At the same time the reason it is "okay" for some people to have more "power" is that the more powerful members do not control, limit, or impose upon other members or the organization. Their power complements and enhances everyone's power. Lally emphasizes the inclusive quality of the power as well:

> The power of the people I see as powerful is really more inclusive than exclusive. It provides an energy, a kind of excitement that allows people to move in whatever way they want to move in.

Gene argues that this power is *power with:*

I see individual members of that group working with other people, and so it's the soliciting of the ideas, of the thinking, of taking what other people say seriously, of drawing them into that group.

She also points out that the group of people who are "more powerful" can be "continually expanded; it's not a closed group." She notes that new people move into that group all the time.

This would appear to be *power with:* co-agency and jointly developing capacities. Lucile agrees with this analysis. She explains that the power of the more powerful individuals, "frequently gives other people in the group a feeling of being empowered as well, because somebody is speaking articulately things that they were thinking." This is synergistic power. Its exercise expands the effectiveness of the individuals in the group and of the group as a whole. She notes that the key is that, "while they speak with conviction, [it is] without the purpose that it necessarily has to win in the end." Thus an important quality, as has been discussed earlier, is the ability to be clear and assertive *and* open to change. This said, it is not hard to see the fragility of these dynamics and the potential for the "wise" person to control, manipulate, and exclude.

Rachel observes that "some people are shy and just don't say their opinions a whole lot, so I don't think they have as much power as other people." These people have less "power because they don't offer as much." She argues that

ESR functions with processes and conditions and meeting structures that foster empowerment. But I don't think anyone just comes to a meeting and feels empowered. It is what you put in. I think if you are not empowered in ESR-type conditions, it is not because other people are empowered. It's because there's something in you that is blocking, you're not taking the risk or you're not offering the support or the questioning or the challenge to someone else, so it is not coming back to you.

While this comment sounds perilously close to an attitude of blaming the victim, the important point, I think, is that empowerment is not a gift bestowed, but rather it is earned through risk and action. This said, it is also important to point out that the distinction between internal and external barriers to empowerment are never clear cut or easily identified.

Gene presents a dramatic example of ineffectuality in the group that illustrates some of these tensions and dynamics. She notes that she was aware of one person who is on the steering committee who "isn't listened to and who knows it." This is true even though "we nod our heads while she speaks." The irony is that several people had spoken to Gene about the situation, saying that other members feel that this woman exerts *too much* power in the group:

> I think we have a situation for the first time on the steering committee where there is someone who doesn't feel powerful and so is using *power over* to be powerful. And people are contributing to that happening by not listening to her, by not taking her seriously and pulling her aside and saying, 'Look, when you do X it makes the meeting less effective and makes me pissed off.' We're not... somehow we haven't had to deal with it and confront it, and we walk on eggshells, and we don't want to hurt people's feelings, and we don't know how to deal with it.

The situation she describes is not one in which a person is being rendered powerless through interpersonal domination. Rather, it indicates a failure of co-agency. The dynamics of synergy and dialogue have broken down in the individual's relationships in the group. There is no integration, and inclusion is difficult. There is a downward negative spiral. Lines of openness and mutuality have closed, and on both sides the dynamics of domination begin to emerge. These dynamics empower no one.

This discussion makes the point that in their experiences of *power with,* not every member of the group participates equally. It would appear that some people are better able to balance openness and conviction, to express their ideas, and to synthesize the group's thinking. Others are more committed to the organization, more willing to act on their own words. Even others are better able to help others understand and act. The crucial distinction is that in this context differentials in abilities and attitudes do not mean that people control others. Rather, the differentials can enhance the capacities of all individuals and the group as a whole.

Power Over and the Experience of Empowerment

In the previous discussion we saw how *power with* played a central role in these six educators' experiences of empowerment, primarily in the power dynamics they experienced as members of the steering committee of Boston Area ESR. However, the interviews also indicated that people experienced *power over* in ESR as well, and they suggest that it played two very different roles in the experience of empowerment.

First, the most common result of situations in which one person sought to limit and control another was disempowerment. Whether the individuals were exerting *power over* or were its victims, feelings of ineffectiveness and powerlessness generally resulted. The example Gene cites above is illustrative. She describes a destructive spiral of controlling behavior in which the group is not listening and the individual who is not being listened to attempts to impose her views. The result is that everybody feels less effective and less empowered.

During the final group interview, the occurrence of *power over* within the organization was discussed in depth. The group agreed that one place where it seemed to occur most frequently was in the curriculum development process. This seems to have occurred for two reasons. First, the time lines that were set up for writing the curricula were very tight. There were intense pressures for quick writing and editing. The time needed for reaching consensus was often not available. Second, it appears that in several instances a process had been set up in which those who wrote sections of the curricula were not involved in the final editing. Because of this, some people had their contributions deleted, edited, or changed without their knowledge or consent. Thus, arbitrary decisions were imposed on a person or group.

As the overall coordinator of the curriculum projects, Shelley intensely felt the pressures of deadlines and questions of quality. Often choices had to be made quickly, and he was the person faced with the responsibility for an immediate decision. This presented opportunities for exclusion and win-lose situations. Rachel remembers an experience while she was working with a small group on a math curriculum. Everyone was committed to trying to complete the curriculum by the end of the summer, and they worked very hard to achieve this goal; however, in the end,

> it wasn't what it should be to be published. But we didn't decide that as a group. We gave the whole thing to Shelley to do some sorting through, some editing.

Shelley made the decision to not publish the curriculum as it was. Rachel does not remember if she was in on the decision making, but she does recall that

Certainly no one else on the committee participated in the decision of whether or not it could be published right at that time. And a lot of other people on the committee felt very disempowered by how the decision was made.

What made the situation disempowering was not that it was a bad or wrong decision, but *how* it was made. Shelley imposed the decision on the group. He closed off participation and voice. As a result the curriculum writers felt betrayed, angry, and impotent. (However, they were still working on the curriculum two years later.)

What is most fascinating about these dynamics is that not only was the experience disempowering for those who had the decision imposed on them, but Shelley did not feel empowered either:

If you are invested with authority by depriving others of authority, then it is not empowering, it is brutal. When I know that I am doing something that is a *power over* thing, I have this inner cringe inside of me; it's like a reticence to do it, and it's a knowing it is not totally right.[1]

Most of the examples of situations in which individuals exerted control over others and imposed their wills on others were of this type (examples were infrequent). They hindered empowerment. That *power over* occurs in any organization should not be surprising, but it is important to note that the group viewed many of these instances as mistakes, as failures of process, and as failures to empower. These examples illustrate, once again, the fragility of *power with*. Always functioning within a larger context of competition and domination and in the absence of institutionalized structures of *power with,* oases of co-agency and synergy are constantly vulnerable to the pressures, the demands, and the pervasive patterns and rules of structures of domination.

However, as the reflective interview process moved into its last stages and as I pursued the role of *power over* in empowerment in more depth, a more positive function emerged. While no one described experiences in which relationships of domination— as either the controller or controlled—were empowering, we began to uncover the fact that there were times when *power over* functioned to help create and maintain empowering dynamics within the organization.

Gene described how as coordinator she felt a responsibility for the organization's success and a desire to create empowering experiences for its members. She saw success and empowerment as reciprocal, one reinforcing the possibilities of the other. In taking this responsibility seriously she sometimes felt "[that] I have to take control, because if I didn't take control of some situations, none of you would have felt empowered by certain situations."

Gene offered an example of a situation in which she asserted control over a fellow member of the staff for just these reasons.

> For instance a task was not getting done, and I finally had to say, 'For the next month you have to do this. This is all you can spend your time with. It's so crucial that this gets done.' If I hadn't done that, then the spring fund-raising would have been a bigger mess than it was.

Exerting control over someone, however, was not empowering for Gene or for the person she was controlling. "It felt lousy to me," she said. Nevertheless, when she saw no other option, she felt it her responsibility to act for the sake of the organization and the other people involved in the work. However, for Gene, such actions were always seen as a last resort, because, unlike *power with*, "*power over* always has a cost."

Another dimension of the positive role of controlling or restricting behavior in experiences of empowerment seems to be the "gatekeeping" function. There are subtle, and sometimes not so subtle, selection processes that determine who joins which committee, who does which workshop, and who will be a paid employee of the organization. These processes are sometimes characterized by *power over*. Shelley calls it a "baseline *power over*" that "allows all the *power with* to happen."

As one of the founders of Boston ESR and as its first coordinator, Shelley had a major role in the development of the chapter and in the recruitment of people to work in the organization. He saw one of his important roles as "creating a safe environment for people to think and work—a productive environment for people to do things." In this role there were times when he felt that he had to exert control over other people. He recounted one instance in which he told a person working on a curriculum revision that the group could not work with him and that he would have to leave it. The members of the group had worked hard over a period of months to collaborate effectively with this person, but the process had stalled and the project was not being completed. It was clear to the other members of the group that if the project was to be finished, this one individual would have to drop out. Shelley was the person who "asked," but actually told, the person that he would have to leave the group.

In this situation, *power over* was used in an effort to make the remaining participants more effective. *Power over* was used to allow *power with* and empowerment to occur and thus for an effective curriculum to be developed. However, the relationship between Shelley and the individual asked to leave was not empowering for either of them. For Shelley, *power over* "never feels good." Once again, *power over* was seen as only a last resort. Nevertheless, no matter how benign the *power over* wielder's motivations may be, this situation always holds within it the possibility of domination—of the oppressive exclusion of another's voice. Distinguishing between the two is by no means a simple task.

Shelley described other ways he exerted control of people in order to create and maintain a situation in which *power with* and empowerment could occur. He describes the role he played in choosing people to serve on the steering committee:

> I specifically never advertised much for the steering committee—I asked people individually. That is the kind of control I had. I chose to ask some people and not others—others who I knew might be interested, because I wanted to keep the process clear and set a tone for what our process would [be]. . . . It wasn't that I didn't feel other people wouldn't be good, but that may not have been the best way they could have helped the organization . . . so I encouraged them to participate in another way. It's not like I said, oh, that person is awful, get them out of the organization, although there were a couple of people I didn't know what to do with, and I was glad that they left.

Once again we see how Shelley used his unique knowledge and position to make unilateral decisions that affected other people, by inhibiting them from doing things they may have wanted to do. This subtle manipulation involved the use of *power over* to maintain empowering dynamics within the organization. Once again Shelley saw *power over* as a last resort, and his goal, always, was to maximize *power with*, not his own *power over* others. Nevertheless, it does remain unclear to what extent these uses of *power over* fulfilled their intended functions of preserving and creating *power with* dynamics. The gatekeeping use of *power over* in an organization can be used to maintain control in an organization by excluding people of diverse opinions and backgrounds, people who are raising or might raise issues or suggest practices that challenge the exisiting norms and patterns in the group. Thus gatekeeping can serve to maintain oppressive patterns and practices. And, while I have no indication that this occurred in ESR, there is no doubt that such use of power can occur and presents another side to the purported positive use of *power over* to promote the empowerment of those who are *permitted* inside a group.

Thus we see that *power over* was a factor in the six individuals' empowering experiences within the Boston area steering committee and in the chapter. Although it apparently never played a directly positive role in their experiences of empowerment, it seems to have had an impact by helping to create and maintain *power with* relationships that were seen as so essential to empowerment. It also appears that *power over* could play this role if the individuals who were exerting control were doing so not out of self-interest but rather in the interests of the whole group after trying other avenues of action. However, despite the fact that *power over* has a potential positive role in relation to empowerment, the group felt strongly that it tends to disempower by creating situations of powerlessness. When it was used, they felt it was a mistake or a last resort.

This discussion of *power over* highlights the fact that, while *power with* is the predominant dynamic in these six indiviudals' experiences of empowerment, *power over* is exerted as well. People do try to have their ideas chosen over others; they do hold onto their positions because of pride, people do feel jealousy and defensiveness. However, all participants in the study insisted that instances of *power over* were minimal, especially in contrast to their experiences in schools and other organizations. To a significant degree the experiences of empowerment described have been supported and nourished by relationships of *power with*. This indicates that the nature of power in the experience of empowerment may include both *power with* and *power over*, but it also suggests that the empowering setting is the one in which *power with* relationships are maximized.

Power and Empowered Action in the World

As we have seen, the knowledge that one was making a difference within the ESR community was an essential part of each person's experience of empowerment. However, working in ESR was empowering not just because it offers opportunities for positive experiences in a supportive community, but because the work of the community is to encourage change in other people and in educational and social institutions as well. Lally expresses this well:

> It is only important that I make a difference in the group if it's all part of where the group is headed. It would feel like having a nice time at a dance party—it was very lively and fun, but once it is over, it is over. And that doesn't affect much except having a good time at that particular party at that moment. That is a very different kind of feeling for me than feeling that what got created at that moment is part of a much larger issue, whether it is change in the schools or change around a social or political issue.

As members of ESR, each individual actively works for change in the content and methods of teaching in schools by working with teachers, administrators, students, and parents within her or his own school and in other schools and communities in the greater Boston area. This work is consciously linked to, informed by, and grounded in the larger social and political realities of our society and in the struggle to create a more just, equitable, and peaceful society and world.

In fact, individuals who are working for social and educational change live and work in a multitude of contexts and are members of a variety of groups, some of which are empowering and many of which are not. In order to understand the nature of power in the experience of empowerment we need to examine individuals' experiences in both kinds of settings. As we have seen, it was critical to examine the interpersonal dynamics within a group in which people experience empowerment. This examination allowed for an exploration of the power relationships that promote and nurture empowerment. However, it is also important to explore how individuals struggle for power and empowerment in settings characterized by relationships of domination and control, for this is much more the norm of our everyday life experience. How do people who feel empowered work for change in contexts that are not empowering? What kinds of power relations do these individuals seek to create when working for change in situations characterized by domination? What form of power do they utilize to effect a process of change? This study offered a limited opportunity to explore the answers to these questions. Based on the interviews, it is possible to begin a discussion of this important area and outline some fundamental questions that emerge from an initial examination of the issues.

Often the various constituencies to whom these individuals reach out feel powerless—these are the teachers, students, parents, and administrators who, despite strong feelings that things need to be changed, feel unable to address important issues in their schools and communities. At other times, these educational activists encounter people who exert significant control over educational, religious, social, and political institutions. At times, interactions with these people are empowering. Experiences in workshops or within a school can be empowering. However, too often, working to bring about change in people and institutions is not easy or empowering in itself. The vested interests, personal and ideological preferences, and accepted norms and assumptions of decision makers and bureaucracies often stand as obstacles to change. In these cases, ESR provided a base of support, encouragement, and empowerment. Vera described this function of ESR as "recharging," and Rachel describes how this recharging function works for her:

> [Where I work] it is very clear who is making decisions, and it is very clear who is not being included in decisions ... because of people's titles. It's very hierarchical, and some people are invited to some meetings, and other people are invited to other meetings, and so it's not a place where you can walk in and have a context for doing challenging things and getting support for that and helping other people clarify their ideas. ... There's a very controlled context. I feel more empowered there now than I did when I started there, because of what I have done, but I think I've done it in spite of the context, not because of it. And that's partly because I get reenergized at ESR, and so I go back downtown full of confidence again. But it's what I feel in spite of the context, not because of it.

Thus we see how ESR functions on two levels to spark empowerment. First, it does so internally through its ability to enhance personal transformation and provide opportunities to work for educational and social change in a supportive community. Second, it provides a vital support base for those who are working directly in the wider community for the changes to which ESR and its members are committed.

Everyone in the group felt that *power with* was integral to the ESR approach to working for change. Rachel explained, "On a grander scale that's why I'm in ESR. It's definitely a *power with* way to change things." In each setting in which members of the study group were active, they tried to achieve effective relationships of co-agency as a means to effecting change. They saw themselves as attempting to recreate the interpersonal dynamics that they had experienced within ESR in the settings in which they were working outside of the group. In Shelley's words, "The methodology that we've come up with around change is really the embodiment of everything we've learned on the steering committee." Rachel describes the process as one in which "we try not to alienate and we try to spread power."

Several people described the workshops that they and others conduct for teachers through ESR's Professional Development Program as one way in which they are working for change. Gene said:

> Right now the most powerful thing we do is our workshops, the long workshops. By actually going through with teachers the process they might use with kids . . . which is people talking with other people about educational issues and finding out how to [listen] to their own ideas and to listen to other people and change their ideas.

Lally described some of what actually happens in ESR workshops:

> It's finding ways of allowing teachers to get in touch with their own ability to question and think about things and to really acknowledge the power of that within themselves and feel good about that and then to help them find ways of acknowledging and recognizing that in students and creating that in students as well. I think first acknowledging it, because all kids have that, or have that potential. And then getting excited by the idea of really creating that kind of community in a classroom where both the teachers and the students are involved jointly in exploring and questioning, challenging. I think that's kind of the core of our approach.

The goal is not to impose but rather to engage teachers in a dialogue concerning important issues of teaching theory and practice. Gene argued that fundamentally this approach seeks to change the way people think about themselves, about society, and about education:

I think we want to make change not by [going] for the top, and not even changing teachers' methods of teaching, but I see us even going back to the very first step, which is to change people's thinking or the way they look at things, which is the way to make change, I think. It's also a really long, long process, but probably the most lasting way to make changes.

Shelley described how the workshops he conducts have changed over the years:

My workshops that I've been leading have really changed since the first workshop I led. The first workshop I led, I talked about techniques of how to teach kids about peace and how to teach kids about nuclear war. You do this, you do that, you do this. 'Let's talk about some of the questions that come up. Let's talk about some of the issues you may deal with in your classroom.' Now what I really talk about is that at the heart of creating a peaceful world is really creating a sense of tolerance, mutual respect, a sense of being willing to tolerate not knowing and being willing to say I may be wrong and being willing to change, and all those are the embodiment of what we've seen on the steering committee . . . that I can empower, that's the greatest change you can create . . . you know, the greatest change you can create is by listening to others.

One of Rachel's main responsibilities in her job in Boston was to connect teachers and museum personnel. She described her approach to her job:

The museum is interested in outreach, and the school is more interested in having resources, so they end up both feeling more powerful. It's nothing I gave them, but I set the conditions so that they would be able to do that.

Rachel brings together two parties and draws out their needs and skills through dialogue. The emerging mutual understanding and collaboration results in a synergistic win-win situation. Rachel's role is to listen, to make connections, to offer suggestions, and to facilitate dialogue.

Gene compares two different approaches to working for change in schools. First, she describes what she sees as an ineffective approach:

We could look at it...that there are all these people we need to win over, and we're in a struggle to get them on our side.... I think that people pick that attitude up, and you sort of get polarized. I've been working in Revere a little bit, you know, [with] this guy named John, and that's his attitude. He's an old union organizer, and, you know, he's in a struggle with the principal of Revere High School even though the principal runs a peace essay contest every year, three years running, and helps read them. The end result is that we'll never get into Revere High School and work with the teachers there. John has made it absolutely impossible for us to do that, because it's all a point system. Who's winning, who's losing. John thinks we're going to lose a point here, the principal wins a point there, and so it'll always just be almost a standoff.

She feels that this win-lose competitive *power over* approach makes the principal defensive and unwilling to listen. In contrast she describes how she worked with teachers at Boston English High School:

I went in and said, 'How can I help? Here's what I have to offer,' and it's moving a lot more slowly than I would want, or any of us want, it to happen. But it's this different attitude, an attitude of supporting and listening and helping teachers to identify the questions, by being there, raising certain questions that get people to look at things a little bit differently. And so the shifts are ever so slight, but you're in it together rather than struggling. It's still a struggle. I mean it's hard, but it's not [an adversarial] struggle.

This description highlights the dynamics of *power with* as a vehicle for change.

Vera describes a very different situation, one in which she is a victim of *power over*. In this situation she is faced with a principal with whom she disagrees and who she feels has made decisions without adequately consulting the faculty. Her response in these situations is to speak out and share her feelings:

All I've done is just speak up and say what I thought. Has that worked? That has worked in that it has either been heard or it's made the person angry. I've had to deal with that anger. Which I have a very hard time dealing with. But I've done it anyway. And in the long run it's worked for the good. I mean on the whole I think people at least knew where I stood and what I felt. Which I think is more important than to go around grumbling or muttering to yourself or talking behind people's backs about them. I think it's important to let people know what your position is about an issue.

In this situation an individual, the principal, is imposing his decisions on Vera. Her first reaction is to make herself heard even though the principal might not want to hear what she has to say. She is asserting herself, but not imposing herself. She is saying,

> you haven't thought about this, and this is how it feels to me, and maybe you didn't intend that, but that is how it is. And you need to hear that.... I think you have a surprising result sometimes when you just speak up.

Her first reaction is to express her voice. To make herself heard. This seems in line with *power with*, but is it effective? What does one do if one's protests are futile? Resort to *power over?* Is *power with* a first resort and *power over* a last resort? These questions take on added significance when we begin to think about empowerment and power in the context of struggles for survival and basic freedoms. How do you effectively engage with individuals, organizations, or governments who withhold basic human rights and are willing to use intimidation and violence to maintain their domination? Can *power with* be used to effectively engage and transform those individuals and social structures that wield unyielding *power over?* Is *power with* a middle-class luxury, useful only for those who can wait for change? Is *power with* only possible when both "sides" are willing to enter into a dialogue? On the other hand, can *power over* effectively transform relationships and structures of domination? *Can* the "master's tools" tear down the master's house?

Conclusion

These are difficult and challenging questions for further inquiry. This discussion has focused on applying, expanding, developing, and more fully understanding the concepts of *power over* and especially *power with* in people's personal experiences of social interaction and empowerment. Indeed, the discussion has shown that *power with* and the *power over/power with* framework offers a potent conceptual tool for effectively describing and understanding the interpersonal power relations through which these six people have experienced empowerment in Boston Area Educators for Social Responsibility. Indeed, we have seen how the discourse of *power with* is reflected in the lived experiences of co-agency of these six teachers. We have seen how the themes of *dialogue, trust, voice, assertiveness and openness,* and *shared decision making* offer a language for the experience of power in the process of empowerment, an experience of power very different from limiting visions of power as domination. We have also seen how *power with* provides a language for describing and understanding the kinds of power relationships these educators seek to utilize and create in their efforts to improve education and make the world safer and more just.

In light of the rhetorical calls for teacher empowerment that ring through current efforts at educational reform, this dicussion of the empowerment of a small group of teachers and the power dynamics that nurtured these experiences suggests some simple, yet radical, aspects essential to teacher empowerment. Empowering schools must be educational communities coalesced around a core of values guided by a sense of hope and possibility, grounded in a belief in justice and democracy. These commnities must nourish the voices of all their members; they must provide contexts in which people can speak and listen, learn and grow, and let go of ideas in order to move on to better ideas. Such learning communities must create climates in which all members are respected and listened to. They must be places in which teachers (but not only teachers) have a voice in decision making and the ongoing impetus to look at themselves, their schools and their world critically. In order to do this, the nature of power in schools must be transformed. The hierarchy of decision making must be transformed, the structure of the school day must be transformed, and the way we interact with colleagues and students must be radically reexamined.

Surely, the interrelationships and dynamics between *power over* and *power with* are complex, especially as they are applied to larger social and political analyses. Nevertheless, this discussion serves as a beginning exploration into the meaning, manifestations, and contributions of *power with* to the development of a language of possibility for educational and social change.

Notes

1. Sharon Welch (conversation 1986) raises the important question of whether some people have a disposition to *power with* and feel "good" in *power with* relationships and uncomfortable in *power over* relationships, while others have a disposition to *power over* and feel "good" controlling other people or even being controlled by others. Alice Miller (1983) and Karl Mannheim (1950) offer two insightful perspectives on this question. They both argue that authoritarian personalities develop in authoritarian cultures and that democratic or nondominating personalities develop in open, accepting, democratic cultures and/or families. Thus, they argue (from different theoretical positions) that the predominant power modality in which one's personality develops has a significant influence on one's predispositions to *power over* and *power with.*

6

Transforming Power:
Power in Empowering Teaching

Our central goal is to enable students to shape their own lives in meaningful ways and to have a commitment to helping all people live in a peaceful and just world.

Excerpt from BAESR funding proposal
(Berman and Kreisberg 1984, 1)

In my introduction I stated that this inquiry is framed and focused by the desire to understand the wise and just use of power in our teaching and to contribute to the development of a pedagogy of empowerment. In order to accomplish this, I have argued for the importance of understanding the nature of power that empowers. As we begin such an inquiry we must ask ourselves: How can we, as educators, contribute to our students' empowerment? What are the dynamics of power in teacher–student relationships that help nurture student empowerment? What is the nature of power in empowering learning environments?[1] So far I have addressed these issues largely in theory and in teachers' experiences of empowerment. In this chapter, I turn more directly to these questions of teaching, learning, power, and empowerment by focusing on Lally, Vera, Gene, Shelley, Rachel, and Lucile's reflections on their teaching and their personal efforts to create empowering learning experiences and relationships with their students.

In chapter 1, I argued that student–teacher relationships in U.S. schools are saturated with relationships of domination, of *power over*. And, in fact, the teachers I interviewed were very aware of the coerced nature of their students' experiences in schools. They recognized that their students are compelled to attend school. They are required to take certain courses. Their movements inside the school are carefully controlled and monitored (often they must be given permission to go to the bathroom). They are often told exactly where they can sit. They are repeatedly assigned homework, compelled to speak on command, and forced to be quiet. The six teachers recognized that fundamental power over students is invested in them by parents, by the school system, by our culture of schooling. This means that they have authority to control student behavior, to choose what students learn and how they learn, to decide the grades students receive, and, ultimately, to determine whether or not students will graduate.

Indeed, the problem of power was a fundamental issue in their desire to understand empowering teaching. They saw the coercive character of schooling, and in particular the traditional power of the teacher, as a major obstacle blocking student empowerment. However, despite the pervasiveness of relationships of domination across society and in schools, they believed in the possibility of creating spaces in their classrooms in which, in however small a way, students could be provided with a web of relationships and experiences that offered opportunities for empowerment. They saw the transformation of *power over* relationships in the classroom as crucial to creating these opportunities. They agreed that one of the greatest challenges for teachers trying to create opportunities for students to experience empowerment is to develop the capacity and ability to enter into *power with* relationships with students; to be able to collaborate with students rather than coerce them. The obstacles to creating such relationships were situated in many places, not the least being *within the teachers themselves*. Relationships of domination not only saturate the structures and norms of schools and the experiences and expectations of students and administrators, but they also lie deep within teachers. The struggle to move beyond relationships of domination is not solely with external forces, it is an internal struggle as well. It means wrestling with our commonsense assumptions about teaching and shaking our taken-for-granted patterns of acting and relating in classrooms. Lucile clearly describes the internal tensions she feels as she seeks to transform the traditional teacher–student relationships in her classroom:

> It's hard. I found it really difficult in the public schools to do it, for a number of reasons. One of which is that while I have always cared a great deal about the kids, I've always been a fairly authoritarian teacher in that I primarily make the rules and grades and curriculum materials. So it's meant a shift for me away from thinking of myself as the central authority for making all of the decisions in the classroom.

[That has meant] trying to decide what are the appropriate ways for students to participate in that.

Yet, despite the daily difficulties in examining controversial social and political issues in their curricula and the ongoing internal and external struggles in seeking to transform the power relationships in their classrooms, these teachers were all committed to making these changes in the most effective and empowering way possible.

Six Schools, Six Groups of Students

During the interviews I asked each person to focus on one specific course, unit, or project they felt was a particularly empowering experience for their students. They described experiences in six very different schools whose combined student population represented a diverse cross section of the social, economic, racial, and cultural communities in the greater Boston area.

Lally: Health Issues at Watertown High School

Watertown is primarily a working-class community with a small handful of minority students, a fairly large ethnic community, and a small handful of kids from progressive families whose families moved into Watertown. It is definitely not a progressive school.

Lally described a unit she taught at Watertown High School in an "experimental" health issues course she offered through the Interdepartmental Studies Program (IDS). IDS is a program of one hundred students in grades 9–12. It consists of three smaller classrooms and a "commons room." Students take one to three courses in the program and the balance of their courses in the regular high school. IDS also conducts a town meeting, which meets once every six weeks. In town meetings, various issues that come up in the program are discussed, and decisions or policies are voted on by the students and faculty.

Lally's course was an attempt to teach about health in a way more relevant to the concerns and interests of students than that of the regular health courses. She achieved this, in part, by expanding the focus of her course to psychological as well as physical health issues. Enrollment was kept small so that students would have ample opportunity to discuss the issues raised in the

course. Of the twelve students in the class, one was a nineteen-
year-old male. The rest of the students ranged from ninth to
twelfth grade and had a variety of verbal and written skills. There
was one Black female student in the class. The others were white
and predominantly from working-class families.

The unit Lally described was designed to encourage the students to explore the difference between debate and discussion,
between argument and dialogue. Lally presented a hypothetical
situation in which an unmarried pregnant teenager was faced with
the choices of keeping her child, giving it up for adoption, or having an abortion. Students were asked to choose which option they
favored. Then they presented their reasoning, first using the discussion approach, then the argument approach. She described
these two approaches to conversation in this way:

> The more familiar of the two ways is *arguing*, which usually
> involves having strong opinions and trying to convince the
> other person that you are right. In a more formal setting this
> is often called *debating*. The less familiar way is what we will
> call *discussing* or creating a dialogue. This approach involves
> communicating your own needs while also trying to under-
> stand what the other person is feeling or thinking.

After each interchange the students took time to reflect on their
experiences, describing and evaluating the similarities and differences between the two ways of talking with one another. Upon
completing this set of activities Lally asked that the next time they
felt themselves slipping into an argument with family or friends
they attempt to have a dialogue rather than a debate. After everyone had completed this assignment they discussed these experiences in class.

On one level Lally's unit problemmatized the issue of abortion
and asked students to understand other positions while formulat-
ing and voicing their own; on another level, the unit sought to help
students to develop their skills in listening to others with whom
they disagree as well as their capacities to enter into dialogue.

Vera: Twentieth-Century History at the Shady Hill School

> Shady Hill is a private, [preschool]-through-ninth-grade
> school. It is about seventy years old. It started as a quite pro-
> gressive school, and still considers itself progressive, but I
> think it is becoming a little more constrained, because it has

a large body of professional upper-middle-class parents who push for that kind of thing. About 40 percent of the school is on scholarship of one sort or another. About 17 percent of the school is minority. So there are working-class kids there but they are definitely, I think, uncomfortable in some ways. It is perceived by the outside as being more elitist than it really is. Kids go from there all over, some to public high schools, and many to private schools, and about 30 percent to the 'cream' prep schools.

Vera chose to describe the twentieth-century history course she taught the previous year at the Shady Hill School in Cambridge. The course was offered to ninth graders:

I don't know whether I'm rationalizing, but it seems to me that teaching twentieth-century history to ninth graders fits their psychological and emotional development really well because it's talking about issues that are very close to the present in time and that all impinge on present-day concerns within the lifetime of their parents and grandparents, so that it seems to have an immediacy that some other history does not have. Ninth graders are living very much in their own developmental concerns and establishing their identities and rebelling against their parents' authority and taking all sorts of risks and trying to sort out their values and making choices.

The course began with the study of the Soviet Union: its history, the nature of communism, and the Russian Revolution, culminating in Stalin's rise to power. Then the class used the *Facing History and Ourselves* curriculum, which, focusing on Armenian and Jewish genocides, seeks to engage students in a historical and personal exploration of issues such as authority, racism, responsibility, and freedom. Next the course turned to the United States just after World War I, studying the 1920s and 1930s up to World War II. During the spring semester the class read Hersey's *Hiroshima* and focused on United States/Soviet relations concerning the nuclear arms race.

Opportunities for decision making were at the heart of Vera's approach to the course. Throughout the year students were asked to make decisions, to take stands through papers, role playing, and in class discussions. She also described how students participated in the daily running of the class:

A lot of the teaching is done by the kids and not by me. I'm responsible for finding the materials and for sort of leading from here to there, but they are the ones who often present the material to each other in class, and they are the ones who do a lot of the explaining, so they feel that they have a real input. They come to me with suggestions ... 'We ought to do such and such,' and 'What do you think if we did this?' So that they feel that they have a stake in the course ... [and] along the way they have lots of chances to have input.

Gene: Town Meeting at the Fayerweather School

Fayerweather is a small independent K–8 tuition school. Over half of the kids receive some sort of scholarship aid. The income range is from working class all the way up to upper middle class. The school as a whole is about 91 percent white, but my particular class, which was sixth, seventh, and eighth grade was 30 percent minority, so almost all of the minority kids in the school were in the middle school. Most of the kids were middle class. The parents were making a decision that they would send their kids to a private elementary school and junior high, thinking that then they would love education and they could then make it in public high school. Most of the kids went on to public high schools. [Fayerweather] is progressive and innovative. It was originally fashioned after the British infant schools, so the classes were three grade levels to one class, and they were all open classrooms where kids were making choices. Another distinguishing feature of my class was that half of them came from divorced families.

Gene chose to talk about her class at the Fayerweather School in Cambridge where she team-taught in a combined sixth, seventh, and eighth-grade self-contained classroom. There were twenty-five students in her class, which was the middle school program. Her areas of expertise were language arts and social studies. The person with whom she taught specialized in math and science. Whenever possible, they tried to develop interdisciplinary units. One example of this is a regular midyear, ten-week unit that integrated all the major disciplines and subject areas. In that ten-week period, the students were asked to be more responsible for their learning, and they spent half their time in learning stations or on projects, working both individually and in small groups. The theme that year was "working," and students participated in community internships for one morning or afternoon a week for eight weeks.

During her interviews, Gene focused on the town meeting which she felt was the core of the curriculum:

> We met once a week for an hour and a half on Tuesdays, and a committee called the 'agenda committee' also met another half hour a week to plan the meeting. Those kids were elected twice a year... one from the sixth grade, one from the seventh, and one from the eighth, three at large. The town meeting was responsible for making all the rules and setting all the policies in the program except for ones that were purely academic.... Although kids made recommendations about courses, they didn't have the power, I guess, to plan courses. That seemed to be okay to them. I know it was okay because in turn we respected their authority on particular issues, mostly the ones that had to do with how the classroom ran and social interactions, structures and rules and that kind of thing.

Shelley: Nuclear Issues at Bromfield High School

> Harvard has a middle-class, small-town atmosphere, where most of the kids in the class, probably with the exception of two, were middle class; the others were living at middle-class standards, but their families were having a hard time. It's a balance between rural kids and [kids] whose parents work in the computer ring around Boston. It's a very small town and the school itself is 7–12 with six hundred students. Everyone knows each other, everybody has a reputation. A lot of the kids work at the few stores right in Harvard. I did not see one person of color in the school, when I was there.... It had more of a rural feel, having taught in Maine, than of a suburban school.... Harvard is a very conservative community, although that is changing.

Shelley chose to describe a course entitled "Thinking Critically about National Security," which he taught at Bromfield High School in Harvard, Massachusetts, a small town one hour west of Cambridge. Shelley was not a full-time teacher at Bromfield; rather he taught once a week after regular school hours for ten weeks while he was coordinator of Boston Area ESR.

The course was created by a group of students who wanted to learn more about the arms race and nuclear weapons. The students went through a long struggle with the administration to have the course offered. After approval of the course initially had been denied by the school committee, the students organized an informational community meeting on teaching about nuclear issues, which was attended by sixty-five students, parents, and teachers. After the meeting, approval was still withheld. At that point Shelley offered to teach a course that would meet once a week for two hours after regular school hours. Shelley remembers:

So they got together twenty kids, and we had an initial meeting three weeks before the course actually started. We sat down as a group, and I said 'Why are you doing this? Why are you here?' And everybody said what brought them there. Then I asked them what kinds of questions they had, and I wrote all of those up on the board so that they could see them. Then I asked, 'Well, if these are your questions, what kind of categories, what kind of topics do you want to cover in the course?' And they sort of categorized those into about eight topics with subtopics that covered most of their questions. And then I said that I would take that information back with me, and bring back an outline with some suggested speakers and things that I thought might fit and that we would review that next time.

The basic structure of the course was that a different topic was covered each week and a speaker was invited in to make a presentation on the topic. For instance, guest lecturers spoke about the history of the arms race, the nuclear freeze proposal, the Strategic Defense Initiative, and the Soviet Union. Speakers represented a broad cross-section of the political spectrum on arms policy from proponents of SDI to advocates of a freeze. The first hour of each session was spent discussing the previous week's speaker and eliciting and discussing students' feelings and thoughts about the issues under discussion. The second hour was devoted to the guest speaker's presentation and questions and answers. Students each kept a journal, and Shelley offered brief readings for each class.

Rachel: A Hunger Project in the Fenway School

Fenway is a [public] alternative school, tenth through twelfth graders, within Boston English High School. The vast majority of the kids come from any of a number of housing projects in Boston. A lot from the Mission Hill projects. So the majority are rather poor. Fenway is probably more diverse than the other programs. They tend to have more whites than a lot of the other schools have. But the majority are Black or Caribbean or Hispanic. Within the Boston system, it tries to be progressive, and sometimes they think they are and sometimes they know they are not.

Rachel described her involvement in a special project at the Fenway School, which is an alternative program of 160 students in Boston English High School, a large Boston public school. The Fenway School was created in 1983 to offer students a more cohesive and intimate learning experience, where they could be more involved in their own education, could address issues of more relevance to their lives, and develop closer relationships with their teachers.

Although she was not a teacher in the Fenway School or at Boston English, Rachel played a central role as an outside facilitator and advisor to students in the project she described. Early in the school year, just before the winter of 1984–85 media blitz about the famine in Ethiopia, Rachel helped to organize a unit on world hunger at the Fenway School. The one-week unit included a variety of speakers addressing local and world hunger; a "hunger banquet," which vividly brought home the disparities in diet between rich and poor, as well as the immensity of the problem; plenty of time for discussion and reflection; and a presentation by an Ethiopian woman who offered ideas for action.

Following this unit a small group of students remained interested in taking action to help alleviate hunger. They persistently badgered their faculty to help them organize a fund-raising event. Finally, late in the winter, the faculty turned to Rachel for help in working with the students. A committee of students was formed, which met once a week with Rachel and faculty advisors to accomplish the overall planning of the project. They ended up with several projects: organizing a fashion and talent show, making and selling buttons, running a car wash, and, since it was the end of the school year, cleaning teachers' rooms for a fee. Fifteen to twenty students had major roles in the planning and execution of the events, and most of the students in the Fenway School were involved in some way. They raised over one thousand dollars.

Rachel describes her role as an advisor or a resource person:

What I did, partly, was offer the larger picture, as much as I could, trying to get the kids to set up time-lines and understand when they had to do things. Also, I had a lot of outside resources available to me so that I could have a few of the kids come to [my office] and get a lesson from our PR man on how to write public service announcements and how to write the news releases. Also I was the one who kept posing the questions that they needed to answer: Who were they going to send the money to? Was it going to be just for Africa, or for the U.S. also? What or how are they going to decide the amounts? Whose opinion were they going to trust? Who did they need to interview? Who did they need to talk to before they could make the decisions? And then calling in those people.

Lucile: English at Arlington High School

Arlington is a middle-class community, in the whole range of the middle class. It's about 100 percent white. The high school is grades 9–12 with about two thousand kids, down from three thousand when I went there [to teach]. I think it is a very typical public school. It has fairly traditional subject matter and has a good faculty and administration who care about education. For the most part it is not an educationally oriented community. The kinds of problems they have are the kinds of problems that kids across America seem to have. They don't like to read, they are not especially good writers. Seventy percent of the students take college preparation course, and a lot of those go to community colleges.

Lucile was the one person interviewed who did not focus on a particular class, course, or project. Rather, her discussion of her teaching included several different courses, including an eleventh-grade course "Survey of American Literature," a non-college-prep course on creative writing, and a tenth-grade college-prep English course. She offered several examples from these courses of ways in which she felt she had begun to empower some of her students. One way was by involving students in classroom decision making. She described several examples, including (1) student participation in deciding whether and how to study vocabulary, (2) a student rebellion against a test she developed on *The Scarlet Letter* and how the students ended up creating their own test, (3) student involvement in devising the final exam, and (4) student discussions of fair grading procedures. She also described how learning to write well can contribute to empowerment.

Student Empowerment and the Empowering Classroom

Vera: I have this feeling that empowerment somehow means energizing [students] so that they feel they have some say in their lives about important issues that affect them, and that they can do something about how these other issues impinge on their lives. That they're not robots nor being manipulated.

Gene: [Students] learn that they can make a difference in the world, that because they walk through the world, the world can be a different place, and they can decide the kind of effect they are going to have. It is not all fate.

It is not surprising that the themes that emerged as central in these six educators' personal experiences of empowerment are similar to those they emphasized in describing the empowerment of students: at the core of the process of empowerment is the experience of making a difference, coming to feel that one has more control over one's life and can act effectively on one's convictions. Paralleling their accounts of their own experiences, they described individual transformations in student empowerment using the metaphor of voice. In Gene's words, "[Students] need to learn to speak, and speak up, and so to speak clearly, and to say what it is they're thinking, clearly, so other people can understand it, to be assertive." Echoing our earlier discussion, Vera identified self-confidence and the ability to communicate as the key elements in the development of voice:

An empowered student is the one who has a degree of self-confidence, a feeling that he has some understanding of what it is he is dealing with and some control over his life, and some way of explaining that to other people and some strong conviction about what he believes.

However, as we saw earlier, empowerment does not just mean self-assertion. Voice occurs in dialogue. It therefore includes the development of the capacity for reciprocity and openness in relationships as well. Gene, Lally, Lucile, Shelley, Vera, and Rachel each emphasized that in the process of student empowerment assertiveness develops concurrently with the ability to be open to others. The ability to speak is complemented by the ability to listen; confidence is balanced by humility. Gene described it this way:

They need to know how to take a stand and have an opinion, and they need to know how to take in new information and change their minds gracefully without embarrassment. . . . They need to know how to say, this is what I think, I'm right, and I may be wrong; and they need to know how to say you're right, I was wrong.

Lally stressed that students

[develop a willingness] to say what they're thinking and the willingness to hear what other kids are thinking, to be willing to challenge and be willing to question with their own thoughts; the willingness to involve other kids and not just be concerned with their act, and I think ultimately the willingness to act on something that they feel real strongly about.

As each of the six teachers' reflections on her or his teaching experiences unfolded, the themes of *dialogue, decision making,* and *supportive community* emerged as central. Each emphasized that dialogue about issues important to students was the core activity that cultivated student empowerment. In fact, dialogue that led to individual and shared decision making seemed to create the greatest opportunities for student empowerment. All six saw the creation of a supportive group in the classroom as essential for successful dialogue, much in the same way that the ESR membership had supported them. The supportive group was the context in which decisions could be made, and action taken. As individuals develop a sense of connection and community, they are ever more willing to take risks, because, increasingly, mistakes are accepted and everyone's contribution is valued by the teacher and students. Repeatedly, the teachers emphasized the importance of creating a context in which students could feel free to share their thoughts, beliefs, and feelings in the process of making decisions about issues that mattered.

Shelley explained that the basic role that a supportive group plays in student empowerment is to offer students "a sense of shared effort, a sense that they aren't alone." This theme, which also appeared in chapter 4, is based on the thesis that shared effort alleviates feelings of isolation. This can be particularly true for adolescents, who often feel that they are the only ones who are afraid, confused, or frustrated. Shelley points out that in a supportive group students discover not only were they not alone in their interest to learn about something, but they weren't alone in some of the missing pieces of logic, the lack of understanding, the struggle to come up with their own opinions, the dealing with their feelings. All of that they could see was shared and that it was okay.

Gene explains why it is important to encourage this type of supportive atmosphere:

It is hard in this culture to make mistakes. It's hard to not be successful and believe there is some success in it. It's hard to not feel like a failure, and it is hard to take risks.

At the same time it is extremely difficult to build accepting and mutually respecting groups of students in a culture in which competition and individual success is promoted and in which domination is the predominant mode of relationship. It is difficult to bring students together to respect and listen to one another when they are divided by cultural, class, race, and gender experiences in this society. It is difficult to encourage students to take risks and trust others when they are constantly reminded of their otherness: be they fat, cool, ugly, beautiful, athletic, 'nerdy,' bright, pimply, quiet, loud, funny, or obnoxious. Nevertheless, for all six teachers, the ongoing struggle—and at least partial success—at creating a supportive atmosphere was seen as absolutely essential for the dialogue and shared decision making so vital to the experiences of empowerment to occur.

As we saw in chapter 5, careful, mutual listening is an essential quality of dialogue. Lucile states why this is so important: "The way that people are generally willing to listen to you is first of all if you are willing to listen to them." This kind of reciprocal listening is similar to that which was discussed in chapter 5. It is the kind of listening that is cultivated in an environment in which people feel able to express their opinions because they feel that their views are respected and valued. Lally describes the climate of mutual respect in her class, where the group accepted that

what everybody has to say is important, that was just assumed and not everybody chooses to contribute all the time, but nobody puts anybody down. They may make a crack every now and then in jest, but for the most part they really respect each other. It was an open, trusting atmosphere.

Gene observes that students' emerging respect for one another reflects their growing respect for themselves and their own ideas and opinions:

> They don't want people to put them down, so they start thinking that maybe they shouldn't put down other people's ideas. It doesn't mean that they have to agree with everybody, but it means that to say something was stupid isn't fair at some level. I think they respected that people took a risk when they brought a proposal to the group.

As this kind of environment develops, students can begin to develop their voices and cultivate their abilities to be both assertive and open to others.

Lally makes the connections between listening, assertion, supportive community, and dialogue:

> I think the discussion mode is at the core of it, interacting with people in a way where you are really making an effort to hear where they're coming from and where you implicitly assume that people have something to contribute. And you may find in the end that you choose not to [agree] with that person. . . . I think it is hard to do that unless you feel that you're worthwhile and that you've been acknowledged and that you've got something to contribute.

An important aspect of dialogue is that through the process of study and discussion students expand their critical awareness of the issues discussed. This awareness, in itself, can help students feel they have more control over their lives. Vera described the effects of expanded awareness of social issues on how students feel about themselves:

> When you have a sense of mastery and control over a topic that you can talk about or that you have an opinion about, it's not just you floundering around with vague feelings and opinions, but you now have a backlog of information and ideas that you've discussed in class, that you've sort of thrown back and forth. I think they have a sense that they can talk sensibly to other people about what they've studied and that they know something they didn't know before. Not just that

they've explored ideas about when it's important to make a
choice, or whatever, but they actually have some factual
information as well, which I think makes them feel they have
a better grip on the world.

Shelley echoed these sentiments:

To be able to understand, to be able to have something be
comprehensible, to have looked at a problem and have said,
'God, what is this about? Why is it this way?' And then all of
a sudden to see, 'That's what it is about!' is a very empowering experience.

Critical awareness is more than an accumulated storehouse
of facts and knowledge. It implies that the student has critically
explored the available facts and interpretations of a particular
issue. Critical awareness requires examining contradictory facts
and interpretations and uncovering their hidden assumptions and
biases. Most importantly, critical awareness involves developing
one's own opinion, one's own interpretation, and one's own integration of meanings. Critical awareness means that rather than sub-
mitting to the knowledge of others, the knower actively engages
with knowledge while creating new knowledge.

Vera emphasized this theme when she stressed the importance of connecting broad historical and social issues with concerns relevant to students. She observed:

I too learned a lot of information and learned it well, but it
was never related to my life in the decisions I would have to
make. It was just something out there, and although those
connections were implicit, they were never made explicit.

In her classroom, issues were treated as living problems for students to engage with and to consider within the contexts of their
own lives.

Through the process of dialogic discussion, students experience the ability to make a difference in a group. They experience
having their opinions valued. In the process of sharing opinions,
and identifying, selecting, and justifying analyses and choices, students are challenged to speak, to listen and to make decisions.
They are encouraged to achieve the balance between assertion and

openness so essential to empowerment. Vera offered an example of the kinds of interactions that can occur in classroom dialogue concerning contemporary issues:

> We were talking about Reagan going to Bitburg, right after we had finished studying about the Holocaust. I had handed out a whole series of articles that I had cut out of the *Globe* and the *Times* and sort of said, read those, and then tell me what you think. The first one to speak was a boy who said, 'Well, I think that Reagan shouldn't go to Bitburg, but I think if I were Reagan, I would probably go to Bitburg, because it would look weak if I were to change my mind.' And then the discussion went on, and different people said, 'But he should change his mind because . . .' and 'He shouldn't change his mind because . . .' or 'There are other things he could do . . .' or whatever. [After this discussion, the same boy] wanted to speak. He said, 'Well, I can see how maybe it wouldn't be weak for Reagan to change his mind,' and I couldn't help but say, 'And none of us thinks you're weak and foolish for changing your mind.' I think that was the general atmosphere of the class, so that people felt free to say what they wanted to say and to change their minds and to accept the kinds of comments that other people made.

Shelley offered another example:

> They learned from each other's struggles. [For example] one kid listened to another kid talking, wrote it in her journal, because she thought it was so important, and then when we were doing the journal readings or talking about the journals, Rachel said, 'Wait Chris, I wrote down what you said.' And she read it and then gave it back to Chris to ask her to explain it. . . . They were able to bounce off each other and learn from each other.

In creating and participating in classroom dialogue concerning political and social issues, the teachers did not impose facts and analyses upon their students. Rather, they engaged their students in a shared inquiry, a mutual exploration of the issues. They listened. They shared thoughts and opinions. They shared information. They encouraged critical thinking. Their goal was not to fill their students with information, but to engage them in the search for insights into the meaning of events and the relationship between events and their lives. Their goal was not to have students know the right answers, but to be able to identify the problems, ask questions and to explore, with others, possible solutions.

While dialogue is the foundation of empowering classroom dynamics, dialogue towards the goal of making choices and reaching decisions seems to be the linchpin in helping students develop their voices. Through the challenge of making personal choices students experience a developing sense of self. They derive a sense of ownership—of ideas, of values, of a vision of the right and the just. They are encouraged to not only express their opinions but to take stands and to be responsible for the stands they take. They begin to feel the contours of their unique identities and to hear the sounds of their unique voices.

One area in which students were encouraged to make decisions was in relation to the various social issues they were addressing. For example, Lally asked her students to decide, Should the pregnant teenager keep her child? Have an abortion? Put the baby up for adoption? Vera describes how personal decision making was central to her course:

All along, most of the assignments over the year ask kids to make a decision, to make a choice, to take responsibility for making a decision, and to defend that decision, either in writing or in role playing or whatever. That's what most of them say they found important. They found they weren't told what to think; they were given an opportunity to figure out for themselves what they would think or what they would do.

Decision making links reflection and action—it is a moment when thought and action meet. The teachers all emphasized that it was important to support student action on their decisions concerning social, political, and personal issues discussed in class. Such actions ranged from trying out new behaviors with friends, as was the case in Lally's unit, to organizing a major fund-raising event to alleviate world hunger, as in Rachel's project. However, in emphasizing the importance of encouraging and supporting students to meaningful action outside the classroom, several of the study participants expressed regret for not doing enough of this. It appears that this aspect of empowerment is among the most difficult for teachers, given the political realities of schools as well as the lack of time and other structural constraints on their teaching.

While action outside the classroom on issues discussed in scheduled classes proved somewhat difficult to promote and support, action within the classroom was central to the teachers' emerging pedagogies of empowerment. It was in the daily functioning of their classrooms that they saw the most immediate possibilities for encouraging and supporting meaningful action by their students. As we have seen, the control of decision making is a fundamental ingredient of teacher domination. In seeking to move away from traditional coercive relationships toward more equal, dialogic, and empowering relationships, the teachers began to share decision making concerning the management of the class or project, the content of the course, and other types of activities in which students would engage. Students were encouraged to make both personal and group decisions, and thereby to participate in a more complicated dialectic of decision making.

In most of the contexts described by the teachers, students were given, to varying degrees, a say in determining how the class would be run and in selecting what the class would focus on for study. In Gene's classroom, decision making occurred in town meetings with regard to the everyday rules, problems, and issues involved in the functioning of the community. In town meetings teachers and students had an equal vote, and a two-thirds majority was needed for a measure to be approved. Gene describes the town meeting as the "hub of the wheel," the core activity around which everything else revolved. In Shelley's course the students created the course, chose the teacher, and determined the topics covered. In Rachel's project students were involved in deciding a whole range of personal, organizational, and policy decisions concerning how to organize the fund-raising events and where to give the money they raised. Rachel described how students took increasing responsibility for decision making and observes that "[they never] thought they could decide anything that important."

Lucile depicted students participating in decisions ranging from the content of tests to whether or not they would study vocabulary lists. In Vera's course students were often asked for suggestions as to course content. She regularly solicited students' opinions on a range of process and content issues and offered opportunities for shared and individual decision making. Lally is the only one who did not implement this kind of decision making with her students. However, she felt it was important and indicated that she was "seriously thinking" about ways to involve students in the future.

Group decisions involved issues over which students were invested with real decision making and implementing power. Unlike their positions on whether they supported SDI, the Freeze, or abortion, which they could take action on but over which they had little immediate control, students were invested with the authority to make decisions that affected their lives directly in the classroom. Through the process of making group choices, students experienced the dynamic process of collaborative decision making. Successful co-decision making is co-agency. By sharing their power to determine class content and policy, the teachers broke down some of the hierarchy of domination and diffused *power over*. They created situations in which students could have real control over concrete issues—that is, they could experience making a difference in a truly meaningful way.

Equally important, in making decisions about their lives in the classroom, students must also take responsibility for the implementation of their decisions and for their consequences. They learn that decisions do, indeed, have consequences, that with empowerment comes responsibility, and that not all decisions work out as planned. Through shared decision making and collaborative action, students must learn to identify their priorities, express their needs and thoughts, listen to others, reach decisions within a group, and work together to effect their decisions. They are engaged in concrete action in which the range of interpersonal skills central to empowerment can be developed and practiced. In the process of considering, deciding, and acting upon classroom procedures and curricula, students expand their awareness of interpersonal relationships, group process, and the nature of education. They consider the meaning and importance of a range of values—such as equality, democracy, responsibility, cooperation, competition, and respect for others—through their immediate challenge to work together. They discover that they should not take everyday occurrences in the classroom for granted, and they learn that they, too, can have a voice in shaping their lives within the classroom.

At their best, the kinds of dialogic interactions described above build confidence, enhance self-esteem, and encourage further participation. Lally describes this process:

I think a lot of times they say things or they have ideas that they didn't even think they had because they just intuitively want to get in on [the discussion]. Then when they hear that they're heard by somebody else, I think that kind of adds to that sense of, 'Yeah, I'm somebody here. I am worthwhile in this class at this moment.' I think that's the experience when someone tries something and they get a positive reaction, whether it's people looking or responding. I think it gets to be kind of a cumulative thing. Kids see that they have ideas and feelings that matter to other people, that they can care enough about themselves to care about other people in the class too, and that it's exciting. It really makes you feel alive when you're interacting with people like that.

Students identify themselves as contributing members of a group. Through dialogue, decision making, and action on issues both outside and within the classroom, students become clearer about their convictions and better able to work with others.

The Field of Empowering Education

The accounts of the participants in this study suggest that there is a "field of empowering education" that encompasses both the commonalities and differences among the different teaching experiences described herein (see figure 1 below).

There are two axes in this field: "praxis" and "content." Praxis reflects the importance all six teachers placed on the interaction of reflection and action in the process of empowerment. Praxis falls into two inextricably related but distinct categories: on the one hand, there is reflection, the development of critical awareness; on the other hand, there is action, taking meaningful steps to change or maintain existing conditions. The two, when most potent, interact dialectically, informing and emerging out of one another. This is praxis.

The second axis—content—captures the diversity of foci for reflection and action that were represented in the teachers' experiences. These content areas fall into two broad categories: classroom issues and social issues (issues related directly to life outside the classroom). Gene's focus on town meetings and Lucile's focus on the issues of tests and grades are examples of classroom issues, while Rachel's students' fund-raising project to help end hunger, Shelley's focus on the nuclear arms race, and Lally's unit on abortion are examples of social issues. Obviously the two can overlap, as when discussing the racist and sexist attitudes that are held by members of a class.

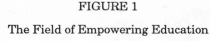

FIGURE 1

The Field of Empowering Education

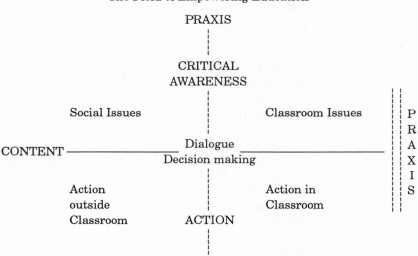

Finally, at the heart of empowering pedagogy are the processes of dialogue and decision making within a supportive group. These processes embody the synergistic dynamics and potential of empowering community and the dynamics through which voice is nurtured and developed. They capture the interactive and inherently social nature of empowerment and its fundamental relationship to the real ability students have to participate in decisions that affect their lives.

This field, taken as a whole, may represent the ideal or "ultimately" empowering educational setting, one in which awareness and action, dialogue and decision making concerning classroom issues and social issues, are encouraged and supported. This would be the truly democratic classroom. However, it is clear that not one of the classrooms described in this chapter embodies the ideal. In fact, it is unclear just how this could be achieved, given the realities of how time and curriculum are organized in the schools in which the teachers work. Thus, within the realities in which these teachers work, the boundaries of the structures and norms are pushed in different ways and in different directions. While Vera's course promotes awareness of classroom dynamics and offers opportunities for students to participate in classroom decisions, she seems to put more stress on developing awareness of social and political issues in both their historical and contemporary contexts while at the same time not placing a strong emphasis on social action on the issues addressed. On the other hand, Rachel's project was geared toward social action and group dynamics, and while reflection is certainly a component of all action, there was relatively little time for concentrated research, reading, and critical reflection on the issue of hunger. Finally, Gene's town meetings encourage both reflection and action on school and classroom issues, while she explores social issues in other contexts (the actual courses).

The important point here is that each person is struggling to create learning environments that, as much as possible, provide opportunities for students in their classes to understand their work and their lives more fully, to develop their own voices in relation to the powers that be, and to experience participation in decisions that relate to and affect their lives. Each has chosen a different way to do this. Their choices are determined by a range of factors that include their own personal priorities, interests, and strengths; the limits of their own emerging understanding of empowerment and empowering pedagogy; the kinds of dialogue and shared decision making with which they feel most comfortable; the limitations of their school settings; and the interests and backgrounds of their students. The result is that individuals emphasize different areas of the field, and some include more of the entire field in their teaching than others. Intuitively, though, they all seem to understand that to maximize the empowering experiences of their students they must encompass as much of the field as possible, and they are struggling to understand the obstacles, both internal and external, that they face along the way.

Power in Student–Teacher Relationships that Nurture Empowerment

For all six teachers, the quality of their relationships with their students is basic to their efforts to create empowering learning communities. As we have seen, too often relationships between teachers and students are constrained by the implicit acceptance of *power over* as a fundamental basis for the relationships. Recognizing this, the six viewed one of their biggest challenges as that of creating alternatives to domination in teacher–student relationships. To accomplish this, they felt it crucial to break down traditional barriers between themselves and their students. Gene explains that, for her, this means creating a classroom where there aren't artificial divisions between teachers and students, where teachers are learning and students are teaching as well as teachers being teachers and students learning from them . . . to not recreate hierarchical, authoritarian structures.

Lucile's description of how she sees herself in relation to her students challenges the traditional power assumptions of her role: "I think that, as much as possible, I feel that I am on a road of inquiry with them." Her language is revealing. She does not see herself as separate and superior to her students. Nor does she see herself necessarily in the front, leading the inquiry. She positions herself *with* her students. They are inquiring together. As the teachers entered into dialogic relationships with their students, they abandoned many of the traditional ways in which instructors maintain distance and control over students. They sought to model, instead, the behaviors that they wanted to encourage in students.

The ethics of assertiveness have not traditionally been a central problem for teachers. However, these are a problem for teachers who are trying to understand how to create relationships with students not characterized by domination. Too often teacher assertiveness has meant imposing control, order, and submission. Throughout the interviews it was clear that the teachers' attempts to nurture student empowerment and to understand the "power that empowers" involved their own personal struggle to free themselves from their traditional role while simultaneously trying to understand what responsibilities and decisions were appropriately theirs. They were asking questions such as: When is a teacher's assertiveness domination? When is assertiveness *power over,* and when is it *power with?* When does the assertiveness of a teacher help empower students, and when is it oppressive? What are the different responsibilities of students and teachers? What is the difference between a teacher and a student in an empowering classroom? In fact, the question of the nature of power in the experience of empowerment was central to their quest to understand and develop a pedagogy of empowerment.

In the experiences of the teachers presented in chapters 4 and 5 and in the description of student empowerment referred to above, we saw how individuals who enter into relationships of co-agency develop the ability to be open and sensitive to the needs of others and the corresponding ability to articulate their thoughts and beliefs clearly and effectively. This balance of assertiveness and openness is captured in the concept of *assertive mutuality*. Lally describes assertive mutuality in the following comments:

> It means being aware of your own feelings and also being aware of the other person's feelings and that one is not exclusive of the other, and that it becomes important to feel for what the other person is saying and to feel where they are, at the same time letting them know who you are.

The experience of assertive mutuality lies at the center of the empowering teacher–student relationship. The qualities that characterize an empowered person are the same qualities that support the empowerment of others. This highlights the reciprocal character of *power with* and the synergistic nature of empowerment.

Given the teacher's traditional domination in the classroom and the distance between teacher and student that it creates, perhaps the most challenging aspect of assertive mutuality is the openness and receptivity—the *vulnerability*—that it demands of teachers in their relationships with students. Lucile describes her struggle to be open:

> It's for me to be continually open to questions about how we're doing things and then to encourage that same thing in them.... That we're all asking questions all the time.... How is this working? Looking back at our goals, are we getting toward the goals? Are these goals really the ones that you really want to work towards? Maybe the first thing that they want is good SAT scores. Well frankly I'd want to press them.... Is that what they really want out of English class? I'm willing to help them with their SAT scores, they want to go to college, that's a legitimate thing, but so I guess it's the sense of our being there to really work together.... How best to discover what we want to have happen in class that year and how to have it happen. And I think the thing that's hardest for me as a teacher in that situation is to just let myself be so open to questions all the time.... It's incredibly vulnerable I think...I feel very worried about it a lot.

Lally echoes Lucile's focus on vulnerability as she describes a core quality of the empowering student–teacher relationship:

[It requires] being willing to be vulnerable, to be able to share your experiences, to not quite know where something's going to go.

Gene offers an example of her own willingness to become vulnerable:

The place that happened for our class one year was during a variety show. None of the kids had ever been on stage before, singing, and the music teacher got them to do it, and got us to do it as teachers, and we were all vulnerable. So you know we practiced, but then at some point in the rehearsals we had to sing alone. It was finally time for us to each do our parts, and I can remember stepping up to the microphone during one of the rehearsals and singing and stepping back to the group, because we were sort of a chorus kind of a situation, and having a seventh grade girl take my hand, sort of pat it and whisper, 'What a nice job.'

By making herself vulnerable with her students, Gene creates a situation in which traditional student and teacher roles are blurred: the teacher risks, the student comforts, the teacher feels supported. Gene's vulnerability encourages more egalitarian relationships with her students. In these relationships mutual support is more likely to occur.

A key quality of vulnerability and openness is listening. Listening has been a recurrent theme throughout this discussion of empowerment and *power with*. Listening is such a common theme of educational rhetoric that it sometimes seems to lose its meaning. The listening Shelley refers to is an ongoing process of attuning himself to students' thoughts, concerns, and needs:

A core part is staying with students' thinking and helping them develop their thinking or their knowledge. It is not a process of filling students with knowledge, it's a process of continually staying in touch with the way they're thinking about things and their concerns.

Listening is much more than hearing words. To truly listen one must acknowledge the value of the person and that person's ideas, feelings, and experiences. To do this one must take a particular stance toward knowledge and the educational enterprise. Staying in touch with students' thinking means trying to avoid imposing on them the requirement that they know solely what the teacher knows and think the way the teacher thinks. It means hearing their concerns and understanding their points of view in order to be able to help them develop their own knowledge and ways of thinking. It means integrating their thinking into the pedagogical approach. Lally described the dynamics of interaction in which there is true listening and mutuality as a "shared kind of dance."

For these teachers vulnerability comes as a result of a struggle to release control of the classroom, to let go of *power over* so that responsive relationships in which co-agency and empowerment can develop are achieved. Openness and vulnerability involve taking risks, sharing one's thoughts *and* one's feelings, and being willing to accept the thoughts and feelings of others. Being vulnerable means being willing to admit one is wrong, that a mistake was made. It means being willing to show that one cares, that one is excited, disappointed, or angry. It means being honest.

When teachers and students successfully develop relationships that are characterized by assertive mutuality, vulnerability, listening, and dialogue, then these relationships become models for the kinds of relationships that students can form with one another. The student–teacher relationship becomes a model for the kinds of relationships that are the backbone of empowering community.

Assertiveness as Imposition: The Role of *Power Over*

It is not easy to transform power relationships in classrooms in most U.S. schools. For Lucile the realities of schooling mean that

in public schools, anyway, the only thing you can do is do less *power over*. There is no way, as long as there are grading systems and things like that, that you are ever going to be able to totally eliminate *power over*.

Vera, too, noted the limits of change while at the same time affirming the potential for a radically different possibility in education:

I think if you want to teach completely as *power with*, I know you can do it. But you have to be in an environment where you have total support, because it's an act of faith. It would mean that you would be building curriculum with the children; there would be no course that you've designed. There would be course development out of the needs of children all the way through. And I believe that that's the best way and the most valid way to teach. But I can't do it unless I would be in a school where everybody believed in it and supported it and where parents supported it and where no one was afraid that children wouldn't learn, children wouldn't pass tests, children wouldn't do this, children wouldn't do that, children wouldn't get into schools, blah, blah, blah. That whole other-world garbage that surrounds a school. If everyone is dedicated to that and is willing to support it, then I'm sure it works, and I'm sure it's probably the most exciting kind of school there can be.... I'm willing to take part of the year and have the kids determine what should happen. But I guess I don't have the courage to ... and I don't think I would have permission to run a whole year that way.

Perhaps the most immediate and troubling challenge facing these teachers is that, given the pervasiveness of domination throughout the schools, students arrive in their classrooms having been shaped by and conditioned to respond to domination. They have internalized the attitudes and behaviors expected of powerless people, and they have learned to survive within a *power over* game over which they have little control. Thus, in their experience of domination they have learned to be passive, deferential, subversive, resistant, and/or submissive. They often feel so powerless, mistrusting, and cynical that creating a supportive context with transformed power relationships is a struggle for both teacher and student. Shelley observed:

I think that empowerment is difficult within the context of schools as they are traditionally designed and I think it raises a lot of questions for teachers about how to create an empowering classroom.... It provides for a very uphill struggle, where you create an empowering classroom and students challenge you and students don't believe you, don't trust you. One of the other difficulties or challenges that is so hard is creating a safe environment; how do you stop the put-downs?

In order to cope with these realities, virtually all the study participants felt they used *power over* in the initial phases of their courses to create a space in which mutuality and co-agency could grow. Shelley said,

I will not allow criticism. I confronted that the first day. I said that in here we're going to consider each other's views with respect and not with critique. And when we hear speakers I'd like us to really listen appreciatively. . . . We don't want to attack.

Vera described a similar approach to creating a supportive environment:

I create it didactically, by simply not allowing anybody to put anyone down. And if it happens, I speak to them after class and say that the next time I am going to ask them to leave.

She noted, however, that the didactic approach only sets the initial boundaries within which she tries to create a climate of trust and respect by modeling mutuality and co-agency.

Rachel noted that, given students' experiences in and out of school, they can "walk into the relationship with you feeling cynical and not trusting adults." In these situations she feels she has exerted control over students: "When I've used *power over*, it has usually been to try to make the transition between what kids are used to and what I want them to experience." What Rachel does is

set up some limits at the very first step until there is a relationship between me and the kids. They have no reason, in a way, to trust me. In a way it is setting up some bounds while they learn to trust me, so that we can do more power sharing and have a more empowering environment later. . . . There seems to be a need for transition. It takes a whole lot of practice to get to *power with*.

The tension Rachel feels is between wanting to enter into *power with* relationships immediately and feeling as if she might "lose control." This is the fear that *power with* instills in teachers: that the students may run wild, or they may do nothing, that rather than the teacher controlling the situation (*power over*) or both the teacher and the students controlling the situation (*power with*), the students alone will control the situation, and the result will be anarchy. Given students' experiences of domination in school and in the rest of their lives, these fears, while often exaggerated, are certainly not totally unfounded. The challenge for the teacher is to structure possibilities, to facilitate the movement from domination to empowerment, from silence to voice, from *power over* to *power with*. Creating an empowering classroom means that the accepted rules of the game have changed. Students (and teacher) must adjust; they must learn new rules. This calls for a curriculum of transition and transformation, for the learning of new skills and new ways of being with others. Quite often it means students undergo a radical change in how they see themselves as students.

Rachel makes some useful distinctions about the kind of power she exerts in the beginning of a course:

> It is not like you are dominating them to get more power so that they have less. It's dominating them so they are protected from whatever; from domination from each other; or problems from outside the classroom; or whatever. Then it's just a matter of being consistent and fair in how you work with those limits. And honest about it, so they share in upholding them or eventually changing them. There is a difference between domination in order to get more power for yourself and domination that is later flexible.

The initial use of *power over* in the classroom resembles the functions of *power over* in ESR that were described in chapter 5. It is utilized to create a space in which *power with* can be cultivated. The group felt, at least in the beginning, that the use of *power over* to protect students from one another and to create conditions in which mutuality and empowerment could occur was an important, if usually distasteful, responsibility of the teacher.

Several people stressed, however, that while there are times when controlling and restrictive actions may seem necessary, they should only be used as a last resort. In fact, such actions are necessary much less often than most teachers assume. Rachel notes that "even the piece about starting a course with requirements and everything like that, it's much more empowering to share that piece. I have done it so that it is actually sharing." Vera observes that even when it comes to students verbally abusing one another there is a nonauthoritarian approach that can be very effective:

> Ideally one shouldn't didactically say anything until the need for it arises. I think the best kinds of discussions you can have about put-downs arise when they just happen and you won't even have to say didactically, 'I don't want put-downs.' You can just say, 'How did you feel?' to the kid who was the

recipient of it. And then have a discussion around what's happening in the classroom, what put-downs do, how they shut down discussion and how they make it hard for people to feel that they are going to be heard, and so on. And never draw a conclusion 'therefore I don't want any put-downs.' The kids will come to that conclusion.

She argues that "whatever kids arrive at by themselves always works better than something you impose." However, she suggests that as a result of such pressures as "efficiency, time, being angry or tired" there is "validity" in using *power over* as a last resort:

I think I am struggling to achieve a situation in which I have to use very little *power over*. But I think that there are times when I do use *power over* and feel I need to use it for the benefit of the larger group, using power over individuals who are having a hard time letting other people have a say or working productively or whatever, and in those cases, after having tried *power with* and having made suggestions that didn't work or whatever, I don't hesitate to use *power over* for the good of the group.

In the situations discussed above, it is clear that the teachers felt that there are times when teacher control can contribute to the creation of an empowering setting, although they emphasize that it is through relationships of co-agency that students are empowered. While recognizing that there are ways to deal with most situations without resorting to authoritarian behavior, they also acknowledge that a range of factors conspire to make the use of *power over* more frequent than they would ideally like.

Assertiveness without Imposition:
The Contours of *Power With*

In trying to create settings and relationships with students that are characterized by mutuality and co-agency, each of the teachers is seeking an appropriate role to play in the classroom. I have already discussed the importance of openness and vulnerability for helping students experience empowerment, and we have seen how there are times when teacher control seems to be an efficient last resort. But another important question these teachers are asking is how to be assertive without imposing on their stu-

dents. They recognize that as teachers they have different responsibilities and expertise than do their students. They believe that
their role of teacher is not to control students, yet that it can and
should involve active participation in classroom activities that may
be different from the way students participate. All feel that becoming an empowering teacher involves more than being responsive
and supportive.

In her thinking about how to be assertive without dominating
the classroom, Gene has identified what she calls the "authority of
expertise":

> I'm becoming more and more convinced that kids can decide
> more of what they should learn, but I still think there is an
> authority of expertise there, where I have more experience.
> Now, I know more about the kinds of communication skills
> that need to be learned simply because I know what they are.
> But I think there is a way to structure it more carefully so
> that you could share that knowledge with the kids and then
> have them decide. It would take a lot more time, and it would
> be harder to teach because you wouldn't be able to plan a
> course in advance as much.

The authority of expertise is not domination because it does not
give the teacher license to control her or his students. Rather, it
means that in a classroom where there is growing mutual respect
and shared decision making, both teacher and students recognize
that the teacher has a wider range of experience and a depth of
formal knowledge both in the subject matter and in working with
people, and that this knowledge and experience are resources for
the group to listen to and learn from. The teacher, however, is not
the only one in the class who has expertise. On a very basic level
the students have an authority of expertise of their own experience, and they develop authority of expertise in a variety of areas.
The authority of expertise within the *power with* paradigm does
not lead to domination, but rather to the fact that people listen
carefully and take wisdom and experience into consideration as
they make decisions. The authority of expertise enhances the capa-
bilities of everyone.

By entering into relationships of co-agency with students, the
teacher does not relinquish control, but rather *shares* control.
Lucile describes how the authority of expertise and shared control
function together:

I have taught for fifteen years. I may not be an expert, but I have some experience, I've seen a lot of different kids, and I've seen a lot of different things that work, and I have a lot of ideas. They might as well not reinvent the wheel. I think that it's important to say, 'Try this out,' and maybe if they don't like the idea, to try it out in a nonthreatening way. They were the ones that wanted vocabulary quizzes. I hate vocabulary quizzes. First of all I think they're stupid. You don't learn vocabulary that way, but that's what they wanted. They liked the concrete grade. So what I managed to do was put in my agenda, which was they took it with another kid, which meant that they had to figure out how to study together; they had to agree about how to take the test together, and they both got one grade for this test.

In this quote we see how in a context of shared decision making the teacher expresses her beliefs and makes suggestions based on her experience and that these suggestions and insights are taken seriously by students and integrated into decisions. The key is that the students' concerns are also integrated into decisions so that as much as possible teacher and students alike feel heard and included. This is reciprocal influence and emergence: the synergistic interaction that characterizes *power with*.

One important role of the teacher in empowering students seems to be that of initiator and facilitator. Several of the teachers observed that while dialogue and shared power hold the potential for empowerment, they also make many demands on students. These demands are not normally made on students in school, and they involve ways of being, relating, and thinking about themselves and their education to which they are totally unaccustomed, and which, in fact, have been discouraged by the system and much of the wider culture. Gene observes that, for students,

it's hard. It means you have to think hard, you have to be honest about what you are thinking and feeling. You have to work it out interpersonally with other people. You have to take risks. You have to take responsibility for the decisions you make, which means you have to evaluate and be honest about that. So it's hard. And also it's hard to listen to other people, especially when you think they are wrong. . . . It's often tedious, time consuming and sometimes it's painful.

Given student difficulty and reluctance to take responsibility, it is up to the teacher to nurture and support the growing desire and capacity to take responsibility. While ultimately students may take on the roles of initiator and facilitator of classroom learning, the teacher often finds her- or himself to be the only one with the skills, knowledge, and commitment to fulfill these functions at a particular point in time. This usually means, especially in the beginning, that the teacher takes on a larger role in finding and suggesting materials and organizing activities for the class. Lucile explains her thinking about this:

> Sometimes at the beginning of the year I'd start by making plans. Because, I'll tell you something, if you give them the plans, they make the most conservative plans I've ever seen, far more conservative that I do. You know, fifty vocabulary words a week. And they don't see an expanded possibility for things like cooperating on tasks, retaking something if they don't do it right the first time so we might learn something. They've been educated by the method of the system so long I think you have to throw some new choices out to them, options anyway.

The teacher also takes special initiative for finding activities that will help students accept more responsibility and that will help them to be able to fulfill the responsibilities they do accept. Lucile notes:

> They are required to take English. Somebody comes in the beginning of the year, they tell them what they're going to do. So they have not thought about whether or not English is valuable to them and for what reason. I think they have to do some thinking about that first, and they have to say to themselves, 'I have to be here for the year. What is it that I hope I can do as a result of being here this year?' And then I get to say some of my thinking about what English is, and we work on what are the ways we can create this end result. What ought to count for what reason, because grades have to be given. I think the encouragement within a classroom in a school system where that hasn't happened before can make them see that they have a right to say something about how they are educated.

The teacher also takes responsibility for coordinating and facilitating discussions. Lally describes this role:

> My role was to pretty much set the ground rules to start with, to shift the focus, and basically to respond when I thought something needed to be a little bit different, when they needed time to stop and reflect, when they needed to move to the next part. If one person is talking too much, to move it to somebody else; if somebody else needs to be brought out, to bring out that person. If I need to add some information or have them read something at some point. . . . I have those kinds of decisions to make. I am older than the rest, so I've had some experiences I can add that they haven't had yet.

Another important assertive role of the teacher is in challenging students—encouraging them to do their best, prodding their thinking, asking them tough questions. Gene examines how she took these roles in her relationship with one student who, over a two-year period, moved from feeling powerless and acting in destructive ways to becoming one of the most active, involved, and constructive members of the class:

> I took her really seriously, and I wouldn't accept the behavior. I just kept on pushing her and pushing her to work on it. And I told her that I thought that she wasn't being challenged and that it wasn't that I wasn't giving challenging work and that she needed to think about it, that she was responsible for her education. I talked with her parents, and I worked in tutorial with her in writing. At the end of the sixth grade I gave her positive feedback, when things were working. Then toward the end of the seventh grade, I remember she sat in the town meeting, and she said, I mean she was becoming more assertive about how she was feeling and stuff, and someone said something, and she said, 'Well I feel attacked.' And I said, 'That's bullshit . . .' in a whisper, . . . I said, 'That's bullshit, they didn't attack you, they just said they disagreed with something you said.' So I was really honest, and called her on it when it was real clear that she was just using it. . . . I said, 'You may feel attacked, but they weren't.' I had to say it, and she started to give sort of a half smile. . . . It was really hard for her when I left, she cried for about half a day.

In the "ideal" *power with* classroom, students are willing and able to initiate, facilitate, challenge and support. However, given the reality of schools, schooling, and society, students come to class with neither the willingness nor the skills to take on these roles. What emerges as the crucial difference in this discussion is not a differential in *power over* but a differential in *responsibility*. When a particular course or project begins, these individuals in their roles as "teachers" take responsibility for the class and for each student in the class. The students, however, do not come in with a similar sense of responsibility. As a result of their past experiences, they most likely have not taken responsibility for their own learning, let alone for the learning of their fellow students. Given this differential in responsibility *taken,* an essential part of the work of the empowering teacher is to consistently offer opportunities and support for students to take more responsibility for their own and others' learning.

The Challenge of Empowering Students

Each of the teachers in this study is involved in an ongoing struggle to understand the nature of her or his *power over* and to create, as well as she or he can, relationships based on *power with.* The concepts of *power over* and *power with* provided them with a language with which to talk about these struggles—it helped them describe and understand their experiences more clearly.

The teachers who have shared their experiences in these pages did not find transforming power dynamics in their classrooms easy. They recognize the paralyzing and oppressive nature of *power over,* but they also recognize that their students and they themselves have been "comfortably uncomfortable" in relationships of domination: *power over* so dominates our experience. Lucile emphasizes how difficult it is to empower students in schools:

> I want to emphasize that I think it is extremely difficult to do it in the public schools. And I am trying to make myself feel satisfied with little, little bits of it; rather than feeling like a failure because I can't really make this entire classroom of kids feel empowered.

Empowering teaching is frustrating and difficult work. Yet it is the "little bits," the small triumphs, that keep these teachers committed.

All the teachers whose experiences and reflections are shared
in these pages seek to create relationships of co-agency and mutuality with their students. Yet all describe the tensions and difficulties
inherent in letting go of control. They all express feelings of vulnerability and doubt in the risks they are taking and in not being sure of
the results. They see the structural forces limiting the possibilities
of transforming power relationships: the resistance in the institutions, in their colleagues, in their students, and in themselves. Nevertheless they remain committed. Their struggle is difficult, full of
doubts, failures, and triumphs. They realize they are limited in what
they can accomplish, yet they rest their commitment to teaching on
their willingness to push the limits and prove the possible. Vera
noted, "I think that kids can go far, they really can go very far."

At one point in her interviews, Gene reflects on the relationships she tries to create with students in her classroom. She
reflects on her desire "to not let [students] think of me as less than
a human being because I am a teacher." This is a moving insight.
It captures a sad and disturbing truth: too often teachers and students dehumanize one another: each sees the other as one-dimen-
sional, as other, as the enemy. At the heart of the rehumanization
of the pedagogical relationship lie acts of human vulnerability and
experiences of human connection. Gene goes on to say,

> And I also admitted when I was wrong, and that was really
> the biggest thing I learned in the last two years, to say 'I did
> that wrong' or 'I overreacted' or 'I let my personal feelings get
> in the way, and you didn't mean it that way, and I shouldn't
> have done that. I shouldn't have reacted that way' or, you
> know, 'You're right, I screwed up . . . I didn't do that, and I told
> you I would have the paper today, and I didn't have it, and
> any excuse I give you won't be good.'

Indeed, such acts of honesty, vulnerability, and respect are the
essence of mutuality and stand at the core of empowering relationships. Deep beneath the hegemony of domination and the saturation of our consciousness with its ideology, transforming power
emerges in those acts and those human interactions that shatter
the boundaries of domination and affirm the possibility of different
forms of relationship. As Giroux (1988) notes,

> To be a teacher who can make a difference in both the lives of
> students and in the quality of life in general necessitates

more than acquiring a language of critique and possibility. It also means having the courage to take risks, to look into the future, and to imagine a world that could be as opposed to simply what is. (p. 215)

Empowering relationships call on each of us to look deep within ourselves and to reach beyond ourselves. Gene sums it up well:

[To] just swallow every ounce of pride that I have and say that I was wrong to a twelve-year-old, I think that that's real empowering. And there were times when I didn't do it consistently. I struggled with it, but I think that's part of empowering relationships. If you ask kids to do it, you've got to be ready to do it yourself.

Notes

1. One of my colleagues is quick to remind me that we (teachers, administrators, parents, whoever) don't empower anyone. In fact the notion of "empowering" someone else is a notion locked in a *power over* vision of the world and change. In fact, we can only empower ourselves and provide community and solidarity with others struggling to participate more effectively and centrally in the decisions that affect their/our lives.

7

Power, Empowerment, and Democratic Education

Throughout this study I have explored the relationships connecting domination, power, and empowerment. The experiences of teachers and students have been situated within the pervasive structures of domination present in our culture and in our schools. In the past decade, the concept of empowerment has emerged as an alternative to domination. Empowerment embodies the idea of self-determination, a process through which individuals and communities increasingly control their own destinies without imposing on others. The link between controlling one's own life and valued resources while simultaneously respecting others' rights to do the same is crucial to empowerment theory. It is this dual dimension of empowerment that makes the nature of power in empowerment such a vital and problematic question.

Although the discussions in this study have ranged over a broad theoretical terrain, my primary focus has been on the dynamics of power in face-to-face human interactions in pairs and small groups, in particular among teachers and between teachers and students. I have justified this focus by arguing that, whereas developing a critical understanding of the role of domination in our institutions and of the effects of hegemony and ideologies of domination on our consciousness and experience are essential to any theory of empowerment and educational and social change, there is a fundamental imperative to understand and nurture those modes of relationship that help people to act purposefully and effectively while at the same time enhancing others' abilities to do the same. My point here is that while consciousness shapes and is inseparably entwined with experience, it is not experience. While social critique can lead to transformed social and material relations, it cannot replace them in theory or practice. We experience power in our relationships with other people. It is on this level that we must understand the alternatives to domination and the power that nurtures and sustains empowerment.

I have argued that dominant discourses of power restrict power to relationships of domination, to *power over*, and that this has confined us to a conceptual straightjacket in which the only way to effective action is through the imposition of one's will on others. This view of power, I have shown, is a limited one, sustained by the hegemony of domination in our culture and filtered through ideologies and material relations of domination that have been shaped by the expansion of Western science, patriarchy, and capitalism. Thus, our understandings of power and how the world works, as well as our extensive experiences of domination, have restricted our abilities to envision and create alternatives to relationships of domination.

In this analysis my work has relied heavily on the social and educational critiques of critical pedagogy and feminist theory, which offer important perspectives into the dynamics of domination and empowerment. In chapter 1, I noted that Aronowitz and Giroux, recognizing the need to expand our conceptions of power and possibility, have argued for the importance of going beyond our critiques of domination and authoritarian education to develop a "language of possibility" that can provide a theoretical basis for the development of a liberating or emancipatory pedagogy. This, they suggest, calls for reconceptualizing basic categories and concepts such as power, social control, knowledge, and curriculum (Aronowitz and Giroux 1985). Nevertheless, although *power with* is an implicit concept in the work of critical pedagogy theorists such as Paulo Freire, Henry Giroux, Ira Shor, Kathleen Weiler, Roger Simon, and Peter McLaren I do feel that critical pedagogy, in particular, has yet to fully construct conceptions of power that are not limited to relations of control and imposition.[1] To be sure, the recent influence of Michel Foucault's work on critical pedagogy and emerging postmodernist discourses of education and society have created new openings for moving beyond limiting notions of power as centralized control and domination, but critical pedagogy as well as postmodernism have also been limited, in many ways, by Foucault's reluctance to imagine and theorize nondominating forms of power.

Elizabeth Ellsworth (1989) addresses some of the negative implications of failing to fully develop a counterconception of power to *power over* when she points out contradictions in notions of "empowering teaching" that invest liberatory potential in teachers:

> As educators who claim to be dedicated to ending oppression, critical pedagogues have acknowledged the socially construct-

ed and legitimated authority that teachers / professors hold over students. Yet theorists of critical pedagogy have failed to launch any meaningful analysis of or program for reformulating the institutionalized power imbalances between themselves and their students, or of the essentially paternalistic project of education itself. ... Strategies such as student empowerment and dialogue give the illusion of equality while in fact leaving the authoritarian nature of the teacher/student relationship intact. (p. 306)

Ellsworth argues that as long as educators and theorists continue to base empowerment on rationalism, "these perspectives that would question the political interests (sexism, racism, colonialism, for example) expressed and guaranteed by rationalism would be rejected as 'irrational' (biased, partial)" (p. 306). In her call for a politicization and an historical understanding of oppression and liberation, Ellsworth rejects "student empowerment [which] has been defined in the broadest possible humanist terms, and [which] becomes a 'capacity to act effectively' in a way that fails to challenge any identifiable social or political position, institution, or group" (p. 307).

While situating this particular project ·within these discourses, I have taken it as my focus and my challenge to move beyond the language of critique and resistance and to expand our language of possibility by seeking to identify the power of possibility both in theory and in the experience of struggle and innovation for empowerment and change. In so doing, I have found that feminist discourses of women's experiences of oppression, community, and struggle for change offer some of the richest insights and perspectives on power relationships that are based on mutual action rather than domination (*power over*). This is the case, in part, because feminists have tended to see the microdynamics of relationships as a more central and important focus for inquiry into the nature of domination and the possibilities of liberation than have critical theorists.

In any case, I believe that the concept of *power with* opens up new possibilities for understanding our experiences and new vistas for action. *Power with* represents a reconceptualization of the nature of power that offers a tool for fulfilling the empowering potential of education. The themes of voice, synergy, synergistic community, balance of assertiveness and openness, vulnerability, assertive mutuality, co-agency, integration, dialogue, and shared decision making are essential in the discourse of empowerment and a reconceived notion of power. Thus they too represent valuable contributions to the vocabulary of the language of possibility.

I want to stress the importance of the empowerment of *both* teachers and students to any movement for educational and social change. I am often asked whether it is possible for teachers to create mutually empowering situations with their students if they themselves are not empowered. I do not believe that it is possible. However, it is *not* essential (although certainly it is preferable) that teachers feel their school is an empowering workplace in order for them to be able to create an empowering dynamic with their students. As we have seen, it is common for people to be empowered in one part of their lives and not in others. For instance, this study has shown how teachers may be empowered in groups such as ESR. Teachers can call on these out-of-school experiences as models and resources for support in their work in their classrooms. More importantly, empowerment is synergistic—through creating experiences with students that are empowering for them, teachers also feel empowered. Teachers who help students to become empowered are experiencing personal empowerment in their classrooms through their relationships with their students. Finally, one is never purely empowered or disempowered, for the reality of our lives is infinitely more complex. We are empowered and disempowered—always. Few individuals are totally disempowered in all aspects of their lives. Powerlessness and empowerment are ever present aspects of all of our lives. The *process* of empowerment can occur anywhere, under just about any conditions. This is not meant to minimize the difficulty of empowering students in school environments that are, on the whole, disempowering for teachers and students. But it does help explain the possibility.

However, a distressing development in education is that many educators are talking about the empowerment of teachers without a corresponding commitment to empowering students. This betrays a managerial cooptation of the concept of empowerment. Any model of teacher empowerment that does not include the goal of empowering students as a central theme is not truly an empowerment model. It merely reflects one group's reorganization that could quite easily lead to the maintenance of broader pedagogical relationships of domination. While these changes may give teachers a greater say in their professional lives and thereby enhance teachers' sense of competence and their ability to make a difference in their schools, the corresponding concentration of power over students in the hands of teachers is contrary to the dual nature of empowerment described at the beginning of this chapter. Because of this, the danger of a rhetoric of teacher empowerment that does not include student empowerment at the center of its work is great.

As this project comes to a close, it is clear that in order to more fully understand the nature of power and the process of empowerment, we must come to see and understand both *power over* and *power with* and the dual human capacities for domination and co-agency, for both limiting and liberating action. This study represents only an initial exploration of these issues. Many questions remain unexplored, and many new questions have emerged. In particular, while the theoretical discussion contained in the early chapters suggests broad implications for the understanding of power, social control, and social change, one's ability to generalize from the interview study is limited. My goal, however, was modest: to examine the concept of *power with,* both in theory and in the experiences of six teachers; in particular to explore the ways *power with* can help us describe and understand the interpersonal dynamics that support the empowerment of teachers and students. The investigation has yielded valuable insights; however, this work is clearly only a beginning—one that I hope has raised some important issues for further inquiry.

While the interview study revealed that *power with* can be an effective tool for understanding personal experiences of empowerment, it also raises the question as to whether empowerment must encompass the development of both *power with* and *power over*. In order to answer this question, we still need to ask how *power with* engages with *power over*. Is it possible to transform *power over* through *power with?* Must force match force, domination meet domination? Is there a way to effectively work for control of one's life with others without dominating and imposing upon those who seek to control others? How do you resist and transform *power over* without resorting to *power over?* Can synergistic communities manifesting *power with* be easily oppressed by other communities and a wider society dominated by the scarcity paradigm and utilizing *power over* (Katz and Seth 1986)?

The difficulty of these questions becomes clearer when one considers that the members of ESR were all middle class and that the issues that they were choosing to deal with did not affect their daily needs for food, shelter, employment, safety, and basic freedoms. (Although the nuclear issue certainly confronts survival issues, ESR has not chosen to deal with the issue through direct political action.) *Power with* may have been effective for ESR members in their work, but what about situations in which everyday domination means everyday suffering? What is the *power with* way to achieve justice and peace in Central America? What is the *power with* way to halt the arms race? What is the *power with* way to achieve freedom for people of color in South Africa? What is the *power with* way to achieve democratic political rights in the People's Republic of China? What is the *power with* way to end hunger and homelessness in the United States?

The discussion of the "constructive" use of *power over* in ESR raises important questions relating to the role *power over* plays in settings that seek to empower people. How can the constructive and destructive use of *power over* be distinguished? How is it determined who has the right to exercise *power over?* Upon what basis do we justify our control of others as being for those others' "own good"? How do we distinguish a teacher's use of *power over* to help create conditions for empowerment and her or his use of power as a mechanism of control? Given the structures of domination in schools, can *power with* and empowering experiences actually be created? What are the implications of *power with* and empowerment for how curriculum is developed? What is a *power with* way to organize a school? A teachers' union? When are students' acts of resistance to domination expressions of powerlessness, and when are they expressions of empowerment? When is resistance characterized by *power over,* and when is it characterized by *power with?*

A central issue raised by the discussion of Boston ESR is whether, as a "peripheral" institution, Boston ESR can sustain its active members over a long period of time, given the fact that members are predominantly volunteers who spend most of their time in, gain their livelihood from, and receive their social status as a result of their involvement in other institutions (i.e., schools) that function with predominantly *power over* dynamics. This question points to the importance of exploring the limitations on organizations such as ESR for creating long-term empowering contexts.

Teacher Empowerment

The discussion of the six teachers' experiences of power in empowerment suggests key themes for developing models for the empowerment of teachers. Teachers must feel control over their schools and their teaching—they must be equal participants in decision making in schools. Teacher empowerment will be supported when teachers come together around shared ideals to solve practical problems and when they have opportunities for support, community, and dialogue. Teachers must be given the opportunity to develop and express their voices through the ongoing praxis of pedagogical reflection and action. This calls for organizational structures and leadership that foster the *spirit of dialogue,* the dispositions and skills necessary to engage in integrative behavior. Empowering schools will provide teachers with ongoing opportunities to develop a critical awareness of their own lives and experiences, of the meaning and impact of their teaching, of their students' lives and learning experiences, and of the nature of our society and the impact of their teaching on this society. To begin a process of empowerment, teachers must enter into a process of personal and institutional change that will lead to the transformation of *both* the structure of schools within which they work and their relationships toward their colleagues and their students.

On another level, this discussion of power and empowerment and education challenges us to resist notions of teaching as a technical process. Teaching is an intellectual, creative, moral, and political endeavor.

Implications for a Pedagogy of Empowerment

Chapter 6 indicates how crucial it is for us to more fully explore how teachers can and do facilitate the movement from traditional authoritarian relationships to increasingly democratic relationships with their students. This transition lies at the heart of the challenge of empowering education. Too often radical educational theory focuses on domination and resistance to domination in the classroom. Although resistance is a potent concept for understanding how students react to structures of domination in schools, it does not provide a lens through which we can understand how teachers who are committed to the empowerment of their students can and do establish connections with students and facilitate processes of empowerment. How do teachers create an empowering dynamic for their students (and themselves) in their classrooms?

This study suggests that empowering teachers seek to establish radically different power relationships with their students than are typical in schools in the United States. These relationships are complex, situated as they are within essentially coercive institutions. The relationships these teachers are trying to create are self-consciously grounded in a commitment to care and connection, to mutuality and vulnerability, and on the authority of expertise rather than on the power of position. Facilitating the transition to these new relationships takes time, skill, and patience. In the process teachers mediate between conventional school and classroom rules and structures and their own and their students' emerging abilities to participate in and create an empowering community. They move to change the rules and structures and to include students in the decision making process, and they nurture the development of a supportive group in which dialogue and critical inquiry can occur.[2]

Who we are as teachers and students in schools is mediated by our cultures of domination and by our social identities and lived experiences that have been forged within them. These cultures, our positions within them, and our experiences must be problematized and critically encountered. But on a more fundamental level these cultures and everyday experiences of domination must be challenged in our daily lives, not solely on the level of critique, but directly on the level of lived experience—in our daily relationships with other human beings and the planet. To a frightening extent *we are our experiences of domination. But we are also our experiences of love and care, nurturance and acceptance, co-agency and mutuality.* We must affirm, cultivate, and nurture these experiences. This means we must struggle with ourselves, with the contradictions of our own experiences in our struggle with our social world, for the struggle is the same: to find within us and our culture the resources, the experience, and the courage to forge not only the possibility of alternatives to domination, but the reality as well.

Taking this struggle and this challenge seriously is not easy. For instance, to what degree is the concept of "dialogue" a culturally limited and potentially oppressive construct? Does dialogue, and thus the conception of *power with* developed here, rely on particular modes of oral discourse that are more characteristic of members of educated elites? Does this put other groups at a disadvantage, and thereby perpetuate inequality and cultural domination? How can dialogue occur among people from very different educational, linguistic, and cultural backgrounds? To what degree is the centrality of oral dialogue to a theory of *power with* and empowerment a culturally specific and ethnocentrically inscribed concept? In terms of my own teaching, these questions mean I must ask myself the degree to which my commitment to dialogue in class serves to maintain domination. On the one hand, answering these questions is vital for understanding the possibilities and the limits of *power with*. Perhaps the particular manifestation of *power with* in Educators for Social Responsibility is but one of many possible forms that *power with* takes? But on a more personal and profound level, committing myself to struggle with these questions means committing myself to an ongoing process of wrestling with my own experiences, my own social identities, and the meanings and qualities of my everyday actions and relationships.

In a recent article, Elizabeth Ellsworth (1989) raises haunting questions concerning this challenge:

> The concept of critical pedagogy assumes a commitment on the part of the professor / teacher toward ending the student's oppression. Yet the literature offers no sustained attempt to problematize this stance and confront the likelihood that the professor brings to social movements ... interests of her or his own race, class, ethnicity, gender, and other positions. S/he does not play the role of disinterested mediator on the side of the oppressed group. (p. 309)

Teacher Education

People come to teacher education programs knowing what teachers do, in a sense knowing how to teach. What we know, in large part we know from our experience. And our experience in this culture is saturated with relationships of domination. Education, as we have seen, is a powerful site for the expression of the hegemony of domination in this culture. Indeed, the experience of teaching and learning that most people have in this culture is strikingly uniform. In this experience, power and knowledge are deeply entwined. What we "know" from our experience is teacher-dominated teaching: Teachers talk a lot; teachers control students; teachers transmit knowledge. Students have little or no voice or control over their learning. Learning is competitive, lonely. Teachers know everything. Teachers have power. Students do not. Learning can be boring, disconnected, alienating. Likewise, what we know about what is worth knowing is equally saturated by a dominant and dominating culture. We know that the history, values, literature, and culture of wealthy, white, and Western men are of supreme value. No matter how deeply and directly we reject this knowledge, this teaching, this educational practice that perpetuates authoritarianism, racism, sexism, and classism and rewards docility, conformity, and passivity, the knowledge still lies deep within all of us in the form of our lived experience of teaching and learning in this culture. For the most part, for most people, and for most people preparing to be teachers, this experience, this knowledge, lies unexamined.

For example, recently Arthur,[3] an extremely quiet and hesitant young man who is a student in our teacher certification program, sat in my office reflecting on his experience in the social studies methods class I was teaching. In general, he was having a positive experience. However, he noted that he couldn't wait to finish the certification program here at the university so that he would never have to sit in a circle again in school. I asked him why he felt that way. As it turns out, when he was a junior high and high school student he was extremely overweight and self-conscious. He told me that he liked rows because when sitting in rows he could more effectively hide from his teachers and his peers.

This prospective teacher's painful experiences of schooling, teaching, and learning are shaping the kind of teacher he will be. I can see this clearly in how he is in my class. These powerful formative experiences appear to be taken for granted and left unexamined. But how might he, and we, make sense out of his experience? What is the meaning of his experience? What caused his fear and discomfort in school? In addition to his weight, how did his experience as a working-class Italian American relate to how he was treated by teachers and his peers? What feelings about teaching and learning is he bringing to his own classroom as a result of these experiences? What assumptions about power and teaching does he bring to his own teaching? What limits do these experiences and assumptions place on his ability to enter into truly mutual relationships with his students and colleagues? It is only when Arthur begins to examine his experiences of school and unpacks their meaning and significance to who he is and who he will be as a teacher that he will be able to move beyond the limiting aspects of these experiences. At that point these experiences may become assets, rather than obstacles to becoming a more sensitive, responsive, and caring teacher. Such an examination will not be easy for Arthur to undertake, nor will it be easy for a teacher educator to help him make sense of his experience. The point here is, however, that these experiences, as well as more generally his experiences of our culture, will powerfully shape the kind of teacher Arthur will become. If left unexamined, they will limit his ability to be an effective and empowering teacher.

Another example, in contrast to Arthur's, is the story of John,[4] a recent graduate of our program. For thirteen years John worked as a forklift operator at a Milton Bradley toy factory in western Massachusetts. As part of his union benefits, John studied part-time and received his B.A. in history with teacher certification. He now teaches social studies at a local vocational high school. In the course of our examination of domination, power, and education in another course I teach on education and U.S. culture, we came to talk about the cultural meanings of clothing. In particular, we came to discuss the significance of male teachers wearing ties and jackets and the complex messages concerning social class and power that such dress conveys. In the middle of this discussion John had a moment of personal insight. He suddenly recognized that one of the reasons he had wanted to become a teacher was to be able to wear a tie and jacket to work. He said he now saw that this desire was connected to his working-class background and experiences and his perception of teachers as having status and power, which he desired. John went on to do an interview study of the attitudes toward work and organizational power relationships of floor workers and white-collar managers at his Milton Bradley factory.

Although John wears a tie and jacket to the school he teaches in today, he has chosen to do so for a variety of reasons, the least being its symbolism to him of status and power attained. I think this example reveals how critical reflection on personal experience can uncover our taken-for-granted experiences and knowledge and offer the possibility of transformed and transforming action. Only through coming to terms with his feelings toward ties and jackets could John begin to unravel his complex feelings about teachers, teachers' work, and the meaning of education.

Our experiences of schooling, saturated with *power over* within a culture saturated with *power over*, have taught us to see the world through a lens of domination and have provided us with clear models of how to exert and respond to such exercises of power. We have too few experiences with *power with*, particularly in our schooling and in our other institutional experiences in our lives. Our experience prepares us for *power over* teaching. But how do we learn to nurture *power with* in the classroom? Where are our experiences of mutuality? Of dialogue? Where do we develop our ability to make ourselves vulnerable to others? To be able to listen to others? When have we learned to effectively share decision making and be a member of an egalitarian and supportive group? These experiences are much rarer, and much more mysterious and difficult for us.

To reiterate, my point here is that our experiences of being students and of what teachers do lie deep within all of us and inform our attitudes towards teaching and our teaching practice. The hegemony of domination affects the very constitution of our identities and personalities. For those of us who want to teach in ways that confront domination, these experiences present major challenges to our ability to do so effectively. Our own experience is one of the greatest obstacles to being empowering teachers.

But our experience is also one of our greatest assets if we reflect on our experience critically—if we in fact commit ourselves to *unlearning* our experience of what it means to be a teacher in this culture so that we can *relearn* what it means to be a teacher. This is no easy task, since we all are in a sense trapped within experiences—prospective teachers, experienced teachers, and teacher educators alike. I think the implication here is that we must commit ourselves to a process of transformation, critical reflection, and risk taking in our educational practice and in our lives.

Teacher education programs must invite prospective teachers to enter into just such a process. This means that formal teacher preparation must encourage prospective teachers to deconstruct their experiences. Prospective teachers must be provided with opportunities to examine their experiences and their meanings. They must be encouraged to become aware of the taken-for-granted and how it has shaped who they are—as people and as teachers. They need to be asked what role traditional education plays in society and encouraged to look hard at how our education has fed race, class, gender, and other oppression in our society. They must be helped to examine the ways in which their voices were, and continue to be, silenced, trivialized, patronized, or ignored in schools and classrooms. They need to be focused on the role of predominant teaching practices in shaping these experiences.

Thus prospective teachers must examine their experiences of domination in schools and in the rest of their lives. They must be helped to identify and express their pain, but at the same time they need to identify those experiences, those teachers, those other individuals, who can serve as models for how we can teach differently. They need to identify and nurture their sides that listen, that are vulnerable, that care, that can let go and share control.

Teacher educators and experienced teachers need to explore these very same issues, on an ongoing basis as well.

But we must do more than just think about our experiences— we must experience learning in different and new ways—ways that, although far from perfect, may offer a sense of possibility and the concrete experience of creative and empowering ways of learning. Teacher education programs must offer opportunities for such experiences. Teacher education is about critique, and it is about possibility—we can ignore neither.

Unlearning fifteen years of experience in one semester of "teacher preparation" courses is no easy task. Combining this with helping prospective teachers to develop the skills necessary to survive in schools as they are while simultaneously offering them experiences, skills, and frameworks to innovate seems an impossible challenge. And it is, if we see the goal of teacher education programs as producing finished products. But this cannot be the goal of teacher certification. In fact we are always learning how to teach. Teacher certification is only the beginning of this process. Teacher certification is, in fact, a foundations of teaching program. We build the structure of teaching the rest of our lives. From this perspective, teacher certification programs should initiate prospective teachers into a lifelong process of critical reflection and personal growth and risk taking.

Toward a Democratic Education

I believe that the concepts of empowerment and *power with* are important for understanding the role education can play in the struggle to create a more just and democratic society. Over seventy years ago, John Dewey argued that education needs to have an anchoring idea and ideal—and that in the United States we had such a concept available—democracy. In placing democracy at the helm of the educational enterprise, Dewey situated education squarely at the center of his theory of democratic society. In his work, he explored the role education could and should play in the maintenance and continued creation of democratic cultures and democratic institutions.

I share Dewey's commitment to democracy and agree with Bowles and Gintis (1986) when they say, "Democracy . . . should provide the fundamental principle ordering the processes by which we become who we are and by which the rules regulating our lives are continually renewed and transformed" (p. 3). Democracy is that form of social organization in which the voices of all members of a community are valued and in which community members participate in the decisions that affect their lives. Democracy involves the "progressive extension of people's capacity to govern their personal and social histories" (p. 3) This commitment to democracy is not a commitment to process alone. It is rooted in and informed by a moral agenda guided by a commitment to human dignity, social justice, and liberation. Through democratic empowerment we can break free from the constraints of domination in our institutions, in our cultures, and in our everyday experiences.

Indeed, empowerment and democracy are complementary ideas. On the one hand, genuine democracy depends on having empowered citizens for its survival. It can only be created and maintained by individuals with the skills, values, and dispositions necessary to fully participate in the lives of their communities. On the other hand, democratic institutions and social processes are uniquely able to provide the conditions for individual and community empowerment. They have a "unique capacity to foster in people the ability intelligently and creatively to control their lives" (Bowles and Gintis 1986, 123). Aronowitz and Giroux (1985) make the link between democracy and empowerment directly: "Democracy is not, for us at least, a set of formal rules of participation, but the lived experience of empowerment" (p. xi).

When democracy is moved from theory to practice, it becomes clear that the concept of democracy, in the same way as the concept of empowerment, is in need of a conception or language of power that can explain effective community action that is not based on relationships of domination. A democratic theory of power must encompass the power that restricts freedom and denies popular sovereignty, the power that is manifest in resistance to domination, and the power that is the expression of liberty and self-determination. Such a theory must be able to describe a power that empowers people to democratic participation. *Power over,* alone, is inadequate to this task. *Power with,* on the other hand, offers a side of power that resonates with the possibility of community, participatory decision making, and democratic empowerment.

In chapter 1, I stated that an underlying tenet of this book was a belief in individuals' and groups' abilities to be agents of change. Bowles and Gintis (1986) make a similar point, arguing that, while it is clear that our social structures and the rules of our institutions shape who we are and how we live, we (individuals and groups of individuals) do have the ability to change the rules of the game and the nature of these structures. Thus the movement toward a more democratic culture involves the interaction of people and the rules that shape their lives:

> The problem of building a democratic society is thus one of the dynamic interaction of rules and actors, with the actors rendering the rules more democratic and the increasingly democratic rules rendering the actors more firmly committed to and skilled at democratic participation and decision making. We term this process a democratic dynamic. (p. 186)

A democratic culture engages individuals' capacities for participation and decision making and nurtures their commitment to democratic processes and forms of community. A democratic dynamic is an empowering dynamic. It is the progressive evolution of peoples' capacities to control their lives and act with others to fulfill individual and community goals. It can only occur through the creation and development of institutions that promote democratic culture and the personal characteristics necessary for the effective maintenance of democratic processes. Thus a democratic dynamic is the mutual development of democratic rules and democratic sentiments and capacities (Bowles and Gintis 1986).

Mannheim (1951) explores the connections among personality, behavior, and society and their implications for democratic theory. He argues that individuals' patterns of behavior, indeed their underlying personality structures, are shaped in large part by the particular society in which they live:

> certain aspects of behavior are conditioned by fields of action, methods of participation in social life, and prevailing notions of right conduct in a society. Besides, the pattern of integrated personality corresponds to the conditioning forces of that society and to the ideal personality to which the individual tries to conform. Environmental conditions—material and ideal— determine the aspirations and motives of individuals. (p. 228)

Authoritarian society, Mannheim argues, "is bound to produce the dominative type of character" (p. 232) who is obsessed with achieving and maintaining superiority and status and incapable of participating in dialogic discussions and democratic processes. Democratic societies or even democratic communities, on the other hand, produce individuals capable of democratic behavior. Thus a democratic dynamic involves the spiraling process through which increasingly democratic social forms shape increasingly democratic individuals who in turn create even more democratic social forms, and so forth.

In Mannheim's discussion of democratic behavior, the link between democracy, empowerment, and *power with* becomes clear. He notes that democratic behavior reflects very basic personality traits that are characterized by an "openness and readiness for co-operation, which not only enables the individual to face disagreement but prepares him to expect substantial enrichment of his own personality by absorbing differences in the process" (Mannheim 1951, 230). He describes democratic behavior as "integrative," and his conception of integration is virtually the same as Follett's and May's presented in chapter 3:

> Integrative behavior is more than compromise. It means that people, though fully aware of the fact that differences of constitution and social position, of drives and interests, shape their experience and attitude to life in different ways, yet transmute their different approaches for the purpose of co-operating in a common way of life. Such transmutation is a creative form of integration: out of the process of common living and co-operative pursuits, a new purpose emerges which the partners come to cherish even more than their original aims. (p. 203)

This is precisely the process of dialogue and openness to growth and change described by the six teachers in my study, and it is remarkably similar to Follett's comments on the mutually influencing, generative, and synergistic nature of *power with*. This suggests that democratic behavior is characterized by the capacity and predisposition to engage in *power with* relationships and directly links a democratic dynamic to the process of empowerment.

Indeed, democratic participation demands that people be capable of thinking critically and speaking for themselves and it depends on people's willingness to uphold their convictions. But learning to govern oneself as an equal member of a community also means developing the ability to be open to others. It requires that people have the capacity to listen to others with care and sensitivity. Democratic citizens must be willing and able to work with others cooperatively and to integrate different viewpoints into their own positions. They must be firm enough to stand up and be heard, yet flexible and secure enough to continue growing and changing.

In order to develop people who are committed and capable of democratic participation, we must create communities, bit by bit, in which democracy is increasingly learned and practiced every day. This is a democratic dynamic: the ongoing interaction between people and the institutions they create and that create them. The dynamic entails, on the one hand, the creation, by people, of social forms and institutions that nurture empowerment through *power with* relationships, and on the other hand, the development, in people, of the skills, knowledge, values, and dispositions necessary to effectively control their lives and participate in *power with* relationships with others. *Power with* thus offers a conception of power central to a democratic dynamic, and the progressive democratization of social institutions and individual personalities and behaviors captures the individual process of change central to democratic transformation.

The relation between education and a democratic dynamic is clear. As key sites in preparing children for participation in society, schools can play an important role in impeding or creating and maintaining a democratic dynamic. Nevertheless, schools cannot and should not be seen as the sole or even primary catalysts for democratic change. Bowles and Gintis (1986) note that "democracy, like domination, knows no single home but is a characteristic of the entire ensemble of social relationships that make up society" (p. 90). Schools are but one in a vast web of interdependent sites of social interaction that shape our actions and our lives (such as the family, the state, the economy, and religious institutions). The structures and guiding norms of these sites are mutually influencing and for democratic change to occur, changes must occur simultaneously throughout them all, or at least among several at once. Thus schools have an important but qualified role to play in social change.

Grambs and Carr (1979) describe the imperative for schools if they are to play a positive role in creating and maintaining a democratic dynamic:

> Democracy is learned behavior. We are not born with it. . . . Democracy is an array of behaviors which regulate how we behave in the privacy of our homes, in our neighborhoods, on the job, and in public places. It is only when young people in school experience over and over again, in thousands of individual incidents, the ways in which democracy works and feels that they are going to be able to act democratically. (p. 111)

Currently schools in the United States play contradictory roles in relation to democracy. On balance, they do much more to perpetuate domination than to create and sustain a democratic dynamic; "it is a contradiction to envision a democratic society when its inheritors, the kids, are forced to live under conditions of unrelieved subordination" (Aronowitz and Giroux 1985, xi). However, Bowles and Gintis (1986) stress the positive and necessary role education can play in democratic transformation:

> We see the possibility of a democratic learning dynamics, one that would inhabit the imperfect realms of democracy and choice in our society and progressively transform ever-wider circles of social life toward democratic ends. (p. 208)

Arguing in a similar vein, Giroux (1988b) believes that schools need to be reconceived as "democratic sites dedicated to self and social empowerment" (p. 185). Within schools students can and should learn the knowledge and skills necessary to participate in an "authentic democracy" (p. 214).

In 1937, John Dewey observed:

> The problem of education in its relation to the direction of social change is all one with the problem of finding out what democracy means in its total range of concrete applications: domestic, international, religious, cultural, economic *and* political.... The trouble, at least one great trouble, is that we have taken democracy for granted; we have thought and acted as if our forefathers had founded it once for all. We have forgotten that it has to be enacted anew in every generation, in every year and day, in the living relations of person to person in all social forms and institutions. Forgetting this... we have been negligent even in creating a school that should be the constant nurse of democracy. (Dewey 1940, 357–58)

The implications of this study for the practice of education are dramatic: to transform our schools from places characterized by human isolation, competition for scarce resources, and relationships of domination and submission into democratic communities in which people enter into critical inquiry characterized by mutual support, cooperative decision making, and synergistic learning. In such learning communities people can meet, express, and act on their concerns for themselves, their communities and the greater global community. They can discover and begin to live the meaning of democracy.

On a fundamental level this calls for changing the dynamics of power relationships within schools. This may sound utopian, but this study has shown that the seeds of such change exist, today, in our educators, students, and schools. Making schools empowering for students and teachers, difficult as it may be, is possible. As teachers, we can contribute to the creation of a democratic dynamic. We can, indeed, become "nurses of democracy" through the wise and just use of power. As teachers, we *can* make a difference.

Notes

1. For instance, when Paulo Freire writes that "dialogue is not A over B but A with B," he is clearly conceiving an alternative mode of power relationship than one of control and domination, one that, it can be argued, fits well within a conception of power as *power with*.

2. One weakness in this discussion of empowering student–teacher relationships is that the voices of students are missing. A most important avenue of further research is to explore the nature of power in students' experiences of empowerment in schools. How do they experience the teacher and their peers in the empowering classroom? How does the empowering classroom affect their lives and commitments outside of the classroom? What is the nature of power in *their* experiences of empowerment? These missing voices must be included in any further research.

3. The name is a pseudonym.

4. The name is a pseudonym.

Afterword

When Seth Kreisberg died on December 6, 1989, he had nearly completed this book. The last chapter, chapter 7—"Power, Empowerment, and Democratic Education"—awaited his final revision. There were concepts that he intended to integrate, new ideas and new ways of saying things to incorporate, and the additional insights of colleagues, students, and family to consider.

Chapter 7 remains just about as Seth left it.

Seth's last draft of chapter 7 contained several sections that had only headings, and there were notes and marginalia scattered throughout, indicating several themes that Seth had wanted to pursue further.

He had wanted to discuss the question of authority and how it might be redefined. From the notes he left, we know that Seth saw authority as an approach both to content and to people, and that a redefinition of authority—one that reflected *power with* relationships—would or could transform what counted as curricular knowledge and how teachers and students defined each other as they pursued a better understanding of the world, themselves, and their participation in the world. Curricular authority would not reside in lists of facts generated by experts, but in the problems pursued by a community of learners and in the connections made between experience and knowledge. Seth especially intended to expand on the concept of the authority of expertise, which he saw as a fundamental grounding for teachers seeking to create empowering classrooms. Seth contrasted teachers' relying on the authority of expertise rather than the power of position, on the mutual acknowledgement by students and teachers of the teacher's greater experience and knowledge within a particular field of inquiry. In addition, the authority of expertise is based on a relationship of mutuality among members of a class, in which a teacher respects the voices and experience of her or his students, and the students in turn respect the teacher's. Seth intended to contrast this concept with authority based on the power of position, where authority is based on institutionally sanctioned and reinforced control over students.

In chapter 7's section "Teacher Empowerment," Seth had
intended to further discuss how listening, vulnerability, collegiality,
mutuality, and risk could be instrumental in changing power relations in schools. Regarding these concepts we know that he was
greatly influenced by feminist discussions. One place where Seth
learned an alternative way of sharing and working is in the work of
feminist theorists who describe the type of self-formation and group
interaction experienced by women as relationships characterized
by vulnerability, openness, and nurturance. It is just those qualities
that our culture has relegated to women and to the private sphere.
The public sphere, the work of business, law, politics, and to a large
extent even education, is governed by rules rather than by flexibility, by rights rather than by compassion. Seth, along with Jean
Baker Miller, Susan Miller Okin, Mary Daly, and Evelyn Fox
Keller, challenged the inevitability and the appropriateness of this
distinction. The values of care, empathy, and vulnerability, when no
longer limited to the private sphere, can and do transform the public sphere. As many feminist theorists point out, it is in these personal experiences of mutuality that we learn alternatives to *power
over* and domination.

Transforming Power is an invitation to mutuality and dialogue. This invitation is clear in the final chapter, where Seth
explores what empowerment in classrooms and in teacher education would mean, what forms it might take, and how teachers and
students might create contexts that truly foster democratic participation. What would an education based on dialogue and empowerment look like across cultures with their various ways of engaging
in talk and learning? What would it mean to take democracy seriously in our daily lives? What kinds of relationships must exist
among teachers and students so that they can respond directly and
forcefully to racism, sexism, and other forms of fascism, and the
violence they bring, without simultaneously disempowering others? What are the possibilities for dialogue in a society that seems
to value "talking at" more than "talking with"? And what is the
role of education and educators in that process?

Seth's research had led him from the search to transform
power to the search to transform classrooms in the United States
and to addressing the problems inherent in fostering such fundamental change. He had begun to focus on what he labeled the
"transition"—the transition that teachers and students had to
undergo to transform traditional or conventional power relationships and teacher-centered pedagogies to democratic and partici-

patory learning and more mutual and caring pedagogical relationships. Seth had begun a new project that focused on talking with and observing teachers and students who are engaged in the process of creating more empowering and democratic classrooms. He wanted to explore the challenges faced by teachers who are undergoing this transition within institutions that are saturated by cultures of control and domination and deeply resistant to change.

Seth observed that educators encounter resistance on all levels. First, in themselves, as they question the value of their efforts and find the depth of their past experiences difficult to transcend and their old patterns difficult to change. Teachers also have to assist their students in the transition, students who may ask why the teacher isn't "teaching," who may feel uncomfortable being asked to think and choose for themselves, and who may be unwilling or unable to take increased responsibility for their learning. Students arrive in their classrooms having been shaped by and conditioned to respond to teacher-dominated teaching and learning. They see school knowledge as imposed from above and detached from their experience. They have internalized the attitudes and behaviors expected of powerless people, having learned to be passive, deferential, subversive, resistant, and/or submissive. Students often come to class feeling so powerless, mistrusting, and cynical that creating a supportive context with transformed power relationships is a struggle for teacher and students alike.

Outside the classroom, teachers face resistance from administrators, colleagues, and parents who question whether "real" teaching and learning is occurring and whether students are learning what they need to "succeed" and "survive" in the "real world." Seth wrestled daily with these same issues in his own teaching at the University of Massachusetts and hoped to have the chance to return to high school teaching to address the challenges there as well.

The search for an empowering pedagogy cannot be separated from the social realities and circumstances of our daily lives, from our individual and community histories, or from a sense of the broader historical moment in which we live. It must emerge from a mutual dialogue that is grounded in our experiences and in action. In creating more empowering pedagogies, students and teachers will need a better understanding of our circumstances and histories, a transforming understanding, what Maxine Greene (1986) calls "repossessing" our history (p. 438).

Greene describes a history of attempts to develop a critical pedagogy in America. She shows that the search for a critical pedagogy, whether it is the pedagogy of Emerson, Thoreau, Douglass, Parker, Dewey, or Freire,[1] reflects both an intellectual climate and social realities, including the realities of resistance. Critical pedagogies are, in part, responses to the "mystification" (Greene 1986, 439) of our lives and their circumstances and to the "speechlessness" (p. 439) of so many people excluded from the processes that might transform inaction to action.

   Transforming Power is, in part, the story of a group of educators who responded to the mystification and speechlessness of our times by struggling against the threat of nuclear war. The arms race, m.a.d. (*m*utually *a*ssured *d*estruction) policies, a powerful military-industrial complex, and the omnipresence of a nuclear threat, are sufficient to make anyone feel helpless, overwhelmed, and speechless. The problem seems huge, above and beyond us. Young people in our society have lived their whole lives under the threat of nuclear war, and many of them believe a nuclear war is probable. The problem makes them and us feel small, nearly invisible. In addressing the threat of nuclear war, these educators found themselves addressing the issues of power in our society, in their daily lives, and in education. They saw that there was a relationship between addressing the problem and how they acted toward one other. Further, they saw that education could play a role in addressing the threat of nuclear war and changing relationships; but for students and teachers to do so, they both had to become empowered and emerge from the invisibility and silence into which they were relegated. The struggle against the threat of nuclear war was not separated from the struggle against the social conditions that disempower people. In struggling against the threat of nuclear war, they transformed themselves, others, and the pedagogies they brought to their classrooms.

   Telling the story of these educators is important for several reasons. What these teachers did is part of *our* history. The history presented to us in school textbooks, the history of wars and heroes, renders us invisible and ahistorical—as if we have no part in history, no agency. Our history, the history of ordinary people and our struggles for democracy and humanity both in our daily lives and in the broader society, is hidden from us. It is part of the way in which we are silenced. Educators find this particularly problematic. We do not learn of our history and come to believe we do not have one. If we are taught any history it is the history of education and policymakers, not the history of teachers. We know little about the people who preceded us, who they were, what they did, how they lived their lives, what they struggled for, and what they accomplished. Knowing our history, "repossessing" it as Greene terms it, helps make us historical and helps us see the possibilities for action and empowerment.

Telling the story of these educators is important for another reason as well. What they did shows us possibilities for redefining power. It is not so much that others will be able to copy what they have done—the fact that we live in different circumstances will require us to determine our own actions—but what they did can give us new insights into the possibilities for redefining power and for what it might mean to take democracy seriously in our society and in education. Telling their story helps inform our vision.

How their story informs our vision depends as much on us and our experiences as on their experiences. Which is merely to say that what we take away from their story, what we learn from it, depends on our past experiences, the possibilities we see for our futures, and how we understand our past and future. Knowledge is not separated from experience, neither ours nor theirs. Rather knowledge is intimately connected to experience. To the degree that we are alienated from our experiences and to the degree we do not reflect on them, we remain ignorant regardless of how many facts we or our students memorize.

We need to ask, how is it we become alienated from our own experience and history? How is it that we have come to accept the hegemony of power as *power over?* How is it that our vision of democracy has become limited to a question of access to *power over?* How is it that we have become silenced? However, it is not enough to ask only about how we have been silenced and alienated or even about the various forms of resistance we have taken. We must also ask about transformation. As Seth asks, we must explore how to "transform our schools from places characterized by human isolation, competition for scarce resources, and relationships of domination and submission into democratic communities in which people enter into critical inquiry characterized by mutual support, cooperative decision making, and synergistic learning" (p. 208). While there is no single answer for all people and all schools, how we answer the questions above depends on the dialogues we are willing to enter, on how we connect our experiences and knowledge, on the vision of democracy we hold, and on changing the dynamics of power relationships within and outside of schools.

We know that Seth planned to conclude chapter 7 with a more detailed discussion of how empowering democratic classrooms can more fully acknowledge the humanity and aspirations of both teachers and students. At the center of creating mutually empowering dynamics is the struggle to break down structures and patterns that dehumanize and disempower and to cultivate forms of relationship that provide affirmation, nurturance, hope, and a sense of possibility. Greene (1986) addresses this:

> We cannot negate the fact of power. But we can undertake a resistance, a reaching out towards becoming *persons* among other persons, for all the talk of human resources, for all the orienting of education to the economy. To engage with our students as persons is to affirm our own incompleteness, our consciousness of spaces still to be explored, desires still to be tapped, possibilities still to be opened and pursued. At once, it is to rediscover the value of care, to reach back to experiences of caring and being cared for (as Nel Noddings writes) as sources of an ethical ideal. It is, Nodding says, an ideal to be nurtured through "dialogue, practice, and confirmation," processes much akin to those involved in opening a public sphere. We have to find out how to open such spheres, such spaces, where a better state of things can be imagined; because it is only through the projection of a better social order that we can perceive the gaps in what exists and try to transform and repair. I would like to think that this can happen in classrooms, in corridors, in schoolyards, in the streets around. (pp. 440–41)

Seth knew, from his research and experience, that we can create such spaces. He hoped to contribute further to our understanding of how teachers and students can and do create spaces in which they encounter one another as persons, spaces in which silenced voices are heard, in which lived worlds are examined, and in which imagined worlds begin to be lived.

Transforming Power is an invitation to an ongoing dialogue, not just between a book and its readers but among a community of educators and students. It is an invitation to a conversation that is optimistic about the possibilities for change despite the difficult times in which we live.

David Bloome
Irma V. González
Amherst, Massachusetts

Notes

1. Although Freire is not American, his ideas about a critical pedagogy have been advocated by some American educators (e.g., Shor, 1980).
Freire (1978) has noted that educational pedagogies cannot be imported
but must develop out of people's historical and political experiences and circumstances. In reference to Freire, Greene (1986) reminds us "that a critical pedagogy relevant to the United States today must go beyond—calling
on different memories, repossessing another history" (p. 438).

Appendix A

The Model for the Research Design: The interview project was modeled on Kieffer's approach of "dialogic retrospection" (Kieffer 1981, 1983/84), which incorporates and builds on the methods developed and discussed in Reinharz (1979, 1983), Giorgi (1970b), Sardello (1971), Von Eckartsberg (1971), Colaizzi (1978), Levinson (1978), and Merton, Fiske, and Kendall (1956). Kieffer (1981) observes that since empowerment is "an interactive and highly subjective relationship of individuals and their environment," it demands "innovation in qualitative/ethnographic methodology" and a "special strategy to capture the intense experience of human struggle and transformation."

In his study "The Emergence of Empowerment: The Development of Participatory Competence among Individuals in Citizen Organizations" (1981) Kieffer interviewed ten citizen activists from a range of organizations across the country. He began with an initial open-ended interview focused on interviewees' personal experiences in developing "participatory competence." He then sent verbatim transcripts to the participants, which "provided opportunity for more intensive and critical self-reflection and follow-up" (Kieffer 1983/84). Follow-up interviews were conducted several months later:

> based on the researcher's preliminary analysis and the subjects' opportunity for self-critical reflection, these dialogues encouraged participants to extend, to correct, and to clarify their earlier conversations and validate and refine emergent interpretations. (p. 15)

Again, Kieffer sent out verbatim transcripts of the interviews to participants for further feedback. As Kieffer's data analysis began, he continued to return to his participants for reflection, correction, and general feedback: "Tentative interpretations constructed throughout the research process were consistently referred back to participants for response and refinement" (Kieffer 1983/84, 14).

Von Eckartsberg describes this process as the "elaboration of meaning through joint inquiry" (1971, 77).

A Note Concerning the Study Participants: While at the outset of the research project these six individuals represented a wide cross section of steering committee members in terms of length and intensity of involvement, as the project wound through a year of interviewing, it became clear that the group was not as representative as it once was. Over that period of time one individual stepped down as a coordinator of the chapter, and another participant replaced him in this role. As the project was completed, another participant in the study was hired as a co-coordinator. As a result, three of the participants have become full-time, paid staff members in ESR. This is clearly not the norm. It has become obvious that the six participants in the project are among the most active and committed members of the organization and that they are among the most empowered.

While this may be a weakness in terms of my ability to generalize the experiences of this group, generalizability is not a goal of this study. Rather, my goal is to understand both the interpersonal and intrapersonal experiences of empowerment of these individuals and to explore the nature of power in their experiences. Given this goal, the fact that the study participants are among the most involved and most empowered individuals in the organization is a strength, rather than a weakness: the central goal is to understand the experience of empowerment, not the steering committee.

These individuals teach or have taught in very diverse settings ranging from the Boston, Arlington, and Watertown public schools to progressive or elite Boston area private schools. Thus they also provide an excellent initial sample for exploring the nature of power in empowering teaching.

Data Collection and Analysis

The following is an outline of the research model used for the interview study:

1. *Preliminary research.* A pilot questionnaire study and extensive participant observation of Boston Educators for Social Responsibility.
2. *The initial interviews.* Focused on each individual's experiences of empowerment in Boston ESR and on her or his attempts to empower students.

3. *Tapes transcribed and then read by participants.*
4. *Primary analysis.*
5. *Introduction to study participants of the concepts of power over and power with.* Participants read paper on *power over* and *power with*.
6. *Follow-up interviews.* Focused on filling out and clarifying the initial interviews and exploring the connections among their experiences and reflections on empowerment and the conceptual framework for power presented in the paper they read.
7. *Secondary analysis.* Concentrated focus on analyzing transcripts using the conceptions of *power over* and *power with* as guide.
8. *Final meeting with study participants.* Meeting of all participants and researcher for reporting and discussing my observations and analyses.
9. Analysis and writing up of findings.
10. Sharing first draft of findings with participants.
11. Revision, editing, and final preparation for publication.

Discussion of Data Collection and Analysis

Preliminary Data Collection: Preliminary research for this project began in 1984. At that time I began to systematically observe Boston steering committee meetings and various subcommittee meetings using a variety of methods in participant observation (Pelto and Pelto 1978, Schatzman and Strauss 1973, Spradley 1980, Bogdan and Taylor 1975). My data collection at that time consisted of taping meetings, taking notes during and after meetings, personally transcribing tapes and adding observations at that time, and collecting all significant documents of the steering committee and Boston ESR.

In addition I conducted the pilot study of empowerment in Boston ESR's 1982 summer curriculum project (Berman 1982). This extensive questionnaire project has proved invaluable in (1) establishing Boston ESR as an excellent context in which to study empowerment, (2) providing support for the viability of conducting research on the nature of power in empowerment, and (3) offering crucial information for developing my interview schedule.

This preliminary research left me with a wealth of data that offered additional perspectives useful for the analysis of the intensive interviews that are the focus of this study.

The Initial Interview: The "initial" interview with participants was actually a set of interviews. The first focused on participants' personal experiences of empowerment within the organization, the second focused on participants' experiences empowering students. In shaping my interview strategy I attempted to create a disciplined yet convivial relationship. Kieffer, relying on Levinson (1978), describes this interview style as "open-ended, flexible, and conversational."

I developed an interview schedule (see Appendix B) based on (1) my understanding of ESR developed through the preliminary field research, (2) my understanding of empowerment theories developed through a literature review, and (3) my theoretical research on and synthesis of the concepts *power over* and *power with*. However, the interviews were not to be limited to the prepared questions. Rather, extensive probing served as a springboard for dialogue.

The overall goal of these initial interviews was to spur participants to (1) recall and describe what they considered to be their experiences of empowerment in ESR and in their teaching, *and* (2) to reflect on the meaning of empowerment and the nature of power as it emerges from and applies to their experiences. As Kieffer (1983/84) describes it, the goal is to prompt the individual "to articulate as fully as possible a description of his/her experience, in his/her own most meaningful terms" (p. 116).

The questions elicited rich description of experiences and thoughtful reflection on the meaning of these experiences. After each interview, participants expressed eagerness to continue with the research process.

Each of these initial interviews was transcribed by a paid typist and sent—unedited—to the interviewee for his or her review. It was explained that they should read through the interview carefully, checking for its accuracy and completeness in describing their experience and in describing their understanding of that experience in terms of empowerment (Kieffer, 1981; Colaizzi 1978, Reinharz 1983).

Primary Analysis: At this point I began analysis of the protocols. This process involved two steps. The first step involved reading the protocols for the completeness and clarity of the individuals' accounts of and reflections on their experiences; the second step involved bringing the analytic categories of *power over* and *power with* to bear on the protocols.

Step One: The first step in the data analysis process was for me to listen to the tapes of the interviews while following along in the transcripts. At this point my goal was *not* to apply the analytic framework of power to the protocols. My goal was to read each protocol carefully to familiarize myself with its content and to search for clarity and completeness. This process involved identifying questions, inconsistencies, and gaps in the accounts of the individuals' experiences. This reading provided initial questions for the follow-up interviews.

For an example of how questions arose from this analysis, in response to the question "How does the steering committee reach consensus?" Shelley answered, in part:

> so I guess that part of the process that we have is that people are willing to suspend their own belief . . . people are willing to consider other forms that really come into somebody else's belief. . . . I think that that's been present all the time with the steering committee. . . . I think that everybody is included in the decisions so that no one feels that they have been pre-empted or that they have not been listened to and that I think we search for some common solutions that would be adequate for everybody.

In reading this protocol for clarity and completeness, two questions arise: What does it mean to "suspend belief"? How does it feel when we suspend our own beliefs? It would also be useful to have a specific example of the process he identifies.

Step Two: It is at this point that I applied my analytic categories of *power over* and *power with* to the protocols. Using my theoretical synthesis of the *power over* and *power with* categories, I began to explore to what degree the experiences and dynamics described in the interviews corresponded to the conceptions of *power over* and *power with* The method was straightforward: a careful reading of each protocol, noting in each those dynamics that seemed to fit into either the *power over* and *power with* definitions and those that did not fit in either category. There were several questions that underlay this entire analysis: Was the *power over/power with* distinction useful for analyzing and explaining people's experiences of empowerment? Is *power over/power with* a real and useful distinction? What did people's experiences tell us about the nature of *power over* and *power with?* The point of the analysis was to identify patterns and to make preliminary interpretations of the data. The goal of this reading was to develop questions for the follow-up interview.

Saving the application of the theoretical categories of power for the second step allowed each protocol to develop an integrity of its own, separate from the analytic frameworks. It is important to note, again, that the goal was not to squeeze people's experiences into my theoretical framework, but rather to see whether the framework is able to lend insight into the nature of the experiences.

Introduction of the Theoretical Framework for Understanding the Nature of Power in the Experience of Empowerment: This step in the research process extended Kieffer's approach in giving pre-interview, researcher-generated theory an explicit and active role in the research process. Kieffer, while conducting an extensive literature review in several areas related to empowerment theory and generating his research questions out of this review, purposely kept his theoretical frameworks and biases submerged throughout his data collection and analysis. At the same time he admitted that his interviews "themselves were shaped, in some degree, by [his] conceptual biases" and that the "same theoretical screen inescapably (if only unconsciously) operated in the data analysis" (Kieffer 1981, 119). My research project attempts to bring the pre-interview theoretical frameworks to the surface of the research process and to engage participants not only in a dialogue concerning their own experience, but in a dialogue concerning the adequacy and accuracy of the *power over/power with* distinction in describing the nature of power in their experiences of empowerment. Thus the dialogue this project seeks to create is not merely between "researcher" and "researched," but between the theory of the researcher and the experience of the researched.

At this point in the research project I introduced the theoretical framework of *power over* and *power with* to the participants in the study. Each participant received a copy of a paper I had written on *power over* and *power with*, which was very similar to chapters 2 and 3 of this book, and a paper describing the research project. They were asked to read the paper carefully and then to reflect on the experiences they described in their transcripts. They were encouraged to consider their experiences in light of the theoretical discussion of *power over* and *power with* in the paper, specifically looking to see whether *power over* or *power with* are applicable distinctions and which seemed better able to help them understand and explain their experience of empowerment.

Follow-up Interviews: I then conducted follow up interviews with each of the participants in the study. These interviews were even more dialogical in nature than the first interviews. They consisted of two parts:

1. In the first part of the interview, interviewees were asked to come prepared to extend, correct and to clarify the earlier conversations (Kieffer 1981). I came to the interview with the set of questions that emerged out of my attempt to fully understand the first interviews and the experiences they describe. Kieffer refers to Von Eckartsberg to describe this process:

> Essentially, the researcher conducting the inquiry engages in a dialogue with the person studied by asking him to elaborate the meaning that the reported components of the protocol have for him. This phase of *elaboration of meaning through joint inquiry* is important in experiential methodology. It allows clarification and specification of meaning—as the person himself experienced it—and it prevents imputation of meaning from an "alien frame of reference" on the part of researchers. The researcher can never really assume that he understands what was said or written, but he has to obtain a clarification from the person studied himself. Only in this fashion can he safeguard against premature and falsifying interpretation. (Von Eckartsberg 1971, 77)

2. The focus of the second half of the interview was to create a dialogue centering on the central research questions:

> Were the concepts of *power over* and *power with* helpful for understanding and explaining individuals' experiences?

> If so, were the experiences that individuals described as empowering characterized more by *power over* or by *power with?*

> In what ways can reflection on these experiences deepen and broaden our understanding of the concepts of *power over* and *power with?*

Both the interviewer and the interviewee came to the interview prepared to discuss our observations concerning the answers to these questions. The study participants were asked to begin the discussion by sharing their thoughts. I pursued the discussion by asking questions and offering analyses that sought to help both of us clarify our thoughts and analyses.

Secondary Analysis: Once again interviews were transcribed, and the process of primary analysis was repeated for each interview. Next the two analyses of interviews with each participant were integrated "creating for each participant a comprehensive ... portrait" (Kieffer 1981, 123).

At this point integrative analysis began. The goal of this analysis was to identify both the common and divergent themes across interviewees' experiences in relation to the research questions.

It is difficult to offer a step-by-step description of this phase of the data analysis. Reinharz (1983) articulates the dynamics of the process well when she observes:

> Data analysis is an activity based on a cognitive mode different from data gathering: reflective rather than active, solitary rather than interactional. The recorded experiences, conversation transcripts, pieces of information are compiled, reduced and examined for their interactions (patterns) and basic themes. The more significant is extracted from the significant within a system of meaning. Parts are strung together to make new wholes—simplicity is sought beneath the complexity. The somewhat imprecise statements are intended to convey the reflective analytic stance taken toward the data, which is humanistic rather than mechanistic. ... As the interpretations are made and recorded the remaining data are examined to see how they corroborate or refute ongoing analysis. There are no rules for data analysis except one—that the analysis draw heavily on the language of the persons studied, i.e., that it is grounded. (p. 183)

It is important to note that whereas I completed much of this analysis before I began writing, much of the analysis also occurred during the actual process of writing. That is, themes were identified, insights occurred, and order emerged as I attempted to organize my analysis and thoughts into a coherent piece of writing.

Final Group Meeting: As my interpretation, integration construction, and writing neared completion I presented my observations to a gathering of five of the six participants in the study (the sixth member of the group could not make the meeting, and we met separately). I asked for feedback and comments, which were then integrated into the final presentation.

Conclusion of the Research: Following the final group meeting I proceeded to finish my first draft of my description and analysis of their interviews. After this was completed, two of the study participants were given copies of the draft to read and comment on (the other four were unable to read it due to time constraints on all of us).

Presentation of Data: My goal in the presentation of the interview study is to vividly recount the experiences of empowerment shared by the participants in the study and to sensitively present our joint and my individual interpretation of the nature of power in their experience of empowerment. In the presentation and analysis I use excerpts from interviews liberally. This project is motivated by a belief in the potential for dialogue to offer insight into our experiences and our world. The book arises out of such a dialogue and the use of extensive quotations is an attempt to give a more direct voice to those who shared their experiences and insights.

Upon reading the transcripts of their interviews, virtually all of the study participants expressed dismay and embarrassment at their perceived verbosity, "umming" and "you know-ing," and lack of clarity. They encouraged me to "clean up" their comments. I have done this while also seeking to maintain meaning, tone, and vernacular. At times I have extended or reconstructed comments by using noncontiguous comments (Kieffer 1981, 133). I have always attempted to keep quotations true to their contextual meaning and intent.

Finally, I have often used excerpts to illustrate patterns that I perceive across interviews. Often one excerpt will be selected to illustrate a pattern. Clearly, each person's experiences and ways of describing his or her experiences are unique, yet it is also the goal of this research to look for common patterns of experience. With this uniqueness in mind, illustrative excerpts have been chosen for both their representativeness and their ability to capture the experience or insight in question.

Reflections on the Interview Study

The six individuals who were involved in the empirical research project were eager participants. First, as friends and colleagues they wanted to support my work. Second, they looked forward to the opportunity to reflect on their experiences. And finally, they all felt that through sharing their experiences they could contribute to the work of ESR and to our understanding of empowerment.

Several times in the interview cycle I asked for comments on the research model. Throughout, study participants felt the process respected their voices, encouraged them to be reflective, and offered them greater insight into their work in ESR and as teachers. All of them recognized that the research model's participatory and dialogic method was consistent with the values of ESR. Rachel noted:

> I think it really does work, and I'm impressed with the consistency. You haven't been just coming over here and chitchatting with me. You've been pushing me, provoking me to think things through more. So it's been the different skills we come with, you also need to hear my experience.

They all appreciated being included in the reflective and analytic aspects of the process. Lally commented:

> I liked the discussions. I don't like reading what I said. That was really hard. I think the process that you're doing for the paper is really crucial, it's really unique and it's fun to be a part of it in this way. Because we're doing what you're writing about and you're including us in the whole process that you're writing about. You're putting into action what you're writing about in the course of writing about it.

In general they all felt that having the opportunity to read their interviews and my theoretical work pushed their thinking and helped them to better understand their experiences. Lucile said:

> I found it interesting to just look at what we uncovered. I mean, I realized that I had learned some things in that conversation about, you know, what empowerment meant and what parts of it were important, and there are some parts of it that I feel like we talked about that I still can't quite articulate.

The interviews, the reflection, and the dialogue also raised many new questions for each person. Gene noted that after each session she understood empowerment better and felt more confused. Perhaps most satisfying to me is that the dialogue of the research process affected, to varying degrees, how each person thinks about her or his experiences and work. Lucile commented during one session:

> Let me say that even this conversation helps me have the perspective that I think I personally need, that I lose and then start to feel disempowered. The conversation helps me rethink and now I already feel more empowered. I feel, "Yeah that really did make a difference."

Rachel described most explicitly how dialogic inquiry can be empowering. Of the research process she said:

> I think it's great! I really do. Especially because this is a planned and provocative time for reflection. That I don't make for myself as much as I would like. So it's been through this process that I have articulated and come to apply that framework [*power over/power with*] to what I know, and I've used it. I've used it with my supervisor, and she was able to understand. She knew what I was saying, that it is not an empowering organization because it's run in a *power over* way. And I used those words many times.

One aspect of the model that I would change is that I asked them to read my sixty-page paper on *power over* and *power with* which was written as a requirement for the doctorate. The paper is academic and long. I think it was unnecessary to give them this paper; it would have been much more effective to write a briefer, less academic paper for them to read. Another lesson I learned from the research project was that, as wonderfully committed and involved as the group was, I had overestimated how committed they would be to the process. Specifically, I had hoped that when each person received their transcripts and the paper on power, they would read each carefully and then do a detailed comparative analysis of the materials. While each did this to some degree, they did not do it with the comprehensiveness I had expected in my abstract construction of the research model.

Although this fact did not affect the success of the research project, because everyone did do reflection and analysis, in retrospect it makes perfect sense that people did as much of the analysis as they did. Textual analysis takes time: they were all busy at

their full-time jobs. Textual analysis takes practice: they had varying degrees of experience doing this kind of analysis. And finally,
the project was mine: as invested as they were in its success, it
was my research project, my interests, and my final analysis that
were leading to, among other things, my doctoral degree. Of course
they were not as committed as I was.

Kieffer (1981) suggests that dialogic research needs to be distinguished from collaborative research, in which the subjects are
involved in developing the research questions, choosing the
methodology, and writing the results. There is joint ownership of
the project, and thus there is true collaboration. In my dialogic
methodology, which built on Kieffer's work, I developed the
research questions, chose the methodology, and wrote the final
analysis. I have sole responsibility for the product. Kieffer suggests that collaborative research is more empowering than dialogic
research because it more thoroughly breaks down the *power over*
relationship between researcher and subjects.

While in general I agree with Kieffer's critique of traditional
research and his call for developing more collaborative models,
my experience with this project indicates that collaboration may
not always be the most empowering methodology. In most
research models, and even in Kieffer's dialogic model, the
researcher's relationship with her or his subjects is created and
defined by the research project itself. Usually there has been very
little contact between researcher and subjects before the research
project starts. As a result, ownership of the project plays a central
role in creating the relationship between researcher and subjects.
This was not the case in this research project. As an active member of ESR and the steering committee, my relationship to the
study participants was neither created or defined by the research
project. Rather, the research took place with the larger context
that I have described in this book: our relationships are equal and
based on mutual trust and respect; they are characterized by
ongoing *power with*. Within this larger context the power implications referred to by Kieffer are much less significant. The participants in this study did not particularly want to be equal owners of
the project. Rather we all saw my research as one of my contributions to the group. They would do their part by entering into the
dialogue, but they did not have the time or the interest to be
"equal owners" of the project. Rather, through the process of dialogic encounter we were able to contribute in the ways with which
we all felt most comfortable. The results were synergistic: we all

learned, we all grew; we all got something out of the process; we all feel we have contributed to ESR.

As I was completing the first draft I asked Shelley if he wanted to read it. He was leaving for a month of conducting workshops and making presentations and did not have the time. I asked if he wasn't concerned about how I had interpreted his experience. He answered, "Seth, I trust you totally. I am not worried." Within the context of trust, mutuality, and co-agency, "ownership" of this particular project was not seen in terms of *power over*. Study participants had participated in the generation and analysis of data and, given their interests and commitments, that was ownership enough. Shelley was contributing to the organization through conducting workshops, and my contribution was this research. We trusted one another to do it honestly and sensitively. None of us feel we need to have a say in everything that happens within the organization.

Given this particular group of people and our varied commitments and interests, I do not see how shared ownership or "true collaboration" would have made this experience more empowering for the group. This is not to say that collaborative research is not empowering or important, given the way research is usually conducted, nor is it to say that *if* the group had been willing to share ownership of the project that the experience would not have been extremely empowering; it is only to say that in this context, with this group of people, this research model seems to have met our needs and interests extremely well.

Reliability: There are, however, several other important aspects of this particular research model that need to be discussed. In reflecting upon the effectiveness of a research methodology the researcher must consider the "reliability" or "informational adequacy" (Zelditch 1969) of her or his data. This refers to the quality of the information generated; to its honesty, comprehensiveness, depth, and integrity. A common argument against "studying" people with whom one has close personal and professional ties is that overfamiliarity compromises the honesty and integrity of the data generated; that difficult questions may not get asked and truthful answers not given when the dialogue is between people with a mutual history and ongoing working relationships; that the data will not reflect the complexity of people's experiences, especially painful and unspoken feelings and experiences in the group.

While this may be true of situations where the relationship between researcher and subjects is characterized by mistrust and competition, it would seem that there is just as good, if not a better chance, that an individual would be willing to reveal her or his deeper thoughts and experiences to someone with whom she or he has an ongoing relationship characterized by mutual trust and respect, than she or he would to a relative stranger. In addition, it is the responsibility of the researcher to ask difficult questions. While it may be easier to ask these questions if one has no involvement in the setting one is investigating, it is unfair to assume that familiarity breeds cowardice. The commitment of the researcher must be to probe deeply, whether in familiar or unfamiliar territory.

I have taken this responsibility seriously. One example of this is that as the interviews developed I recognized that the six individuals' experiences were fitting into the *power with* paradigm. While this was an exciting development, it caused me reason to wonder if I was not asking the right questions to elicit discussions of *power over* dynamics. This led me to pursue with extra diligence the presence of *power over* in ESR and in the individuals' teaching. I added questions, I looked for small indications of *power over* dynamics that I could explore in more depth. I went as far as to share experiences I have had in ESR in which I thought *power over* was being used. The result of my steady pursuit of *power over* is that I uncovered real and important functions of *power over* in both ESR and individuals' teaching and that I feel confident in describing the heart of the empowering experience for these six individuals as being characterized by *power with*. I would not have uncovered the role of *power over* had I not pressed the issue, and as a result I would not feel as comfortable as I do with my discussion of the role of *power with* in empowerment.

Freire (1973) writes:

> Born of a critical matrix, dialogue creates a critical attitude (Jaspers). It is nourished by love, humility, hope, faith, and trust. When the two "poles" of the dialogue are thus linked by love, hope, and mutual trust, they can join in a critical search for something. Only dialogue truly communicates. (p. 45)

As a result of the kinds of relationships I have with each of the participants in the study, dialogue was possible. In this dialogue individuals shared exceptionally open and honest reflections on their experiences. I believe that the overall honesty, depth, comprehensiveness, and integrity of the data have been enhanced as a result of my established and continuing relationships with the study participants. It would seem, in fact, that the only assurance one has of the integrity of someone's story is found in one's confidence in the relationship one has with the individual.

Validity: Another concern for the researcher reflecting on her or his research methodology relates to the quality of the data analysis. Traditionally this question is raised around issues of "objectivity" and "validity"; within the phenomenological perspective, the possibility of objectivity is questioned, and the problem is rephrased to focus on the attempt to remain true to the "fidelity to the phenomena" (Kieffer 1981, 481). At the heart of this concern is the fear that one's analysis may be biased. Once again, overinvolvement with the individuals and the setting investigated has traditionally been seen as holding too great a potential for "contamination," for the blurring of vision and the biasing of analyses. Presumably distance provides critical perspective, detachment allows for objectivity, and both allow for unbiased and therefore more accurate analysis. However, the counterargument to this position is that distance blurs vision; that detachment encourages insensitivity; and that together, distance and detachment can lead to the distortion of people's experiences in the service of the ends of the researcher. This counterargument suggests that one's understanding of the experiences of others is enhanced when one shares in the living of those experiences.

One way in which this research model allows for confidence in the interpretation of data is through involving the study participants in the reflection and interpretive process. In this way the researcher's interpretations are continuously compared to the interpretations of the study participants. In this study I went as far as to share rough drafts of my analysis and synthesis with several study participants.

However, as a researcher investigating an important context in my own life, my challenge has been to work with the tensions between intimacy and critical distance. I believe that out of the creative friction of these tensions I have been able to delve more deeply and see more clearly than if I had chosen to opt for any one stance alone. However, if I erred to one side, it was on the side of side of intimacy.

Telling Our Story: Richard Katz (1985) tells how the !Kung healers he was living with enjoined him to "tell our story" and how, in order to know something of their "story," he had to let go of his world view and enter into the world of the !Kung. He argues that in fact it was only through making himself vulnerable, through opening himself up to relationship and experience with the !Kung, that he could learn anything about their story.

This book represents my attempt to "tell our story"; in my case the story is in fact "ours," in many ways my story as much as the story of the study participants. I see this as a unique advantage for research. My challenge in conducting this research has been to live both inside and outside of our mutual experiences in ESR. My goal has been to offer an opportunity for the six participants to share their experiences, to provide a vehicle for their voices to be heard, to try to add some perspective, and to explore the insights and lessons their experiences offer for our understanding of power and empowerment. Although the challenges of maintaining critical perspective are real, they seem to pale in view of the benefits our common experience and ongoing relationships offer the research project.

At this point this discussion of method begins to become somewhat of a tangled web. My methodology has emerged out of the same questions and analyses as my theoretical work on power and empowerment. Clearly, the dynamics of dialogue lie at the heart of the entire project. Dialogue, as we have seen, is preeminently about the quality of relationships between people. It is in dialogue that true communication becomes possible, thus it is dialogue that I have chosen as my central tool of research.

The themes I have uncovered through my research have emerged as important themes in my methodology. As I reflect on the research experience I realize that my methodology has tried to create relationships of co-agency. In order to do this I have maintained mutual relationships with the study participants; that is, in order to do my research well I have had to be both assertive and open. I have had to practice the very qualities that emerged as the central dynamics in our understanding of dialogue, *power with* and empowerment.

I have had to listen carefully; listen in the sense described in this book. One of the temptations of working with people with whom one has shared experiences is to assume that they have had the same experiences. In order to not fall prey to this illusion I have had to remain continually open to hearing the experiences of the study participants. I have also had to remain open to changing my thinking about power and empowerment and altering my conceptual framework for understanding power. This sounds easier than it is, and I have struggled to let go and learn. In asking the study participants to be open and vulnerable I have had to make myself vulnerable as well. This has meant sharing my feelings and experiences as well as listening to their feelings and experiences.

I have also played an assertive role. I conceived and implemented the project. Much like the teacher's role discussed in chapter 7, I took responsibility for initiating and facilitating the project. I presented my analysis of power to the group for feedback and reflection. The key, I think, is that my assertiveness (offering the paper on power) was complemented by openness (the willingness to change, broaden, or deepen my thinking). Both were crucial; it was important for the group to have the paper to respond to, and it was vital that I be willing to change my thinking. Out of the tension, out of the dialogue, insight emerged.

The balance of assertiveness and openness was crucial for the interview process as well. I identified and asked the questions, but I always offered individuals a chance to say whatever they felt they wanted to say. I came to the interviews with an agenda of questions that I was always willing to change. Many times I did not get through all the questions I came prepared to ask. I challenged individuals' thinking by asking tough questions, yet tried to remain nonjudgmental in listening to their responses. The continuing challenge for me was to be both assertive and open so that true dialogue could occur, so that through the process of our "reciprocal influencing" new insights, greater clarity, and expanded understanding could emerge.

In the end the question of the objectivity of this study is not the most important question to me. The research will be affirmed as other questions are answered: Do my analyses resonate with the study participants' understanding of their experiences? Have I been able to convey their experiences with power and insight? Does my analysis have relevance and resonance in the lives of the people who read this book? Can the concepts and experiences explored and shared help people to better understand their experiences of power and empowerment? Does this exploration help ESR understand its work better and do it more effectively? I feel that in the answering of these questions the "truth," the "accuracy," even the "objectivity," of my analysis will become evident.

Appendix B

Framework of Questions for the Initial Interviews

Session One:
Focus on Empowering Experiences in Boston ESR

I. Description of the Research Project:

    1. Explain that my interest is in empowerment: your own and what you try to do in your classroom
(Note: I do *not* say that I am specifically interested in the nature of power in their experiences of empowerment—this comes later)

    2. Describe the research model:
        a. Describe criteria for participation in the study
        b. Describe the steps in the research model

        Interview
        Reading the initial interviews
        Reading my paper
        Follow-up interview
        Final group meeting

II. Questions: Description and Reflection on Their Experiences in ESR

(A general follow-up question for many of these questions is to ask for specific examples.)

Why did you become a teacher?

If or when you are asked by a close friend why you are involved in ESR and what you have gotten out of your involvement, how would you or do you respond?

I wonder if you could go back and describe how you got involved in ESR and how you feel you have grown and changed through your involvement. Extensive probing, for instance:

Why did you get involved in ESR?
What attracted you to the organization?
What were you seeking that ESR seemed to offer?

What I would like you to do is to go back to your earliest days in ESR and try to capture what you were like, what you were feeling, learning, hoping for, experiencing. Please try to follow yourself and your changing feelings and experiences over the past three years. I will interrupt to ask pertinent questions as you speak. (Extensive probing to bring out descriptions of key experiences in the organization.)

What has been the role of your relationships with other ESR members in the changes and rewards you have had in ESR?

How would you describe these relationships?

What role has your participation on the steering committee had on your experience in ESR?

How would you describe your role in the steering committee? In the Boston chapter?

Describe how the steering committee functions. How are decisions made in the steering committee? Example.

How does the steering committee develop new programs? How does it reach consensus? Do you think it works effectively? How come? (Focus on getting examples.)

What are your relationships with steering committee members like?

How would you describe your influence in the steering committee and the organization? How does your influence come to be felt?

Do you feel that you have power in the steering committee? How would you describe this power and how it functions? (Press for examples.)

What do you think steering committee members value most about their involvement in ESR?

What do you value most about your involvement in ESR? Is there competition for this?

Have you experienced competition within ESR?

Who are the most powerful members of the steering committee? Why do you say they are powerful? What is the nature of their power? How do they exercise their power? What effect does their exercise of power have on you? How is power exercised on the steering committee? What does it mean to have "power" in the Boston chapter? Do people try to control other people on the steering committee? Do you ever feel imposed upon by others? Do they try to control the development of the organization?

Do you feel that, in general, there is tension for you in trying to fulfill your goals and needs in the organization while also trying to let others fulfill their goals and needs?

What skills have you developed as a result of your involvement in ESR?

Have you experienced personally or in others any jealousy or envy?

How open and accessible do you feel decision making is in the organization?

Has ESR been effective as an organization? Why?

How do we bring about change? What is the "ESR approach" to change, if you can say there is one?

How has ESR affected your ability to bring about educational and social change?

Has your experience in ESR made you a more powerful person?

III.   Reflection on Their Experiences in Terms of Their Conception of Empowerment

Overall, would you say that your experience in ESR has been empowering?

Why do you say that it has been empowering?

Are there particular projects, or relationships, or contexts or settings within Boston ESR that you feel are or were particularly empowering?

What has ESR empowered you to do? In what areas of your life are you now more empowered? Can you give examples?

What are the most important factors that have lead to your feeling empowered?

How important would you say your relationships with other ESR members have been in your process of empowerment?

Do you think that in general, participation in ESR, and on the steering committee in particular, empowers people?

Are people empowered at the expense of others' not being empowered on the steering committee? Within the organization?

What is the difference between the way an empowered person works for change and a powerless or disempowered person works for change?

Can you describe how you understand the process by which empowerment has emerged as a central concept in ESR's work?

How do you define empowerment?

What would you say is the nature of the power that is developed in the process of empowerment?

Session Two: Description and Reflection on
Their Experiences with Trying to Empower Students

How has ESR affected your teaching?

What does it mean to empower students?

At this point I would like you to identify one class, course, or unit you have taught that you feel was a particularly empowering for your students.

Please describe the school in which you taught this course. Who were the students? (Probe for specifics on race, class, gender, the communities they come from, etc.)

What was the name of the course? Please describe the structure and content of the course. What were the key ingredients that lead to the empowerment of students?

What happens to individuals in an empowering classroom? How would you describe the process of empowerment?

What do students learn about themselves when they are empowered? What do students learn about other people when they are empowered? What do students learn about society when they are empowered?

How would you describe your relationships with your students that were empowering? What is an empowering relationship like?

Could you give me an example of one student who you felt was empowered in your classroom last year? How do empowered people act?

How would you describe your relationship with this student?

What is the nature of the power students get when they are empowered?

What are relationships among students like in an empowering situation?

Do some students get empowered at the expense of others not getting empowered? Is empowerment a scarce resource?

Are there any skills that students need to develop in order to be empowered?

I want to talk a little about the connection between curriculum and empowerment. Before I ask any specific questions, do you have any thoughts concerning the relationship between curriculum and empowerment?

What is the role of specific content in the process of empowerment of students?

Does it matter who chooses the curriculum in an empowering classroom?

Are there ways of approaching content that are particularly conducive to empowerment?

What are some of the crucial issues you are facing as you try to understand empowerment in relation to your students?

Bibliography

Albert, M., and R. Hahnel. 1981. *Socialism today and tommorow.* Boston: South End Press.

Americas Watch. 1982. *Report on human rights in El Salvador.* New York: Vintage Books.

Apple, M. 1979. *Ideology and curriculum.* Boston: Routledge & Kegan Paul.

Apple, M. 1982. *Education and power.* Boston: Routledge & Kegan Paul.

Arendt, H. 1970. *On violence.* New York: Harcourt, Brace & World.

Aronowitz, S., and H. Giroux. 1985. *Education under seige: The conservative, liberal, and radical debate over schooling.* Hadley, Massachusetts: Bergin & Garvey.

Asante, M. K. 1987. *The afrocentric idea.* Philadelphia: Temple University Press.

Ashcroft, L. 1987. Defusing "empowering": The what and the why. *Language arts* 64 (February): 140–56.

Ayers, W. 1986. Thinking about teachers and the curriculum. *Harvard Educational Review* 56 (1): 49–51.

Bacharach, S., and E. Lawler. 1980. *Power and politics in organizations.* San Francisco: Jossey-Bass.

Bachrach, P., and M. S. Baratz. 1970. *Power and poverty: Theory and practice.* New York: Oxford University Press.

Bailey, K. 1978. *Methods of social research.* New York: Free Press.

Barnet, R. 1972. *The roots of war.* New York: Penguin Books.

Barnet, R., and R. Muller. 1974. *Global reach: The power of the multinational corporations.* New York: Simon & Schuster.

Bateson, G. 1972. *Steps to an ecology of mind.* New York: Ballantine Books.

Beauvoir, S. de. 1974. *The second sex.* New York: Vintage Books.

Belenky, M. F., B. McV. Clinchy, N. R. Goldenberger, and J. M. Tarule. 1986. *Women's ways of knowing.* New York: Basic Books.

Benedict, R. 1970. Synergy: Patterns of the good culture. *American Anthropologist* 72: 320–33.

Berger, P. L., and T. Luckmann. 1966. *The social construction of reality.* New York: Doubleday.

Berger, P. L., and R. J. Neuhaus. 1977. *To empower people: The role of mediating structures in public policy.* Washington, D.C.: American Enterprise Institute for Public Policy Research.

Berman, S., coordinator. 1982. *Dialogue: A teaching guide to nuclear issues.* Cambridge, MA: Educators for Social Responsibility.

Berman, S., coordinator. 1983. *Perspectives: A guide to teaching about the concept of peace.* Cambridge, MA: Educators for Social Responsibility.

Berman, S., and S. Kreisberg. 1984. *Boston Chapter of Educators for Social Responsibility Funding Proposal.*

Berman, S., J. Corro, E. Greene, J. Hammerman, V. Nordal, R. Poliner, and L. Stowell. 1984. *Making history.* Cambridge, MA: Educators for Social Responsibility.

Bierstadt, R. 1974. *Power and progress.* New York: McGraw-Hill.

Blau, P. 1964. *Exchange and power in social life.* New York: Wiley.

Bogdan, R., and S. J. Taylor. 1975. *Introduction to qualitative research methods: A phenomenological approach to the social sciences.* New York: Wiley.

Bookchin, M. 1982. *The ecology of freedom.* Palo Alto, CA: Cheshire Books.

Bowles, S., and H. Gintis. 1976. *Schooling in capitalist America.* New York: Basic Books.

Bowles, S., and H. Gintis. 1986. *Democracy and capitalism.* New York: Basic Books.

Braverman, H. 1974. *Labor and monopoly capital: The degradation of work in the twentieth century.* New York: Monthly Review Press.

Brenkman, J. 1987. *Culture and domination.* Ithaca, NY: Cornell University Press.

Brumbaugh, R. 1982. *Whitehead, process philosophy and education.* Albany, NY: State University of New York Press.

Buber, M. 1975. *Between man and man.* New York: Macmillan.

Burgest, D. R. 1982. *Social work practice with minorities.* Metuchen, NJ: Scarecrow Press.

Capra, F. 1975. *The tao of physics.* Berkeley, CA: Shambala.

Capra, F. 1982. *The turning point.* New York: Simon & Schuster.

Carroll, B. A. 1971. Peace research: The cult of power. *Conflict Resolution* 16 (4): 585–616.

Carson, R. 1962. *Silent spring.* New York: Fawcett Crest.

Champlin, J., ed. 1971. *Power.* New York: Atherton Press.

Chesler, P. 1978. *About men.* New York: Bantam.

Chodorow, N. 1978. *The reproduction of mothering.* Berkeley, CA: University of California Press.

Christ, C., and J. Plaskow. 1979. *Womanspirit rising: A feminist reader in religion.* San Francisco: Harper & Row.

Clegg, S. 1975. *Power, rule, and domination.* Boston: Routledge & Kegan Paul.

Clegg, S. 1979. *The theory of power and organization.* Boston: Routledge & Kegan Paul.

Coates, G. 1981. *Resettling America: Energy, ecology and community.* Andover, MA: Brick House.

Cohen, J., and J. Rogers. 1983. *On democracy: Toward a transformation of American society.* New York: Anchor Books.

Colaizzi, P. F. 1978. Psychological research as the phenomenologist views it. In *Existential phenomenological alternatives in psychology,* ed. R. S. Valle, and M. King. New York: Oxford University Press.

Coles, R. 1967. *Children of crisis: A study of courage and fear.* Boston: Little, Brown.

Craig, J. and M. Craig. 1979. *Synergic power: Beyond domination and permissiveness.* 2d ed. Berkeley, CA: Proactive Press.

Cummins, J. 1986. Empowering minority students: A framework for intervention. *Harvard Educational Review* 56 (1): 49–51.

Dahl, R. 1957. The concept of power. *Behavorial Science* (July): 201–15.

Dahl, R. 1968a. A critique of the ruling elite model. In *C. Wright Mills and the power elite. See* G. W. Domhoff and H. B. Ballard, 1968.

Dahl, R. 1968. Power. In *The international encyclopedia of the social sciences,* ed. D. Sills. New York: Collier & Macmillan.

Dahl, R. 1976. *Modern political analysis.* 3d ed. Englewood Cliffs, NJ: Prentice Hall.

Daly, M. 1973. *Beyond God the father.* Boston: Beacon Press.

Daly, M. 1978. *Gyn/ecology: The metaethics of radical feminism.* Boston: Beacon Press.

Davis, A. 1981. *Women, race and class.* New York: Random House.

Delpit, L. D. 1988. The silenced dialogue: Power and pedagogy in educating other people's children. *Harvard Educational Review* 58 (3): 280–97.

Dewey, J. 1916. *Democracy and education.* New York: Macmillan.

Dewey, J. 1940. *Education today.* New York: G. P. Putnam's Sons.

Diamond, I., and L. Quinby, eds. 1988. *Feminism and Foucault: Reflections on resistance.* Boston: Northeastern University Press.

Dinnerstein, D. 1976. *The mermaid and the minotaur: Sexual arrangements and human malaise.* New York: Harper Colophon Books.

Domhoff, G. W., and H. Ballard, comp. 1968. *C. Wright Mills and the power elite.* Boston: Beacon Press.

Eisenstein, Z., ed. 1979. *Capitalist patriarchy and the case for socialist feminism.* New York: Monthly Review Press.

Ellison, R. 1952. *The invisible man.* New York: Random House.

Ellsworth, E. 1989. Why doesn't this feel empowering? Working through the repressive myths of critical pedagogy. *Harvard Educational Review* 59 (3): 297–323.

Emmet, D. 1954. The concept of power. In *Power. See* Champlin 1971.

Fanon, F. 1963. *Wretched of the earth.* New York: Grove Press.

Fiske, E. 1988. Grass-roots reform in Miami experiment. *The New York Times,* January 15.

Follett, M. P. 1918. *The new state: Group organization the solution of popular government.* New York: Longmans, Green.

Follett, M. P. 1924. *Creative experience.* New York: Longmans, Green.

Follett, M. P. 1942. *Dynamic administration.* New York: Harper and Brothers.

Foucault, M. 1972. *Archeology of knowledge.* New York: Harper Torchbooks.

Foucault, M. 1979. *Discipline and punish.* New York: Vintage Books.

Foucault, M. 1980a. *Power/knowledge: Selected interviews and other writings 1972–1977.* New York: Pantheon Books.

Foucault, M. 1980b. *The history of sexuality.* New York: Vintage Books.

Foucault, M. 1982. The subject and power. *Critical Inquiry* 8: 777–95.

Freire, P. 1970. *Pedagogy of the oppressed.* New York: Continuum.

Freire, P. 1973. *Education for critical consciousness.* New York: Continuum.

Freire, P. 1978. *Pedagogy in process: The letters to Guinea-Bissau.* New York: Continuum.

Freire, P. 1985. *The politics of education: Culture, power and liberation.* Hadley, Massachusetts: Bergin & Garvey.

French, M. 1985. *Beyond power.* New York: Ballantine Books.

Fromm, E. 1947. *Man for himself.* New York: Fawcett.

Fromm, E. 1955. *The sane society.* New York: Fawcett.

Fuller, B. 1963. *Ideas and integrities.* New York: Macmillan, Collier Books.

Galbraith, J. K. 1983. *The anatomy of power.* Boston: Houghton Mifflin.

Gilligan, C. 1982. *In a different voice.* Cambridge, MA: Harvard University Press.

Gilman, C. P. 1973. *The yellow wallpaper.* New York: The Feminist Press. (Originally published in 1899.)

Giorgi. A. 1970a. *Phenomenology as a human science.* New York: Harper & Row.

Giorgi, A. 1970b. Toward phenomenologically based research in psychology. *Journal of Phenomenological Psychology* 1 (1): 75–98.

Giorgi, A. 1975. Phenomenology and the foundations of psychology. In *Nebraska symposium on motivation, 1975,* ed. W. J. Arnold. Lincoln, NE: University of Nebraska Press.

Giorgi, A., W. F. Fisher, and R. Von Eckartsberg, eds. 1971. *Duquesne studies in phenomenological psychology.* Vol. 1. Pittsburgh: Duquesne University Press.

Giroux, H. A. 1981. *Ideology, culture, and the process of schooling.* Philadelphia: Temple University Press.

Giroux, H. A. 1983. *Theory and resistance in education.* Hadley, Massachusetts: Bergin & Garvey.

Giroux, H. A. 1988a. *Teachers as intellectuals.* Hadley, Massachusetts: Bergin & Garvey.

Giroux, H. A. 1988b. *Schooling and the struggle for public life.* Minneapolis: University of Minnesota Press.

Giroux, H. A., and D. Purpel. 1983. *The hidden curriculum and moral education*. Berkeley, CA: McCutchan.

Good, C. V. 1954. *Methods of research: Educational, psychological, sociological*. New York: Appleton-Crofts.

Goodlad, J. 1983. *A place called school*. New York: McGraw-Hill.

Goodman, J. 1987. Key factors in becoming or not becoming an empowered elementary school teacher: A preliminary study of selected novices. Paper presented at the annual meeting of the American Educational Research Association, Washington, D. C.

Gorden, R. 1980. *Interviewing: Strategy, techniques and tactics*. Homewood, IL: Dorsey Press.

Gordon, S. 1985a. Anger, power, and women's sense of self. *Ms.*, July, 42–44.

Gordon, S. 1985b. From theory to practice. *Ms.*, July, 112.

Gore, J. M. 1989. Agency, structure and the rhetoric of teacher empowerment. Paper presented at the annual meeting of the American Educational Research Association, San Francisco, CA.

Gottlieb, D., and A. Heinsohn. 1971. *America's other youth: Growing up poor*. Englewood Cliffs, NJ: Prentice-Hall.

Grambs, G., and L. Carr. 1979. *Modern methods in secondary education*. New York: Holt.

Gramsci, A. 1972. *Selections from the prison notebooks*, ed. and trans. Q. Hoare and G. Smith. New York: Irvington Press.

Greene, M. 1978. *Landscapes of learning*. New York: Teachers College Press.

Greene, M. 1986. In search of a critical pedagogy. *Harvard Educational Review* 56 (4): 427–41.

Griffin, S. 1978. *Woman and nature*. New York: Harper Colophon Books.

Gross, S. 1985. Personal power and empowerment. *Contemporary Education* 53 (3): 137–43.

Harrington, M. 1962. *The other America*. New York: Macmillan.

Harrington, M. 1984. *The new American poverty*. New York: Holt, Rinehart & Winston.

Hartsock, N. 1983. *Money, sex, and power*. Boston: Northeastern University Press.

Hobbes, T. 1962. *Elements of philosophy. The first section concerning body*. Ed. W. Molesworth. Aalen, Germany: Scientia.

Hobbes, T. 1984. *Leviathan.* New York: Penguin Books.

Hunnius, G., G. D. Garson, and J. Case. 1973. *Workers' control.* New York: Vintage Press.

Hunter, F. 1953. *Community power structure.* Chapel Hill, NC: University of North Carolina Press.

Jervis, K., and A. Tobier, eds. 1987. *Education for democracy: Proceedings from The Cambridge School Conference on Progressive Education.* Weston, MA: The Cambridge School.

Jordan, J. 1984. Meaning of mutuality, *Work in progress #16.* Wellesley, MA: Stone Center Working Papers Series.

Karabel, J., and A. H. Halsey, eds. 1977. *Power and ideology in education.* New York: Oxford University Press.

Katz, R. 1982. *Boiling energy: Community healing among the Kalahari !Kung.* Cambridge, MA: Harvard University Press.

Katz, R. 1983/84. Empowerment and synergy: Expanding the community's healing resources. *Prevention in Human Services* (Special Issue on Empowerment) 3 (2/3): 201–25.

Katz, R. 1985. Hearing healers: The contributions of vulnerability to field work. In *The scientist and the shaman: The interplay of rational thought and spiritual feeling,* ed. A. Schenk and E. Kalawit. Munich, Germany: Dianus-Trikont Verlag.

Katz, R. 1986. Healing and transformation: Perspectives on development, education and community. In *The cultural transition: Human experience and social transformation in the Third World and Japan,* ed. M. White and S. Pollak. London: Routledge & Kegan Paul.

Katz, R., and N. Seth. 1986. Synergy and healing: A perspective on Western health care. *Prevention in Human Services* 4 (3/4).

Keller, E. F. 1985. *Reflections on gender and science.* New Haven, CT: Yale University Press.

Kieffer, C. 1981. *The emergence of empowerment: The development of participatory competence among individuals in citizen organizations.* Ph.D. diss., University of Michigan, Ann Arbor.

Kieffer, C. 1983/84. Citizen empowerment: A developmental perspective. *Prevention in Human Services* (special issue on empowerment) 3 (2/3): 9–36.

King, M. L. 1963. *Why we can't wait.* New York: Mentor.

King, M. L. 1967. *Where do we go from here: Chaos or community?* New York: Bantam.

Kirp, D. L. 1989. Education: The movie. *Mother Jones*, January, 36–45.

Korda, M. 1975. *Power: How to get it, how to use it.* New York: Ballantine Books.

Kreisberg, S. 1984a. Teaching for peace and justice: Toward a pedagogy of empowerment. *Boston Area Educators for Social Responsibility Newsletter*, December.

Kreisberg, S. 1984b. *Perspectives: An ESR research report.* Manuscript, Harvard University Graduate School of Education, Cambridge, MA.

Kreisberg, S. 1985. Transforming power: Toward an understanding of the nature of power in theories of empowerment. Qualifying Paper, Harvard Graduate School of Education, Cambridge, MA.

Kreisberg, S. 1986. *Transforming power: Toward an understanding of the nature of power in the experience of empowerment.* Ph.d. diss., Harvard University Graduate School of Education, Cambridge, MA.

Kreisberg, S. 1988. Creating a democratic classroom. *Democracy and Education* 3 (2): 13–19.

Kuhn, T. S. 1970. *The structure of scientific revolutions.* 2d ed. Chicago: University of Chicago Press.

Kvale, S. 1983. The qualitative research interview. *Journal of Phenomenological Psychology* 14 (2): 171–95.

Lappe, F. M., and J. Collins. 1978. *Food first: Beyond the myth of scarcity.* New York: Ballantine Books.

Laswell, H., and A. Kaplan. 1950. *Power and society.* New Haven, CT: Yale University Press.

Levinson, D. J. 1978. *The seasons of a man's life.* New York: Ballantine Books.

Lorde, A. 1981. The master's tools will never dismantle the master's house. In *This bridge called my back: Writings by radical women of color*, ed. C. Moraga and G. Anzaldua, 98–99. Watertown, MA: Persephone Press.

Lukes, S. 1974. *Power: A radical view.* London, England: Macmillan.

M: the civilized man 1986. 8, (June).

Machiavelli, N. 1971. *The prince.* New York: Norton.

Macy, J. 1978. *Interdependence: Mutual causality in early Buddhist teachings and general systems theory.* Ph.d. diss., Syracuse University, Syracuse, NY.

Macy, J. 1983. *Despair and empowerment in the nuclear age.* Philadelphia: New Society Publishers.

Maeroff, G. I. 1988. *The empowerment of teachers.* New York: Teachers College Press.

Maher, F. A. 1987a. My introduction to 'Introduction to Women's Studies': The role of the teacher's authority in the feminist classroom. *Feminist Teacher* 3 (Fall–Winter): 9–11.

Maher, F. A. 1987b. Toward a richer theory of feminist pedagogy: A comparison of "liberation" and "gender" models for teaching and learning. *Journal of Education* 169 (3): 91–98.

Mannheim, K. 1951. *Freedom, power and democratic planning.* London: Percy Lund, Humphries.

Marcuse, H. 1955. *Eros and civilization.* Boston: Beacon Press.

Marx, K. 1967. *Capital: A critique of political economy.* New York: International.

May, R. 1972. *Power and innocence.* New York: Norton.

McAllister, P., ed. 1982. *Reweaving the web of life: Feminism and nonviolence.* Philadelphia: New Society.

McCall, G. J., and J. L. Simmons, eds. 1969. *Issues in participant observation: A text and reader.* Reading, MA: Addison-Wesley.

McLaren, P. 1988. On ideology and education: Critical pedagogy and the politics of education. *Social Text,* 19–20, Fall 1988, 153–85.

McLaren, P. 1989. *Life in schools.* New York: Longman.

McNeil, L. M. 1988a. Contradictions of control, part 1: Administrators and teachers. *Phi Delta Kappan,* January, 333–39.

McNeil, L. M. 1988b. Contradictions of control, part 2: Teachers, students and curriculum. *Phi Delta Kappan,* February, 432–38.

McNeil, L. M. 1988c. Contradictions of control, part 3: Contradictions of reform. *Phi Delta Kappan,* March, 478–85.

McRobbie, A. 1978. *Working class girls and the culture of femininity.* London: Hutchinson.

Meadows, D. 1972. *The limits to growth.* Washington, D.C.: Patonic.

Memmi, A. 1965. *The colonizer and the colonized.* Boston: Beacon Press.

Merchant, C. 1980. *The death of nature: Women, ecology and the scientific revolution.* San Francisco: Harper & Row.

Merton, R. K., M. Fiske, and P. L. Kendall. 1956. *The focused interview.* New York: Free Press.

Miller, A. 1983. *For your own good: Hidden cruelty, child-rearing and the roots of violence.* New York: Farrar, Strauss & Giroux.

Miller, J. B. 1976. *Toward a new psychology of women.* Boston: Beacon Press.

Miller, J. B. 1982. Women and power. *Work in progress #82–01.* Wellesley, MA: Stone Center Working Papers Series.

Mills, C. W. 1956. *The power elite.* New York: Oxford University Press.

Mills, C. W. 1959. *The sociological imagination.* Oxford, England: Oxford University Press.

Nassaw, D. 1979. *Schooled to order.* New York: Oxford University Press.

Niehardt, J. G. 1932. *Black Elk speaks.* New York: Pocket Books.

Noddings, N. 1984. *Caring: A feminine approach to ethics and moral education.* Berkeley, CA: University of California Press.

Nyberg, D. 1981. *Power over power.* Ithaca, NY: Cornell University Press.

Okin, S. M. 1979. *Women in Western political thought.* Princeton, NJ: Princeton University Press.

Oliver, D. 1976. *Education and community: A radical critique of innovative schooling.* Berkeley, CA: McCutchan.

Oliver, D., and K. W. Gershman. 1986. Cosmology as curriculum: Toward a theory of process education. Manuscript, Harvard University, Cambridge, MA.

Oliver, D., and K. W. Gershman. 1989. *Education, modernity, and fractured meaning: Toward a process theory of teaching and learning.* Albany, NY: State University of New York Press.

Olson, L. 1988. Work conditions in some schools said "intolerable." *Education Week,* September 28, 1, 21.

Pelto, P., and G. Pelto. 1978. *Anthropological research: The structure of inquiry.* 2d ed. New York: Cambridge University Press.

Piven, F. F., and R. A. Cloward. 1982. *The new class war.* New York: Pantheon Books.

The Power Elite. 1989. *Regardies,* January, 50–124.

Rappaport, J. 1977. *Community psychology: Values, research and action.* New York: Holt, Rinehart & Winston.

Rappaport, J. 1981. In praise of paradox: A social policy of empowerment over prevention. *American Journal of Community Psychology* 9 (1): 1–25.

Reich, W. 1976. *The mass psychology of facism.* New York: Pocket Books.

Reinharz, S. 1979. *On becoming a social scientist.* San Francisco: Jossey-Bass.

Reinharz, S. 1983. Experiential analysis: A contribution to feminist research. In *Theories of women's studies,* ed. G. Bowles and D. Klein. London: Routledge & Kegan Paul.

Rich, A. 1976. *Of woman born.* New York: Norton.

Rimer, S. 1988. Paterson principal: A man of extremes. *The New York Times,* January 14, B1–2.

Rosenman, M. 1980. Empowerment as a purpose of education. *Alternative Higher Education: The Journal of Non-Traditional Studies* 4 (4): 248–59.

Rubin, L. B. 1976. *Worlds of pain.* New York: Basic Books.

Russell, B. 1938. *Power.* New York: Norton.

Ryan, W. 1976. *Blaming the victim.* New York: Vintage Books.

Sardello, R. J. 1971. A reciprocal participation model of experimentation. In *Duquesne studies in phenomenological psychology,* vol. 1. *See* A. Giorgi, W. F. Fischer, and R. Von Eckartsberg, eds., 1971.

Schatzman, L., and A. Strauss. 1973. *Field research: Strategies for a natural sociology.* Englewood Cliffs, NJ: Prentice Hall.

Schell, J. 1982. *The fate of the earth.* New York: Avon.

Schlafly, P. 1977. The power of the positive woman. In *Taking sides,* ed. K. Finsterbusch and G. McKenna. 110–16. Guilford, NC: Dushkin.

Schon, D. A. 1983. *The reflective practitioner.* New York: Basic Books.

Sennett, R., and J. Cobb. 1972. *The hidden injuries of class.* New York: Vintage Books.

Sharp, G. 1980. *Social power and political freedom.* Boston: Porter Sargent.

Shor, I. 1980. *Critical teaching and everyday life.* Boston: South End Press.

Shor, I., and P. Freire. 1987. *A pedagogy for liberation.* Hadley, Massachusetts: Bergin & Garvey.

Silberman, C. 1970. *Crisis in the classroom.* New York: Random House.

Simon, H. 1957. *Models of man, social and rational; mathematical essays on rational behavior in a social setting.* New York: Wiley.

Sizer, T. 1984. *Horace's compromise: The dilemma of the American high school.* Boston: Houghton Mifflin.

Skolimowski, H. 1983. Power: Myth and reality. *Alternatives* 9: 25–49.

Snow, R., coord. 1983. *Decision making in a nuclear age.* Wilmington, MA: ZBR.

Solomon, B. 1976. *Black empowerment: Social work in oppressed communities.* New York: Columbia University Press.

Spencer, M. 1988. What are we teaching our kids? *Nuclear Times* 7 (September–October): 17–20.

Spradley, J. P. 1980. *Participant observation.* New York: Holt, Rinehart & Winston.

Spretnak, C., ed. 1982. *The politics of women's spirituality.* Garden City, NY: Anchor Books.

Stamps, J. 1980. *Holonomy: A human systems theory.* Seaside, CA: Intersystems.

Starhawk. 1982. *Dreaming the dark.* Boston: Beacon Press.

Starhawk. 1987. *Truth or dare.* San Francisco: Harper & Row.

Strom, M. S., and W. S. Parsons. 1982. *Facing history and ourselves: Holocaust and human behavior.* Watertown, MA: Intentional Educations.

Surrey, J. L. 1987. Relationship and empowerment. *Work in progress.* Wellesley, MA: Stone Center Working Papers Series.

Terkel, S. 1972. *Working.* New York: Avon Books.

Text of Carnegie report. *Education Week,* 21 May 1986, 11–18.

Thomas, L. 1974. *The lives of a cell.* New York: Bantam.

Tucker, R., ed. 1972. *The Marx-Engels reader.* New York: Norton.

Von Eckartsberg, R. 1971. On experiential methodology. In *Duquesne studies in phenomenological psychology.* vol. 1. *See* A. Giorgi, W. F. Fischer, and R. Von Eckartsberg, eds., 1971.

Weber, M. 1946. *From Max Weber.* Ed. H. H. Gerth and C. W. Mills. New York: Oxford University Press.

Weber, M. 1968. *Economy and society.* Ed. G. Roth and C. Wittich. New York: Bedminster Press.

Weiler, K. 1988. *Women teaching for change: Gender, class and power.* Hadley, Massachusetts: Bergin & Garvey.

Welch, S. 1985. *Communities of resistance and solidarity: A feminist theology of liberation.* Maryknoll, NY: Orbis.

Wigginton, E. 1986. *Sometimes a shining moment: The Foxfire experience.* Garden City, NY: Anchor Books.

Willis, P. 1977. *Learning to labor.* New York: Columbia University Press.

Winter, D. 1972. *The power motive.* New York: Free Press.

Woodhead, A. G. 1970. *Thucydides on the nature of power.* Cambridge, MA: Harvard University Press.

Wright, R. 1945. *Black boy.* New York: Harper and Brothers.

Wright, R. 1966. *Native son.* New York: Harper & Row.

Zelditch, M. 1969. Some methodological problems of field studies. In *Issues in participant observation: A text and reader. See* G. J. McCall and J. L. Simmons, eds., 1969.

Zukov, G. 1979. *The dancing Wu li masters.* New York: Bantam.

Index